In accordance with the latest syllabus prescribed by the
Council for the Indian Certificate of Secondary Education Examination, New Delhi.

A TEXT BOOK OF
ICSE ECONOMIC APPLICATIONS

CLASS X

V. N. NIGAM
A. BANERJEE

OSWAL PUBLISHERS
1/12 Sahitya Kunj, M. G. Road, Agra-282 002

No part of this book can be reproduced in any form or by any means without the prior written permission of the publisher.

Edition : 2021

ISBN : 978-93-89937-96-1

OSWAL PUBLISHERS

Head office	:	1/12, Sahitya Kunj, M. G. Road, Agra-282 002
Phone	:	(0562) 2527771-4, +91 75340 77222
E-mail	:	contact@oswalpublishers.com
Website	:	www.oswalpublishers.com
Printed at		

Preface

We are pleased to place before the Students this page to page thoroughly revised edition of 'Economic Applications', Which meets the requirements of the new course structure introduced by Council the Indian School Certificate Examinations (CISCE).

Each day economic issues impact our lives in various ways. The students must therefore equip themselves with the basic principles of Economics and the manner economic decisions affect progress and development of society. This book is designed to achieve this goal.

Economics by its very nature is considered both - as Art and Science. Often it has to deal with abstract ideas which need to be related to practical experience. Teachers would do well to develop in the students insights and perspectives, through dissemination of information concerning institutions and acquaint them with concrete situations. For example, field visits and area studies can be conducted to acquire first hand information and to gain experience of the working conditions and environment. Visits to textile mills, factories, small-scale and cottage industries, banks and other similar commercial institutions, stock exchanges, transport undertakings, consumers' co-operatives, local markets, etc., can be periodically organised for better understanding of these institutions and the useful role they play.

Salient Features of This Revised Edition of the Book

- Specially designed to meet the requirements of ICSE students.
- Strictly written in accordance with the latest syllabus prescribed by the Council for ICSE, New Delhi.
- Based on new examination pattern.
- Hints have been given as and where necessary.
- Up-to-date study material incorporating most reliable and latest data taken mostly from government journals relating to the Indian Economy.
- Comprehensive coverage of the prescribed course.
- Case Studies given at the end has been specially designed for the students.
- The topics have been organised strictly in accordance to the syllabus, so as to strenghen the continuous and cumulative development of knowledge.

The subject matter has been presented in a very simple, lucid and interesting manner and every attempt has been made to relate theoretical knowledge with actual life. The Exercises at the end of each chapter are designed to test students' understanding of the text and to stimulate further study. The Exercises include both Short and Long Type questions.

Constructive suggestions and comments will be appreciated and thankfully acknowledged.

—**PUBLISHER**

SYLLABUS CLASS X
ECONOMIC APPLICATIONS

There will be **one** theory paper of **two hours** duration of 100 marks and Internal Assessment of 100 marks.

The paper will consist of Part I and Part II.

Part I (Compulsory) will contain short answer questions on the entire syllabus.

Part II will consist of questions that will require detailed answers. There will be a choice of questions.

THEORY — 100 Marks

1. **Demand and Supply: Basic Concepts**

   Demand – Meaning and Types of Demand Supply – Meaning

   Law of demand and supply: Demand and supply schedule and curve (both individual and market); movement and shift of the demand and supply curve; determinants of demand and supply; exceptions to the law of demand.

   Meaning of Demand and Supply. Types of Demand (Joint Demand, Derived Demand and Composite Demand).

   A basic understanding of the law of demand and supply in which demand and supply schedules are to be used to explain the demand and supply curves. The individual demand and supply curves must be distinguished from market demand and supply curves. Determinants of demand and supply are to be specified. Exceptions to the law of demand are to be discussed.

   Elasticity of demand and elasticity of supply. Meaning, types; percentage, method of measuring elasticity of demand and elasticity of supply, Factors affecting elasticity of demand and elasticity of supply.

   The concept of price elasticity of demand and supply are to be explained with percentage method. The factors affecting the elasticity of demand and supply are to be specified. (Simple numericals should be taught)

2. **Factors of Production: Basic Concepts**

   Factors of production–Land, Labour, Capital and Entrepreneur.

   Land–meaning and characteristics, functions and its importance, factors affecting productivity of land.

   Destruction of ecosystem due to changing patterns of land use, migration, industrialization, shifting cultivation, dwelling units, mining, urbanization, construction of dams, etc.

   Labour–meaning and characteristics. Division of labour–meaning, types, advantages and disadvantages. Efficiency of labour- meaning, reasons for low efficiency of Indian labour.

   Capital–meaning, types and characteristics.

   Capital formation–meaning, factors affecting capital formation.

   Entrepreneur–meaning, functions and role of entrepreneurs in economic development.

3. **Alternative Market Structures: Basic Concepts**

   Nature and structure of markets– Perfectly competitive market, Monopoly market, monopolistically competitive market, concept of product differentiation, Monopsony market.

The main features of the following market structures are to be discussed in the context of present business scenario.

Perfectly competitive market, Monopoly market, monopolistically competitive market, Monopsony market (meaning to be highlighted).

4. **The State and Economic Development**

   The role of State in promoting development; the instruments of State intervention–fiscal policy and monetary policy; The Public sector enterprises–their role and problems; the issue of privatization of public enterprises.

   A basic understanding of the role of the State in the economy needs to be highlighted in the context of Indian economy. The meaning of fiscal policy. Direct and Indirect Taxes (meaning, merits and demerits), Types of Taxes (progressive, regressive, proportional and degressive–meaning with examples). Monetary Policy–meaning only. Public sector–its role and problems. Reasons for Privatization.

5. **Money and Banking: Basic Concepts**

   Money: meaning, functions of Money; Inflation–meaning, effects of inflation on the functioning of the economy (in brief). Banking : Commercial Banks–functions; Central Bank–functions; quantitative and qualitative credit control measures adopted by RBI.

   A basic understanding of the concepts of money, its functions. Meaning and types of inflation to be discussed (Creeping, Walking, Running and Hyper-inflation). The impact of inflation on various economic entities such as debtors and creditors, fixed income groups and producers are to be explained very briefly. Functions of commercial banks and functions of RBI–qualitative and quantitative controls used by the RBI as part of its credit control measures should be explained.

   NOTE : It is suggested that case studies may be discussed on the following topics:
   - Factors of Production
   - Banking
   - Inflation

INTERNAL ASSESSMENT   100 Marks

Candidates will be required to do a minimum of **four** assignments during the year, as assigned by the teacher.

Suggested list of assignments:

1. Take a fast moving consumer good (FMCG) like washing machine detergent. Analyze the factors that determine the demand of this product. Present your findings in form of a class presentation.

2. Develop a hypothetical table of information for coffee that shows quantity demanded at various prices and supply of coffee at these prices. Draw a demand curve and supply curve and show an equilibrium price at which market is cleared of its supplies.

3. Make a list of products for which you think demand is price inelastic and

price elastic. Specify the reasons you may think relevant for your analysis.

4. Take a case of public enterprise which is about to be privatized or has been recently privatized. Analyze the pros and cons of such an exercise undertaken by the government. (The case of VSNL or BALCO can be taken up)

5. Take a case of a nationalized bank– visit any one of its branches in your city. Analyze the main functions of this bank's branch. Make a presentation to this effect.

6. Recently rates of interests have been reduced on all the saving instruments. Carry out a survey of 30 people in your area as to what is their reaction to this cut. The sample may consist of salaried people, business people and professionals.

7. Take a case of five FMCGs–fast moving consumer goods–bathing soaps, toothpastes, facial creams, shampoos, ball pens. Analyze as to how the market for these products is characterized by product differentiation.

8. Take the case of a company and analyze the production process in which all the factors that you studied in your class, are used by the company to produce a product.

EVALUATION

The project work is to be evaluated by the subject teacher and by an External Examiner. The External Examiner shall be nominated by the Head of the school and may be a teacher from the faculty. **but not teaching the subject in the relevant section/class.** For example, a teacher of Economics of Class XI may be deputed to be the External Examiner for Class X Economic Applications project work.

The Internal Examiner and the External Examiner will assess the candidate's work independently.

Award of marks   (100 marks)

Subject Teacher

(Internal Examiner)   50 marks

External Examiner   50 marks

The total marks obtained out of 100 are to be sent to the Council by the Head of the School. The Head of the school will be responsible for the online entry of marks on the Council's CAREERS portal by the due date.

CONTENTS

1.	Theory of Demand	9 – 27
2.	Elasticity of Demand	28 – 39
3.	Theory of Supply	40 – 52
4.	Elasticity of Supply	53 – 60
5.	Factors of Production	61 – 65
6.	Land	66 – 71
7.	Destruction of Ecosystem	72 – 88
8.	Labour	81 – 99
9.	Capital and Capital Formation	100 – 110
10.	Entrepreneur	111 – 117
11.	Alternative Market Structures : Basic Concepts	118 – 130
12.	The State and Economic Development	131 – 137
13.	Instruments of State Intervention	138 – 153
14.	Public Sector Enterprises	154 – 161
15.	Privatisation of Public Enterprises	162 – 169
16.	Money and Inflation	170 – 185
17.	Banking : Commercial Banks and Central Bank	186 – 204
	• Case Study	205 – 211
	• Assignment	212 – 216

01 Theory of Demand

All the economic activities of this world are based on the demand and supply of the commodities and services. Demand is made by the consumers to fulfill their everyday requirements. It is the result of the choices exercised by the consumers to select commodities to fulfill their needs. The practice of this concept can be seen in our surroundings. We demand notebooks, bread, vegetables, clothes and movie tickets in our everyday life. But to appreciate this concept better we must understand its meaning.

We know that people have numerous wants which vary in intensity and quality. Just desiring or wanting things is not enough to create a demand. Suppose, a mill worker desires or wants to have a car but does not have the necessary means to buy it. This desire is ineffective and will not become a demand. Similarly, a miser may desire to have the car, has means to purchase it, but will not spend the money. His desire would also not constitute a demand. Thus, we define demand for a commodity or service as an effective desire, *i.e.*, a desire backed by means as well as willingness to pay for it.

OVERVIEW

The terms 'Desire', 'Want' and 'Demand' are generally confused with each other, but all these have different meanings in Economics. The 'Demand' for the commodities or services is the ultimate outcome of unlimited human 'wants'. It is the fundamental factor which regulates all economic activities. The 'Demand' from the consumers encourages the suppliers and producers to participate in economic activities.

In fact, the country's economic planning is based on the present and future estimated demands of various types of goods and services. However, the price of commodity, the taste of people, quality of product, social customs, etc., also determine the demand of a particular commodity.

The demand arises out of the following three things:
- Desire or want of the commodity.
- Willingness to pay.
- Ability or purchasing power to buy.

Only when all these three things are present then the consumer presents his demand in the market.

We can therefore, define demand in the following way:

"Demand for a commodity is the quantity which a consumer is willing to buy at a particular price at a particular time."

"The demand for anything at a given price is the amount of it, which will be bought per unit of time, at that price."
—**Prof. Benham**

"By demand, we mean the quantity of a commodity that will be purchased at a particular price and not merely the desire of a thing."
—**Hansen**

Thus, demand for a commodity refers to the quantity of the commodity which a consumer is willing and able to buy at a particular price and place and within a particular time period.

Distinction between Want and Demand

Want	Demand
1. Desire of a good or service by a consumer.	1. Demand is the quantity of a good or service that a consumer is willing and able to buy at a range of prices.
2. This cannot be communicated to the sellers through price mechanism.	2. It can be communicated to the sellers through price mechanism.
3. It is not related with actual purchase of a commodity at any given price.	3. It is related with the actual purchase of a commodity at any given price during any particular time period.

It must be remembered that demand in Economics is always stated with reference to a particular price. Any change in price will normally bring about a change in the quantity demanded. Demand is also mentioned in the context of a place or boundary. Otherwise it will be difficult to ascertain the relationship between magnitude of demand and consumers. In addition to price and place, demand is also used in reference to a particular period of time. For example, demand for umbrellas will not be as high in winter as during rains. The demand for any commodity or service, therefore, must be stated with reference to the price, place and the relevant point of time.

TYPES OF DEMAND

It has been assumed that demand of a particular commodity is quite independent of demand for other goods. But in actual life, most of the demands are closely interrelated. From a practical point of view, the interrelated demands can be classified as:

1. Joint Demand,
2. Direct Demand and Derived Demand, and
3. Composite Demand.

Joint Demand: When several items are demanded together for one particular purpose, such demand is known as Joint Demand. In such demand no item can do without the other items. Demand for complementary goods is also known as Joint Demand. For example, for making sweet coffee, we use milk, sugar and coffee powder together. If any of the items in this combination remains unavailable, the sweet coffee cannot be prepared. That is why it is called a Joint Demand. The Joint Demand for coffee is denoted by the given line diagram *(Fig. 1·1)*.

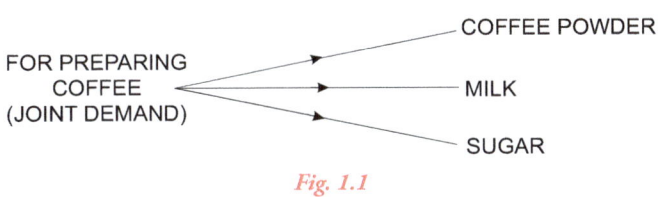

Fig. 1.1

Direct Demand and Derived Demand: Whenever several items are required to make a particular commodity, the demand for various commodities is termed as the Derived Demand and demand of ultimate commodity is called as Direct Demand. So under the derived demand the demand for items (raw material) is dependent on the demand of some other item (finished good). For example, the demand of building is a direct demand and demands for cement, bricks, sand, timber, etc., are called as derived demands. It is denoted by the given line diagram *(Fig. 1.2)*.

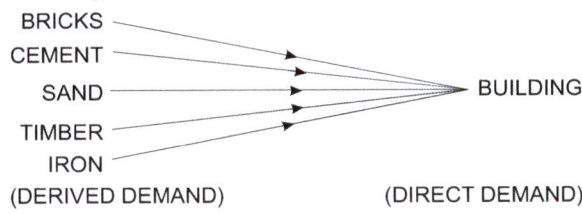

Fig. 1.2

Composite Demand: A commodity can be used for several purposes and its demand is directly linked to its various uses. Such a demand is known as Composite Demand. for example, milk is used for making tea, coffee, butter, cheese, curd, sweets and for direct consumption. The total demand of milk in the market is for all such purpose and it is a composite demand, denoted by given line diagram *(Fig. 1.3)*

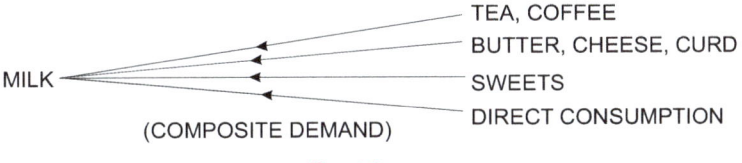

Fig. 1.3

DETERMINANTS OF DEMAND OR FACTORS AFFECTING DEMAND

Demand is not dependent on price alone. There are many other factors which affect the demand of a product. These factors are as follows:

Price of the Product: Demand for a commodity depends on its price. As price rises, for a normal good, its quantity demanded falls and vice-versa. However, there are exceptions, *i.e.*, for giffen goods, as the price rises its quantity demanded also rises.

Income of the Consumer: A key determinant of demand is the level of income of a consumer, *i.e.*, the higher the level of income the higher the demand for a given commodity (except inferior goods). Consumer's income and demand are generally positively related. It means that when income of the consumer rises he wants to have more units of a commodity and when his income falls he reduces the demand.

In case of inferior goods, however, the relationship is opposite, *i.e.*, increase in income reduces the demand because the consumer shifts his consumption to superior goods and forgoes his existing inferior product, thus reduces its demand.

For example, inferior good might be commuting by the bus. As income rises, people are less likely to use the bus and more likely to own an automobile.

Prices of Related Goods: Consumption choices are also influenced by the alternative option available to users in the relevant market place. Market information regarding alternative products, quality, convenience and dependability all influence choices.

The two products may be related in two ways. Firstly as complementary goods and secondly as substitute goods.

Complementary goods are those goods which are consumed or used together like tennis-ball and a racket, petrol and car, etc. Here the relationship between the price of a product and the demand for another is inverse. For example, if the price of petrol increases, it will be costlier for the people to use their personal vehicles. Hence very less people would choose to buy and use cars and they would like to switch to public transportation. So the demand for petrol would decrease and under these circumstances the demand for the complementary good *i.e.,* cars would also decrease. It has happened recently in the past when due to rising petrol prices, the demand for cars fell and companies had to give discounts to increase the sale of the cars. The vice-versa will happen, if the cars get costlier the demand for petrol will fall.

Goods which are perceived by the consumer to be alternative to each other are termed as substitute goods. There is direct relationship between the demand for a product and the price of its substitute. Examples are scooter and motorcycle, tea and coffee, Coca Cola and Pepsi, etc.

The increase in price of Coca Cola would decrease its quantity demanded and people would switch over to its substitute commodity *i.e.,* Pepsi.

Consumer's Tastes and Preferences: Demand for a product is also affected by the tastes and preferences of the consumers. Taste and preference refers to the choices and likings of the consumers regarding goods and services. As tastes and preferences shift from one commodity to the other, demand for the first commodity reduces and that of the other commodity rises. For example, consumers' preference has shifted from simple Java phones to Smartphones. This has resulted into the fall of demand for Java phones and rise in the demand for Smartphones.

Expectation of Future Prices: The current demand of a product also depends on its expected price in future. If future price is expected to rise, its present demand immediately increase because the consumer has a tendency to store it at low prices for his future consumption. If, however the price of a product is expected to fall then he has a tendency to postpone its consumption and as a result the present demand would also fall.

This is often the case on budget day, when consumers rush to fill their petrol tanks prior to an expected increase in taxation, and therefore the price of fuel. The reverse is also true, in that an expectation that prices are about to fall, will decrease current demand, as consumers await the expected price reduction.

Population: An increase in population of a region will result in an increased demand of various goods. Also, the composition of population determines the demand of certain goods proportionately. For example, an increased number of females in the region will generate more demand for sarees, ornaments, cosmetics, etc.

Weather Conditions: The demand for various household goods depends upon the changes in weather conditions. For example, the demand for woollen clothes, coal and electric heaters increases during winter and the demand for cold drinks, ice creams, room coolers, etc., goes up during hot weather.

Consumer Credit Facility: Easy availability of credit to consumers whether from banks, businessmen or any other source increases the purchasing capacity of the consumers. This increases the demand for the commodities. If this credit facility is reduced either by increasing the rate of interests on loans or by increasing the margin money requirements, then the demand of the consumers fall because their purchasing capacity gets curtailed.

Government Policy: Economic policy adopted by the government also influences the demand for commodities. If the government imposes taxes on various commodities in the form of sales tax, excise duties, octroi, etc., the price of these commodities will increase. As a result, the demand of such commodities is very likely to fall.

DEMAND FUNCTION

Demand function expresses the functional relationship between the demand of a commodity and its various determinants. This relationship is shown in the following manner:

$$D_X = f(P_X, P_R, Y, T, E, O)$$

D_X = Demand of a commodity
P_X = Price of the commodity
P_R = Price of related goods (Substitutes and Complementary)
Y = Income of the consumer
T = Taste and preference of the consumer
E = Consumers' future expectations about the price
O = Other factors

DEMAND SCHEDULE

"Demand schedule is a list of prices and quantities." —**Prof. Alfred Marshall**

"The table relating to price and quantity demanded is called the demand schedule."

—**Samuelson**

In other words, the demand schedule is the tabular representation of the relationship between price and quantity demanded of a commodity.

The demand schedule in the table represents the different quantities of commodities that can be purchased at different prices during a certain specified period (it can be a day or a week or a month). As such, the demand schedule is actually a link between series of prices and quantities of a commodity demanded.

The demand schedule can be classified into two categories:
1. Individual demand schedule;
2. Market demand schedule.

Individual Demand Schedule

It represents the demand of an individual for a commodity at different prices at a particular time period. The adjoining *Table 1.1* shows a demand schedule for oranges on 7th July, 2008

Table 1.1 Individual Demand Schedule

Price of Orange (₹ per kg.)	Quantity of Oranges Demanded (kg.)
15	2
12	3
9	4
6	5
3	6

Market Demand Schedule

In a market, there are several consumers, and each has a different liking, taste, preference and income. Every consumer has a different demand. The market demand actually represents the demand of all the consumers combined together. Thus, a market demand schedule is a table showing different quantities of a commodity that all the buyers in the market are ready to buy at different possible prices of the commodity at a point of time. When a particular commodity has several brands or types of commodities, the market demand schedule becomes very complicated because of various factors. However, for a single item, the market demand schedule is rather simple. Study the market demand schedule for milk in *Table 1·2*.

Table 1·2 : Market Demand Schedule

Price of Milk per litre (in ₹)	Demand of Mr. X (in litres)	Demand of Mr. Y (in litres)	Market Demand (in litres)
5	1	2	1+2 = 3
4	2	3	2+3 = 5
3	4	4	3+4 = 7
2	4	5	4+5 = 9
1	5	6	5+6 = 11

Distinction between Individual Demand Schedule and Market Demand Schedule

Individual Demand Schedule	Market Demand Schedule
1. It represents the desired demand of particular commodity which an individual stands ready to purchase at different possible prices.	1. It indicates the total demand (by all individuals) for a particular commodity in the market at which all the buyers are ready to purchase at different possible prices at a given moment of time.
2. The income of an individual affects the individual demand schedule of particular commodity.	2. The income variations and its distributions among different groups of individuals, directs the overall market demand schedule of a commodity.
3. Individual demand schedule depends upon the taste, liking and desire to consume a commodity.	3. The market demand schedule depends upon the number of individuals desiring that commodity. With the increase in number of consumers, the demand increases and vice-versa.
4. This schedule can be conveniently represented by individual demand curve.	4. This can be represented by market demand curve.

DEMAND CURVE

The demand curve is the graphical representation of the relationship between price and quantity demanded of a commodity. Demand curve does not tell us the price. It only tells us how much quantity of goods would be purchased by the consumer at various possible prices. The demand curve can be; either (1) Individual Demand Curve (2) Market Demand Curve depending upon the demand schedule. These can be defined as follows:

1. Individual Demand Curve: An Individual Demand Curve is a graphical representation of the quantities of a commodity that an individual (a particular consumer) stands ready to take off the market at a given instant of time against different prices. In *Fig. 1.4,* an Individual Demand Curve is drawn on the basis of Individual Demand Schedule given in *Table 1.1.*

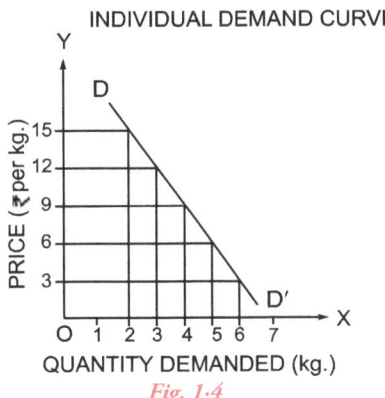

Fig. 1.4

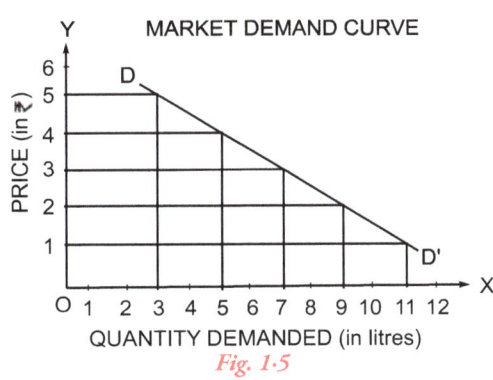

Fig. 1.5

2. Market Demand Curve: A Market Demand Curve is a graphical representation of the quantities of a commodity which all the buyers in the market stand ready to take off at all possible prices at a given moment of time. In *Fig. 1.5,* a Market Demand Curve is drawn on the basis of Market Demand Schedule given in *Table 1.2.*

The quantities and prices of milk have been shown along X-axis and Y-axis respectively and the curve DD' has been obtained by joining various points. It will be clear from the curve DD', that at a higher price, the quantity demanded is low while at lower price, the quantity demanded of a commodity has increased.

Both, the individual consumer's demand curve and the market demand curves slope downwards to the right. Hence, showing an inverse relationship between the price and quantity demanded of the commodity.

It is not necessary, that the demand curve is always a straight line or a convex curve or a concave curve, it may take any shape provided it is negatively sloped.

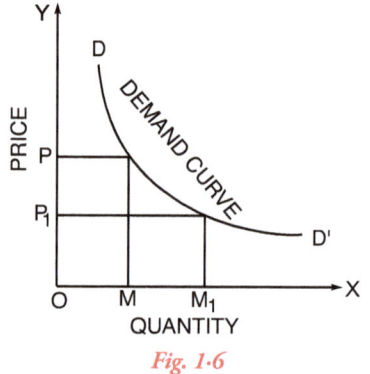

Fig. 1.6

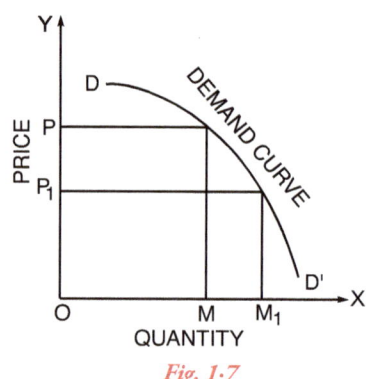

Fig. 1.7

LAW OF DEMAND

The law of demand expresses functional relationship between price and the quantity demanded of a commodity. It has been universally observed that persons buy more quantity of goods when, they are available at a lower price and the quantity purchased declines with an increase in its price.

"A rise in the price of a commodity or service is followed by a fall in quantity demanded, and a fall in price is followed by an increase in quantity demanded, other things remaining constant." Thus, lower the price, the larger is the quantity demanded of a commodity and vice-versa.

The law of demand states that as the price of the commodity falls, its quantity demanded increases and as the price increases, its quantity demanded falls, other things remaining constant. Hence this law expresses the inverse relationship between the price and quantity demanded of a commodity.

We can see the application of this law in our everyday lives. When there is a "Discount Season" in any of the renowned Mall in our city, we go to buy more of the quantity of the commodities. Our father likes to buy more of the petrol if it is cheaper. Our mothers like to buy more of gold and silver if it is cheaper in the market, etc. Similarly, if some of the required commodities get costlier we like to postpone our demand if possible and wait for it to be cheaper. For example, we wait to buy refrigerators or televisions on Diwali because that time we expect to get good discounts on these commodities.

BASIS OR ASSUMPTIONS OF LAW OF DEMAND

The law of demand hold good only when certain assumptions are fulfilled. They are following:

- The income of the consumer remains same during the period under consideration.
- The prices of other closely related and similar goods remain unchanged during the period.
- The preferences and tastes of consumers must remain the same during the period of consumption.
- The quality of similar goods available in the market is almost unchanged.
- During the period under study, it is presumed that prices are not likely to change in near future.
- The commodity under study does not have any prestige value.

MOVEMENT ALONG THE DEMAND CURVE AND SHIFT IN DEMAND CURVE

Generally, a distinction is made between the Movement along the Demand curve and Shift in the Demand curve. The distinction is due to the impact of various determinants on the demand of the commodity in different ways.

MOVEMENT ALONG THE DEMAND CURVE

When due to change in its own price, the quantity demanded of a commodity gets changed and it is expressed by different points on the same demand curve, it is called movement along a demand curve. It is also called extension or contraction in demand or change in quantity demanded. It can be understood as follows:

Extension and Contraction of Demand

The price variations play important role in determining the extension and contraction of demand. The extension and contraction indicate the changes in the demand of a commodity when its price changes in the market, while other factors remaining same. When a buyer purchases more quantity of an item because of reduction in its price, it is known as an extension of demand. Similarly, when less quantity of an item is being purchased due to a rise in price, it is termed as contraction of demand.

The above facts can be denoted graphically as shown in the figure.

The quantity demanded and the corresponding price are taken along X-axis and Y-axis respectively as shown in *Fig. 1.8* At price K, the quantity demanded is L. When the price falls to K_1, the quantity demanded increases and it is represented by L_1. This phenomenon is known (also denoted on graph along curve DD') as extension of demand. Similarly, the quantity demanded is L_2 when price increases to K_2 and the contraction of demand occurs.

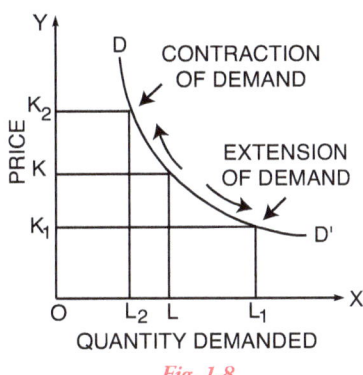

Fig. 1.8

Shift in Demand Curve

In this case, the entire demand curve shifts either upward (rightward) or downward (leftward). This type of change takes place when the demand changes due to change in any of the factors other than own price of the commodity. It is expressed as Increase and Decrease in Demand or Shift in the Demand Curve or Change in Demand.

It can be understood as follows:

Increase in Demand—Upward (Rightward) Shift in Demand

Suppose conditions on which demand for a product depends, such as the number of consumers, the level of income and wealth of consumers, etc., change for the better. Then there will be an upward shift in demand curve which is known as increase in demand. Increase in demand is illustrated by *Fig. 1.9.*

Consider *Fig. 1.9 (a)* first. On the *x*-axis, we represent quantity of commodity and on the *y*-axis, we represent price. We take a demand curve DD_1, which is prepared on the basis of a given number of consumers, a given level of income or wealth of consumers, given tastes, preferences, etc.

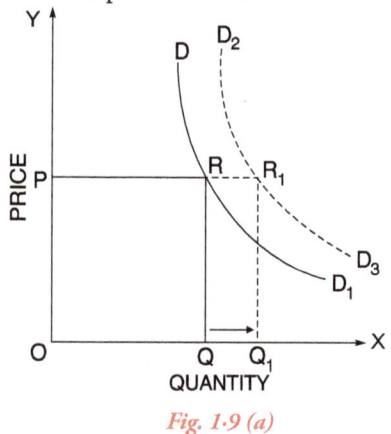
Fig. 1.9 (a)

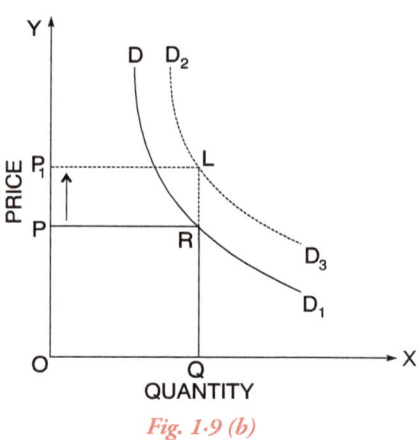
Fig. 1.9 (b)

At the price OP, consumers demand OQ quantity. But suppose the assumptions change. For instance, there are now more consumers in the market; their income and wealth have gone up; they like the commodity more, and so on. As a result of these changes, the old demand curve DD_1, is gradually pushed upward and a new demand curve, viz. D_2D_3 comes into existence. D_2D_3 is given as a dashed (or dotted) curve to distinguish it from the old demand curve. At the price OP, consumers demanded OQ quantity; but now they demand OQ_1 quantity. Why do people demand more of the commodity now? Is the increase in demand (by QQ_1) the result of fall in price? It may be observed that people demand more, not because the price has fallen, but because of large income and wealth, or because of greater preference for this commodity and so on. An upward shift in demand curve is, therefore, known as increase in demand. This increase in demand may be due to some or all of the following conditions:

- The number of consumers in the market may have increased;
- The level of income and wealth of the consumers may have risen;
- The taste, preference, customs and habits may have changed considerably;

- Substitute may not be available in the market or they may have become more expensive; and
- People may anticipate a price rise or reduction in supply.

Fig. 1.9 (b) explains precisely the same point but in a different way, quantity demanded is OQ. The consumers initially demanded this quantity at OP price but are now prepared to pay a higher price than OP. Increase in demand, therefore means that either:

- Consumers are prepared to buy more at the same price; or
- They are prepared to pay a higher price for a given quantity.

Difference between Extension of Demand and Increase in Demand

Under extension of demand, the consumers demand more because the price of the commodity has fallen by keeping all other factors unchanged.

But increase in demand refers to an increase in quantity demanded as a result of changes in any of the other conditions (such as income, fashion, climate, etc.) while prices remain the same.

Difference between Extension of Demand and Increase in Demand

Extension of Demand	Increase in Demand
1. This is caused only by change in own price of the commodity.	1. This is caused by change in determinants other than own price of the commodity.
2. Decrease in own price of the commodity is the only cause.	2. Several causes like increase in income, decrease in price of complementary good or increase in the price of substitute goods, etc.
3. Diagrammatically this is shown as a downward movement on the same demand curve.	3. Diagrammatically this is shown as an upward (rightward) shift in demand curve.

Decrease in Demand—Downward (Leftward) Shift in Demand

Let us now consider downward shift in demand. The decrease in demand is due to an adverse change in demand conditions. For instance:

- The number of consumers in the market may decline;
- The level of incomes and wealth of consumers may be reduced;
- The tastes, preferences, customs and habits may have changed adversely;
- New substitutes may be available or their prices may have come down;
- Consumers may anticipate a fall in price and hence may postpone their demand;
- The commodity may be going out of fashion; and
- The total volume of money in the community may be coming down and hence the demand for goods in general may come down.

As a result of any or all these factors, a new demand curve at a lower level will have to be drawn. The new demand curve, given in dashed (dotted) line in *Fig. 1.9 (c)* and *(d)* refers to the decrease in demand. In *Fig. 1.9 (c)* DD_1, is the normal demand curve and the new demand curve is D_2D_3. At a given price of OP, the consumers demanded OQ quantity; but now they demand OQ_1 quantity, *i.e.*, they demand less at a given price. *Fig. 1.9 (d)* is the same as *Fig. 1.9 (c)*. But in *Fig. 1.9 (d)*, we have taken a given quantity OQ. This quantity was originally demanded at OP price, but now it is demanded at a lower price, viz.; OP_1 price.

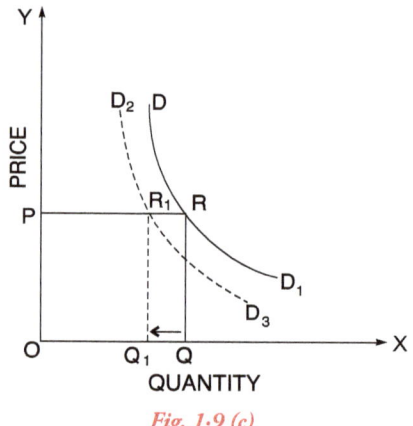
Fig. 1.9 (c)

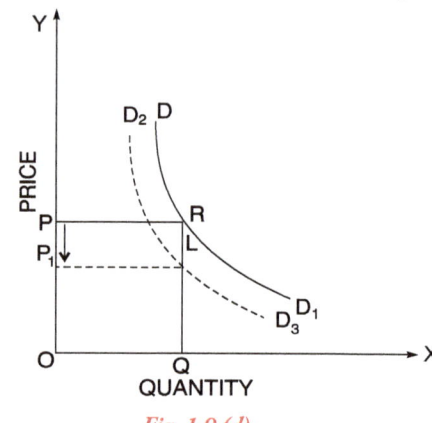
Fig. 1.9 (d)

Therefore, downward shift in demand implies two things:

- The consumers are willing to buy a smaller quantity, at a given price, or
- They are willing to pay lower prices for a given quantity.

Difference between Contraction of Demand and Decrease in Demand

Decrease in demand is different from contraction of demand. While contraction of demand is due to a rise in price, decrease in demand is the result of change in the conditions affecting demand.

Difference between Contraction of Demand and Decrease in Demand

Contraction of Demand	Decrease in Demand
1. This is caused only by change in own price of the commodity.	1. This is caused by change in determinants other than own price of the commodity.
2. Increase in own price of the commodity is the only cause.	2. Several causes like decrease in income, decrease in price of the substitutes, etc.
3. Diagrammatically this is shown as an upward movement (right to left) on the same demand curve.	3. Diagrammatically this is shown by downward (leftward) shift in demand curve.

Exceptions to the Law of Demand

There are certain exceptions to the law of demand. It means that under certain circumstances, consumers buy more when the price of a commodity rises and less when the price falls. In such cases, the demand curve slopes upward from left to right *i.e.* demand curve has a positive slope as is shown in *Fig. 1.10.* Many causes can be attributed to an upward sloping demand curve.

Ignorance: Sometimes consumers are fascinated with the high priced goods from the idea of getting a superior quality. However, this may not be always true. Superior/ deceptive packing and high price deceive the people. This can be called as 'Ignorance effect'.

Speculative Effect: When the price of a commodity goes up, people may buy larger quantity than before, if they anticipate or speculate a further rise in its price. On the other hand, when the price falls, people may not react immediately and may still purchase the same or less quantity than before, waiting for another fall in the price. In both the cases, the law of demand fails to operate. This is known as speculative effect.

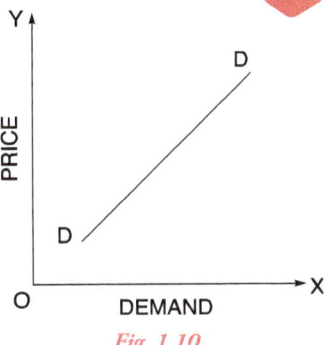

Fig. 1.10

The Giffen's Paradox: Giffen goods are highly inferior goods; showing a very high negative income effect. As a result, when price of such commodities fall, their demand also fall. A fall in the price of inferior goods (Giffen Goods) tends to reduce its demand and a rise in its price tends to extend its demand. This phenomenon was first observed by **Sir Robert Giffen,** popularly known as Giffen's paradox. He observed that the working class families of U.K. were compelled to curtail their consumption of meat in order to be able to spend more on bread. Mr. Giffen, British economist, observed that rise in the price of bread caused the low paid British workers to buy more bread and not less. These workers lived mainly on the diet of bread, when price rose, as they had to spend more for a given quantity of bread, they could not buy as much meat as before. Bread still being comparatively cheaper was substituted for meat even at its high price.

Fear of Shortage: The people may buy more of a commodity even at higher prices when they fear of a shortage of that commodity in near future. This is contrary to the law of demand. It may happen during times of war and inflation and mostly in the case of goods which fall in the category of necessities of life like sugar, kerosene oil, etc.

Prestigious Goods: This is explained by **Prof. Thorstein Bunde Veblen**. If consumers measure the desirability of a good entirely by its price and not by its use, then they buy more of a good at high price and less of a good at low price. Diamond, Jewellery and big cars, etc., are such prestigious goods. In their case demand relates to such consumers who use them as status symbol. As their prices go up and become costlier, rich people think it is more prestigious to have them. So they purchase more. On the other hand, when their prices fall sharply, they are bought less, as they are no more prestigious goods. This is known as *Veblen effect* or conspicuous consumption.

Conspicuous Necessities: Another exception occurs in use of such commodities, as due to their constant use, they have become necessities of life. For example, in spite of the fact that the prices of television sets, refrigerators, washing machines, cooking gas, scooters, etc., have been continuously rising, their demand does not show any tendency to fall. Earlier they used to be considered the "Luxuries" but now they have become inalienable part of individual's life. So they have become necessities now.

Bandwagon Effect: Bandwagon effect takes place when a consumer's demand for a good is affected not by his own choice but by the tastes and preferences of the social class to which he belongs. For example, if a student's friends keep costly smart phones with them, then the student may also like to have a costly smart phone just to show the belongingness to the group.

LESSON AT A GLANCE

Demand: In Economic Applications demand is constituted by three things: (i) Desire or want of the commodity; (ii) Willingness to pay; and (iii) Ability or purchasing power to buy. **Prof. Benham** defined it as a demand for anything, at a given price is the amount of it which will be bought per unit of time at that price.

Types of Demand: The interrelated demands can be classified as: (i) Joint demand; (ii) Direct demand and Derived demand; (iii) Composite demand.

Determinants of Demand or Factors affecting Demand: (i) Price of the product; (ii) Income of the consumer; (iii) Prices of related goods; (iv) Consumer's tastes and preferences; (v) Expectation of future prices; (vi) Population; (vii) Weather conditions; (viii) Consumer credit facility; (ix) Government policy.

Demand Schedule: A tabular statement of price-quantity relationship is known as the demand schedule.

Individual Demand Schedule: Individual demand schedule refers to the quantities of a given commodity which a consumer will buy at all possible prices at a given moment of time.

Market Demand Schedule: Market demand schedule is defined as the quantities of a given commodity which all consumers will buy at all possible prices at a given moment of time.

Demand Curve: The demand curves are the graphical representation of demand schedules.

Individual Demand Curve : Individual demand curve is a graphical representation of the quantity demanded by an individual consumer at different level of prices.

Market Demand Curve : A market demand curve represents graphical representation of cumulative (or combined) demands of different consumers at different prices.

Law of Demand: The law of demand states the relationship between the quantity demanded and price. According to **Dr. Marshall**, "the amount demanded increases with a fall in price and decreases with a rise in price."

Basis or Assumptions of Law of Demand: The main assumptions of the law of demand are : (i) No change in income of the consumer; (ii) Price of the related commodities should remain constant; (iii) No change in tastes and preferences of the consumer; (iv) No change in the quality of similar goods; (v) No change in distribution of income and wealth; and (vi) No prestige value of good.

Movement Along the Demand Curve and Shift in Demand Curve:

Extension in Demand: Extension of demand is a rise in demand due to a fall in price.

Contraction in Demand: Contraction of demand is a fall in demand due to rise in price.

Increase in Demand: Increase in demand means more demand at same price or same demand at more price.

Decrease in Demand: Decrease in demand means less demand at same price and same demand at less price.

Exceptions to the Law of Demand: The exceptions to the law of demand are:

(i) Ignorance; (ii) Speculative effect; (iii) The giffen's paradox; (iv) Fear of shortage; (v) Prestigious goods; (vi) Conspicuous necessities; and (vii) Bandwagon effect.

PROJECT WORK

Conduct a survey of a market in your town and prepare the list of price of vegetables over a period of one month.

On the basis of information so collected and compiled, make an individual and market demand schedule and draw demand curves.

(i) Mention any change that has occurred in demand that can be called as (a) extension or contraction or (b) increase or decrease.

(ii) Mention change in demand that is influenced by the factors like population, substitutes, weather condition, pattern of income or speculation.

QUESTIONS

A. Short Answer Type Questions:

1. Mention two determinants of demand.
2. State the 'law of demand'.
3. State 'demand schedule'.
4. Briefly explain demand schedule and demand curve.
5. State any two factors, other than changes in price which bring about a change in demand.
6. List any four determinants of change in demand.
7. What is a 'demand curve'?
8. Briefly explain the 'law of demand' with the help of a demand schedule and a demand curve.
9. State any two factors on which a demand for a commodity depends.
10. What is meant by Giffen goods?
11. Why are goods demanded?
12. If the demand for good 'Y' increases as price of another good 'X' rises, how are the two goods related?
13. Distinguish between:
    (i) Extension of demand and increase in demand.
    (ii) Contraction of demand and decrease in demand.

14. Give two determinants of demand of a commodity.
15. Give two examples of a pair of commodities that are:
    (i) Substitutes of each other.
    (ii) Complementary to each other.
16. What does the demand curve given below show?

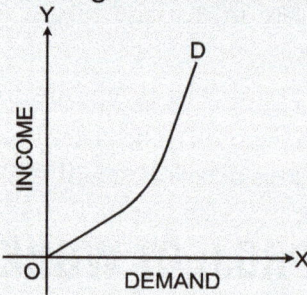

17. Draw graph to depict the following:
    A movement on the demand curve, where both price and quantity change.
18. If the quantity demanded of commodity X decreases as the householder's income increases, what type of a commodity is X? Give an example.
19. Differentiate between derived demand and composite demand using suitable example.
20. Differentiate between Giffen goods and inferior goods.
21. State two reasons for the shift of the demand curve to the left.
22. The following table shows a change in the demand. Read the table carefully and answer the question that follows:

Case	Price (₹)	Quantity (kg.)
I	10	20
	10	10
II	10	20
	5	20

What type of change is it—decrease in demand or contraction in demand? Give a reason.
23. With the help of a suitable diagram explain extension in demand.
24. Explain the following diagram:

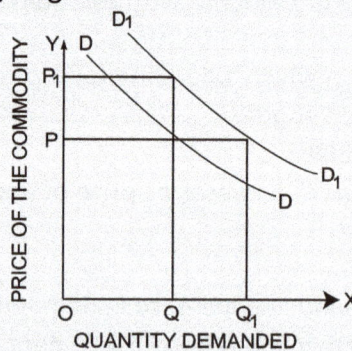

Theory of Demand 25

Recent Year Questions:
1. Mention two assumptions of the law of demand. [ICSE 2011]
2. Explain in brief 'ceteris paribus' assumption of the law of demand. [ICSE 2012]
3. Explain one exception to the law of demand. [ICSE 2012]
4. With the help of a diagram show how a market demand curve can be obtained from individual demand curves. [ICSE 2013]
5. Distinguish between joint demand and composite demand. [ICSE 2013]
6. State whatever the following statement is true or false:
   If prices are expected to fall in the future, current demand rises. [ICSE 2013]
7. If price of X increases, then demand of Y too increases. What is the relationship between goods X and Y? Give an example. [ICSE 2015]
8. Complete the following individual demand schedule: [ICSE 2015]

Price (in ₹)	Quantity of Sugar Demanded (in kgs.)
5	20
6	
7	
8	
9	

9. What are complementary goods? Explain its impact on demand. [ICSE 2016]
10. State whether the following statement is true or false. Give one reason for your answer.
    The demand for inferior goods rises when the income of a consumer increases. [ICSE 2016]
11. Draw a neat labelled diagram of demand curve. [ICSE 2018]

B. Long Answer Type Questions:
1. Explain the Law of Demand with the help of a demand schedule and demand curve. State its two assumptions and two exceptions.
2. With the help of appropriate diagrams, write relevant points of distinction between movement along a demand curve and shift of demand curve.
3. What are the determinants of changes in demand? Describe any five in detail.
4. Explain four factors which lead to an increase in demand for a commodity.
5. (i) Draw demand curve for the following demand schedule for apples on a particular day.

Price per kg. (₹)	20	18	15	13	12	10
Quantity Demanded (kg.)	2	3	4	5	6	10

(ii) Explain the law of demand and point out circumstances under which the law does not operate.
6. Under which exceptional conditions, the Law of Demand deviates? Explain with the help of diagram, giving suitable examples.
7. (i) Does a demand curve always have a negative slope? Justify your answer with four reasons.
   (ii) Describe the nature of the slope of the demand curve.
   (iii) Prepare a demand schedule of your family for milk.
8. How is the market demand curve derived from the individual demand curve?
9. Explain with the help of diagrams, the effect of following changes on the demand of a commodity:
   (i) A rise in the price of complementary goods.
   (ii) A rise in the price of substitute goods.
10. Complete the following table:

Price (₹)	Meenu	Veenu	Sheenu	Market Demand
3	7	(i)…	8	20
4	6	4	(ii)…	16
5	4	3	3	(iii)…
6	(iv)…	2	1	5

11. State whether the following will cause a shift of demand or movement along the same demand curve. Justify your answer giving one reason for each:
    (i) The effect of rise in the price of petrol:
        (1) On demand for cars.
        (2) On demand for public transport.
    (ii) The effect of a sharp increase in air fare due to rise in aviation fuel:
        (1) On tourism.
        (2) On business travel.
12. Explain four circumstances under which the law of demand does not operate.
13. Explain the law of demand with the help of assumptions, a diagram and a schedule. How does demand differs from want?
14. Many a time the inverse relationship between price and the amount purchased does not hold good. Explain this statement giving four reasons.

Recent Year Questions:
1. With the help of a suitable diagram explain the difference between decrease in demand and contraction in demand. [ICSE 2011]

2. Define composite demand. Clearly explain any three determinants of demand in a market. [ICSE 2012]
3. Define Joint demand. With the help of diagrams explain the difference between individual demand and market demand. [ICSE 2014]
4. State the Law of Demand. Explain three exceptions to this law. [ICSE 2015]
5. What is demand? Explain how quantity demanded of a commodity X will be affected by:
    (i) An increase in the price of its substitutes.
    (ii) Consumer credit facility.
    (iii) Government policy. [ICSE 2016]
6. (i) What happens to the demand curve when there is an increase in demand.
    (ii) Discuss three instances when demand will increase. [ICSE 2018]
7. Does a demand curve always have a negative slope. Give three reasons to justify your answer. [ICSE 2019]

02
Elasticity of Demand

We have so far studied the Law of Demand which simply represents the qualitative nature or behaviour or tendency of change in quantity demanded of a commodity with respect to a change in price. But it does not inform about the magnitude of change that how much is the change in quantity demanded due to change in price of the commodity. Hence, it is important to know exactly the quantitative behaviour of changes in quantity demanded when prices change, *i.e.*, whether the change in quantity demanded is proportional to change in price, or the change in quantity demanded is comparatively more than the change in price or it is less. It is equally important to understand, to measure and to determine this change. It should, however, be clearly borne in mind that change in quantity demanded with change in prices is not the same for all types of commodities. Different commodities have different degrees of responsiveness (elasticity) of demand with change in prices.

> **OVERVIEW**
>
> Elasticity of demand is the change in quantity demanded as a result of a change in price. There are various types of elasticity of demand—as perfectly elastic demand, perfectly inelastic demand, income elasticity of demand, cross elasticity of demand, etc. Elasticity of demand may be measured by proportional method. Elasticity of demand is affected by various factors.

Elasticity of demand refers to the "Percentage change in Quantity Demanded due to one Percentage change in the Price of a Commodity". So the Elasticity of Demand is that attribute according to which the demand contracts or extends under the pressure of changes in prices of a commodity.

"The elasticity of demand is a measure of the relative change in amount purchased in response to a relative change in price on a given demand curve." —**Prof. A. L. Meyers**

Mathematically it is represented as:

$$\text{Elasticity of Demand } (E_D) = \frac{\text{Percentage Change in Quantity Demanded}}{\text{Percentage Change in Price}}$$

Or,
$$\text{Elasticity of Demand } (E_D) = \frac{\Delta D}{\Delta P} \times \frac{P_0}{D_0}$$

where, D_0 is the Quantity Demanded prior to change in price and P_0 is Previous Price of the commodity and ΔD ($D_0 - D_1$) and ΔP ($P_0 - P_1$) represent the changes in Quantity Demanded and Price. D_1 and P_1 are the New quantity demanded and New price respectively.

"The elasticity (or responsiveness) of demand in a market is great or small according as the amount demanded increases much or little for a given fall in price, and diminishes much or little for a given rise in price."
—**Dr. Marshall**

TYPES OF ELASTICITY OF DEMAND

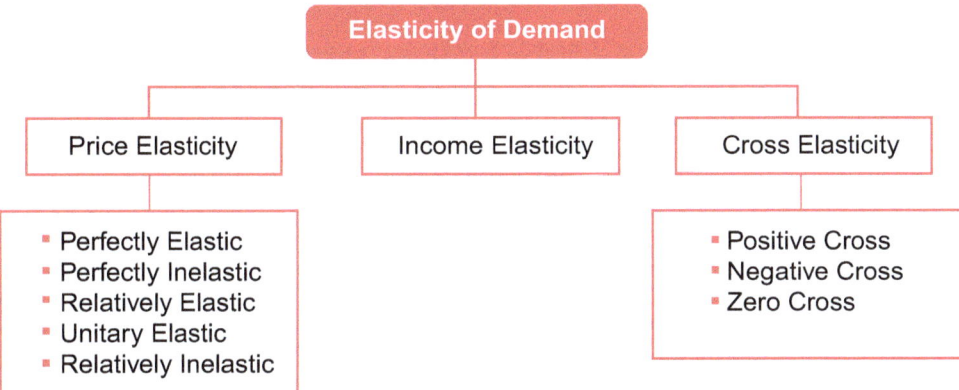

Price Elasticity of Demand (E_p): Price Elasticity of Demand may be defined as the percentage change in the quantity demanded of a commodity divided by the percentage change in the price of that commodity. When we represent the measurement of proportional change in demand (quantity demanded) due to change in price, is called price elasticity of demand.

Therefore,

$$\text{Price Elasticity of Demand } (E_p) = \frac{\%\text{ Change in Quantity Demanded of Commodity}}{\%\text{ Change in Price of Same Commodity}}$$

Or, Price Elasticity of Demand $(E_p) = \dfrac{\Delta D}{\Delta P} \times \dfrac{P_0}{D_0}$

Basically there is no difference between Elasticity of Demand (E_D) and Price Elasticity of Demand (E_p). They are mentioned separately because of subsequent mentioning of Income and Cross Elasticity of demand under elasticity of demand.

Income Elasticity of Demand (E_Y): This relates to the changes of demand in response to changes in income of an individual for a particular commodity. The income elasticity of demand represents the degree of responsiveness of the quantity of a particular commodity demanded by an individual when there is a change in his income. It is measured as a ratio between proportionate change in demand of a commodity in response to proportionate change in the income of the consumer. Therefore,

$$\text{Income Elasticity of Demand } (E_Y) = \frac{\%\text{ Change in Demand of a Commodity}}{\%\text{ Change in the Income of the Consumer}}$$

Or, Income Elasticity of Demand $(E_Y) = \dfrac{\Delta D}{\Delta P} \times \dfrac{P_0}{D_0}$

where, D_0 is the Demand of the commodity prior to change in income and Y_0 is income prior to the change and ΔD and ΔY represent the changes in Demand and Income of the consumer.

Example: Suppose the income of a person increase from ₹2,500 per month to ₹2,700 per month. As a result of this, his consumption of Cold drinks has increased from 30 bottles to 50 bottles per month.

$$\text{Income Elasticity of Demand } (E_Y) = \frac{\Delta D}{\Delta Y} \times \frac{Y_0}{D_0}$$

So, $\Delta D = 30 - 50 = -20$, $\Delta Y = 2{,}500 - 2{,}700 = -200$, $D_0 = 30$, $Y_0 = 2{,}500$

So, $\text{Income Elasticity of Demand } (E_Y) = \dfrac{-20}{-200} \times \dfrac{2{,}500}{30}$

$$= 8 \cdot 33 \text{ (more than unity)}$$

Cross Elasticity of Demand (E_C): Sometimes the price of one good will shift the demand for another good. For example, an increase in the price of Dove soap will increase the demand for Pears Soap. We measure this response by the cross elasticity of demand.

$$\text{Cross Elasticity of Demand } (E_C) = \frac{\text{\% Change in Demand of Commodity A}}{\text{\% Change in the Price of Commodity B}}$$

Example: Suppose the price of Dove soap goes up by 10% and as a result the demand of Pears soap increases by 2%, with no change in the price of Pears soap or anything else that would influence the demand for Pears soap. Then the cross elasticity of demand for Pears soap, with respect to the price of Dove soap, is 2%/10% = 0·2.

If the cross elasticity is positive, it means that an increase in the price of one good will increase the demand for the other goods. When we observe a positive cross elasticity, we say that the two goods are substitutes, as with Dove soap and Pears soap. Conversely, butter and margarine, tea and coffee are substitutes, so we would expect their cross elasticities to be positive.

If the cross elasticity of demand is negative, that means that an increase in the price of one good cuts the demand for the other. For example, if the price of motorcycles went up, we would expect to see a decline in the demand for bike helmets. In this type of cases, we say the goods are complementary.

DIFFERENT MAGNITUDES OF ELASTICITY OF DEMAND

(i) Perfectly Elastic Demand ($E_D = \infty$): When no change in price causes an variation in quantity demanded of a commodity, it is known as perfectly elastic demand. But in reality, such demand rarely occurs. It is just an extreme condition. *Fig. 2.1*

Table 2·1 : Perfectly Elastic Demand

Price (₹ per kg.)	Quantity Demanded (kgs.)
10.0	100
10.0	110
10.0	120

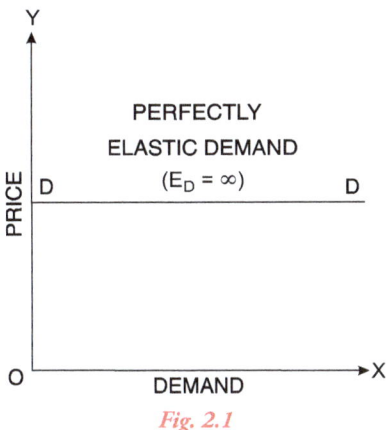

Fig. 2.1

(ii) **Perfectly Inelastic Demand ($E_D = 0$):** When there is no change in quantity demanded in spite of substantial increase or decrease in price, the demand is said to be perfectly inelastic. Such type of demand is observed in the case of necessities. *Fig. 2.2*

Table 2.2 : Perfectly Inelastic Demand

Price (₹ per kg.)	Quantity Demanded (kgs.)
10	100
8	100
6	100

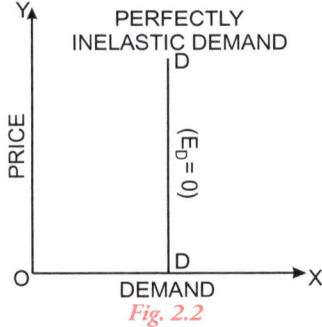

Fig. 2.2

(iii) **Relatively Elastic Demand ($E_D > 1$):** When a price change is small and change in quantity demanded is considerable, it is the situation of relatively elastic demand. The demand of luxuries, e.g., jewellery is an example of highly elastic demand. Its demand has considerable extension or contraction with relatively minor price changes. *Fig. 2.3*

Table 2.3 : Relatively Elastic Demand

Price (₹ per kg.)	Quantity Demanded (kgs.)
10	100
8	140
6	200

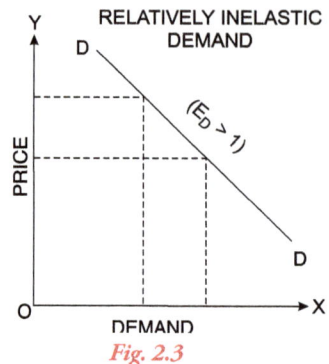

Fig. 2.3

(iv) Unitary Elastic Demand ($E_D = 1$): When the extension or contraction in quantity demanded is equally proportional to price changes, it is a case of unitary elastic demand. The demand for commodities of comforts, *e.g.*, electric fan, umbrella, raincoat, torch, etc., belong to this class. *Fig. 2.4*

Table 2·4 : Unitary Elastic Demand

Price (₹ per kg.)	Quantity Demanded (kgs.)
10	100
8	120
6	150

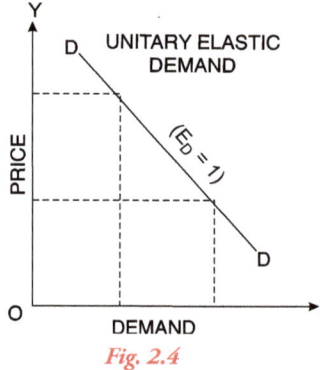

Fig. 2.4

(v) Relatively Inelastic Demand ($E_D < 1$): When a substantial change in prices has little effect on extension or contraction in quantity demanded of the commodity, the demand is known as relatively inelastic demand. The demands of salt, shoes, needles, etc., belong to this class. *Fig. 2.5*

Table 2·5 : Relatively Inelastic Demand

Price (₹ per kg.)	Quantity Demanded (kgs.)
10	100
8	95
6	90

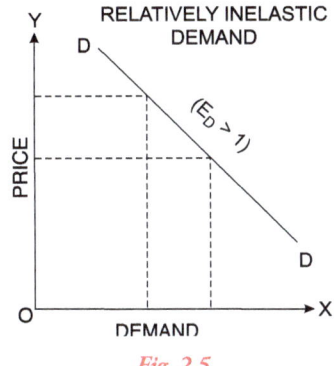

Fig. 2.5

METHODS OF MEASURING OF PRICE ELASTICITY OF DEMAND

Whenever, the elasticity of demand is referred to or mentioned as relatively elastic or relatively inelastic, it is considered as a vague expression. In order to explain this concept, there must be some method to measure the elasticity of demand of a commodity. The economists have proposed the following methods to measure the elasticity of demand:

(i) Percentage method
(ii) Total expenditure method
(iii) Geometrical (or Point) method
(iv) Arc method

Here, as per our syllabus requirement, we will discuss only the percentage method.

Proportional (Percentage) Method: In this method, the percentage change in demand is compared with percentage change in price. This method of determining the elasticity of demand was proposed by **Prof. A. Marshall.**

If the percentage change in demand (extension or contraction) is equally proportional to percentage change in price, the elasticity is said to be unity. If the percentage change in demand is more than the percentage change in price, the elasticity is more than unity and if the percentage change in demand is less than percentage change in price, the elasticity of demand is less than unity.

MATHEMATICALLY, THE ELASTICITY OF DEMAND IS REPRESENTED AS:

$$\text{Price Elasticity of Demand } (E_P) = \frac{\%\text{ Change in Quantity Demanded of Commodity}}{\%\text{ Change in Price of Same Commodity}}$$

Or, Price Elasticity of Demand $(E_P) = \frac{\Delta D}{\Delta P} \times \frac{P_0}{D_0}$

where, D_0 is the Quantity demanded prior to change in price and P_0 is Previous Price of the commodity and ΔD $(D_0 - D_1)$ and ΔP $(P_0 - P_1)$ represent the changes in Quantity demanded and Price. D_1 and P_1 are the New quantity demanded and New price respectively.

Solved Examples:

1. The price of milk increases from ₹12 per litre to ₹15 per litre and its consumption decreases from 4 litres per day to 3 litres per day. Calculate the elasticity of demand of milk.

Calculation:

$$\text{Increase in Price } (\Delta P) = ₹(12 - 15) = |-| ₹3 \text{ per litre}$$

[**Note :** (–) sign is ignored while calculating Price Elasticity of Demand as it shows the inverse relationship between price and quantity demanded.]

$$\% \text{ Increase in Price } = \frac{3}{12} = 25\% \qquad \ldots(A)$$

Decrease in Quantity Demanded $(\Delta D) = 4 - 3 = 1$ litre per day

$$\% \text{ Contraction in Demand } = \frac{1}{4} = 25\% \qquad \ldots(B)$$

$$\therefore \quad \text{Elasticity of Demand } (E_D) = \frac{25\%}{25\%} = 1 \text{ (Unity)}$$

2. The price of an umbrella reduces to ₹40 each from ₹50 each and consequently the demand of an umbrella increases from 100 pieces to 150 pieces per day. Calculate the elasticity of demand of umbrella.

    Calculation:

    $$\text{Reduction in Price } (\Delta P) = ₹50 - ₹40 = ₹10 \text{ each}$$

    $$\% \text{ Reduction in Price } = \frac{10}{50} = 20\% \qquad \ldots(A)$$

    Increase in Quantity Demanded $(\Delta D) = 100 - 150 = |-| 50$ pieces

    [**Note :** (–) sign is ignored while calculating Price Elasticity of Demand as it shows the inverse relationship between price and quantity demanded.]

    $$\% \text{ Increase in Quantity Demanded} = \frac{50}{100} = 50\% \qquad \ldots(B)$$

    $$\text{Elasticity of Demand } (E_D) = \frac{50\%}{20\%} = 2 \cdot 5 \text{ (Greater than Unity)}$$

3. The price of shirt buttons decreases from ₹4 per dozen to ₹3 per dozen. But the demand changes from 100 dozens to 105 dozens per day. Calculate the elasticity of demand of buttons.

    Calculation:

    Increase in Quantity Demanded $(\Delta D) = 100 - 105 = |-| 5$ dozens per day

    $$\% \text{ Change in Demand } = \frac{5}{100} = 5\% \qquad \ldots(A)$$

    $$\text{Reduction in Price } (\Delta P) = ₹4 - ₹3 = ₹1$$

    $$\% \text{ Reduction in Price } = \frac{1}{4} = 25\% \qquad \ldots(B)$$

    $$\therefore \quad \text{Elasticity of Demand } (E_D) = \frac{5\%}{25\%} = 0 \cdot 2 \text{ (Less than Unity)}$$

FACTORS AFFECTING PRICE ELASTICITY OF DEMAND
OR
DETERMINANTS OF PRICE ELASTICITY OF DEMAND

In fact, several factors are to be considered before deciding whether a demand for a particular commodity is *inelastic, relatively elastic or highly elastic*.

Nature of Commodity: The demand for the items of necessities (*i.e.,* essential items) is generally less elastic or inelastic. Such commodities are bought in certain fixed quantities irrespective of their prices. The demand for salt, wheat and rice will remain practically the same. In the similar way, the demands for the items of comforts are relatively elastic whereas for luxuries, the demands are highly elastic. The demand for an electric fan (a commodity of comfort) is relatively elastic while the demand for a car (an item of luxury) is highly elastic. With minor changes in prices, more people are motivated to avail of the advantage in fulfilling their demands.

As already pointed out earlier, the necessities, comforts and luxuries are relative terms and differ from person to person, depending upon the level of income and various conditions of their economic activities. For example, a car is an item of luxury for an office peon, an item of comfort for a college professor, but it may be a necessity for a doctor.

Proportion of Total Expenditure Involved: When the expenditure to be incurred for a particular commodity is a small portion of the total expenditure (or say income), the demand will generally be inelastic or less elastic. Any change in price will not alter the demand of that commodity. The newspaper and the matchbox belong to such type of commodity. On the other hand, the demand for milk is elastic, because it absorbs a good proportion of total expenditure. Its demand is more, when prices are low.

Availability of Substitutes: The commodities, for which other substitutes are available in the market; have more elastic demands as compared to commodities without many substitutes. A good example is that of tea for which coffee is generally available as a substitute. A change in the price of tea causes almost proportional change in demand of coffee. Contrary to the above, the common salt has no substitute and so any increase or decrease in the price of salt does not affect its demand.

Multipurpose Use of a Commodity: If any commodity can be used for several purposes, its demand is generally elastic. As compared to this, the commodity, having one or two uses only, has less elastic demand. For example, the electricity has many types of uses and when its price goes down, people get encouraged to use it more and more. On the contrary, a pair of shoes or a shirt has a specific use only and so its demand is less elastic.

Price Level: When the price of a commodity is very high or very low, the demand is generally less elastic or inelastic. For example, a car is priced at about ₹2 lakh and a change of price by ₹500 will have almost no effect on its demand. Similarly, needles, shirts-buttons and matchboxes are cheap commodities and even 100% changes in the price of these goods does not affect the demand to any noticeable degree. However, the commodities having moderate prices have an appreciable change in demand with changes in prices. For example, woollen clothes, raincoats, etc., belong to the category of commodities having moderate price and the demand of such items is relatively elastic.

Distribution of Income: If the distribution of income in the society is not equitable, the demand from the poor section of society is more susceptible to price change whereas that from rich section is almost unaffected by price variations. The poor people would prefer to have cheaper commodities, so that they are able to derive maximum satisfaction from their low (or say meager) income. On the contrary, the rich people are in a position to fulfil their demands irrespective of the price changes of the goods and can derive maximum satisfaction because of their high income.

However, when there is equitable distribution of income in the society, there is no such class as very rich people or very poor people. Under that condition, the demand of the commodities is generally elastic, because there is nobody who will remain unaffected by price changes. Majority of people will be affected by price changes and accordingly large-scale variations in demand are very likely to take place.

Habits, Tastes and Customs of the People: Some people have a habit of using a particular type or variety of commodity or have a preferential taste for it. Besides, some commodities are consumed because of prevailing customs in the society. Such commodities generally have inelastic demands. These will be consumed irrespective of price variations.

Possibilities of Postponement of Consumption (or Use): If the use of a commodity cannot be postponed or deferred, its demand is usually inelastic or less elastic. For example, as the consumption of raincoat or umbrella cannot be postponed during the monsoon, its demand is usually inelastic because it will have to be purchased on whatever price it is available. On the contrary, the demand of shoes and clothes can be postponed and can be purchased at a time when the prices are low. So the demands of such items which have greater possibilities of postponement, are usually more elastic in nature.

Determinants of Price Elasticity of Demand

Factors	Elasticity of Demand is more when
1. Nature of commodity	1. High priced luxuries are available.
2. Proportion of total expenditure involved	2. A good proportion of total expenditure is involved in the commodity.
3. Availability of substitutes	3. More substitutes are available.
4. Multipurpose use of a commodity	4. The number of uses of the commodity is more.
5. Price level	5. The price of the good is high.
6. Distribution of income	6. The income of the consumer is low.
7. Habits, tastes and customs of the people	7. Commodity is not consumed as per the habits and customs of people.
8. Possibility of postponement of consumption (or use)	8. The commodity has greater possibility of postponement.

LESSON AT A GLANCE

Elasticity of Demand: **Prof. A. L. Meyers** has defined elasticity of demand in the following words: "The elasticity of demand is a measure of the relative change in amount purchased in response to a relative change in price on a given demand curve".

Types of Elasticity of Demand: (i) Price elasticity of demand; (ii) Income elasticity of demand; (iii) Cross elasticity of demand.

(i) Price Elasticity of Demand: This relates to the measurement of proportional change in demand due to change in price.

(ii) Income Elasticity of Demand: This relates to the changes of demand in response to changes in income of an individual for a particular commodity. The income elasticity of demand represents the degree of responsiveness of the quantity of a particular commodity demanded by an individual when there is a change in his income.

(iii) Cross Elasticity of Demand: The cross elasticity of demand of a commodity is the responsiveness of its quantity to the change in the price of the other commodity (the substitutes and complements).

Different Magnitudes of Elasticity of Demand: (i) Perfectly elastic demand; (ii) Perfectly inelastic demand; (iii) Relatively elastic demand; (iv) Unitary elastic demand; and (v) Relatively inelastic demand.

Methods of Measuring of Elasticity of Demand: The Proportional (percentage) method for measurement of elasticity of demand.

Factors Affecting Price Elasticity of Demand: (i) Nature of commodity; (ii) Proportion of total expenditure involved; (iii) Availability of substitutes; (iv) Multipurpose use of a commodity; (v) Price level; (vi) Distribution of income; (vii) Habits, tastes and customs of the people; (viii) Possibilities of postponement of consumption (or use).

PROJECT WORK

Prepare a list of items of different categories like luxury goods, goods of comfort, goods of daily need, etc.

Conduct a survey of market in your locality and prepare a list of price of these commodities over a period of six months.

Mention any change that occurred in the demand of the items listed by you.

On the basis of the information gathered by you, classify the items on the basis of elasticity of their demand.

QUESTIONS

A. Short Answer Type Questions:
1. Define elasticity of demand.
2. What is perfectly elastic demand?

3. Name the types of elasticity of demand.
4. What do you understand by relatively elastic demand?
5. What is income elasticity of demand?
6. Explain cross elasticity of demand
7. What will be the elasticity of demand for goods to which the consumer is habituated?
8. Why is the demand for water inelastic?
9. What would be the shape of demand curve of a commodity when its price elasticity of demand is zero?
10. What is the elasticity of demand for jointly demanded goods like car and petrol, pen and ink?
11. When the price of a commodity changes by 80%, the quantity demanded increases by 100%. Find out the price elasticity of demand.
12. For each of the following state whether it has inelastic demand or elastic demand:
    (i) Luxury cars.   (ii) Life saving drugs.   (iii) English textbook of class X.
13. Study the table given below and state whether demand is elastic or inelastic. Give reasons for your answer.

Price (in ₹)	Total outlay (in ₹)
20	25
30	18

14. The nature of a commodity determines its price elasticity of demand. Explain.
15. If commodity X and Y are complementary goods, what will be the cross elasticity of demand.

Recent Year Questions:

1. Indicate the degree of elasticity of demand of the following demand curves:
   [ICSE 2013]

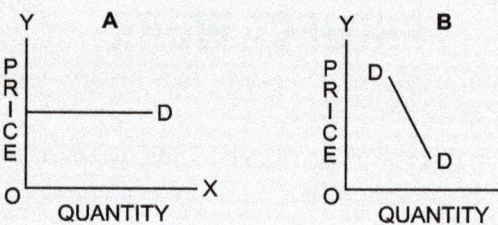

2. The price of milk rises from ₹26 to ₹30 per litre and its demand falls from four litres per day to two litres per day. Calculate the elasticity of demand for milk.
   [ICSE 2013]
3. State whether the following statement is true or false. Give reasons.
   "The price elasticity of demand for commodities, having close substitutes is relatively high."
   [ICSE 2014]
4. Give a reason for the following statement:
   The demand for newspaper is inelastic.
   [ICSE 2015]

5. A consumer purchased 10 units of a commodity when its price was ₹5 per unit. He purchases 12 units of the commodity when price falls to ₹4 per unit. Calculate the price elasticity of demand for the commodity. [ICSE 2015]
6. When is the demand for a good said to be perfectly inelastic? [ICSE 2016]
7. State the formula for calculating the price elasticity of demand using the percentage method. [ICSE 2019]

B. Long Answer Type Questions:

1. What do you mean by elasticity of demand? Explain briefly.
2. What is the relation between slope and elasticity of demand?
3. Explain the income elasticity of demand and cross elasticity of demand.
4. Describe the factors affecting the elasticity of demand.

Recent Year Questions:

1. (i) Define price elasticity of demand. Give the percentage formula of price elasticity of demand.
   (ii) As a result of 5% fall in the price of a good, its demand rises by 12%. Find the price elasticity of demand
   (iii) What type of goods is this? Give reasons.
   (iv) Give two examples of such a goods. [ICSE 2009]
2. Define price elasticity of demand. Explain how the following factors determine price elasticity of demand:
   (i) Existence of substitute goods.
   (ii) Nature of the commodity.
   (iii) Proportion of expenditure incurred in a household budget. [ICSE 2013]
3. What do you understand by price elasticity of demand? With the help of diagrams explain the conditions when:
   (i) $\sum_p > 1$ (ii) $\sum_p < 1$ (iii) $\sum_p = 1$ [ICSE 2015]

C. Numerical Type Questions:

1. Price of an item X rises from ₹20 to ₹30 per unit. Consequently its demand falls by 10 units and becomes 100 units. Determine price elasticity of demand. [Ans. 0·33]
2. Determine price elasticity of demand using percentage method:

Price (in ₹)	Total outlay (in ₹)
20	100
30	200

3. Price of rice falls from ₹5 to ₹4 per kg. this leads to an increase in the demand from 10 kg to 20 kg in a month. Comment on its elasticity of demand. [Ans. 5]
4. A consumer spends ₹80 on a commodity at a price of ₹1 per unit and ₹100 at a price of ₹2 per unit. What is the price elasticity of demand?
5. Originally, a product was selling for ₹10 and the quantity demanded was 1000 units. The product price changes to ₹14 and as a result the quantity demanded changes to 500 units. Calculate the price elasticity. [Ans. 1·25]

03 Theory of Supply

Demand represents the consumers' side of the market while the supply shows the sellers' side of the market. The equilibrium price and quantity in the market is determined by both the force of demand and supply. In the previous chapters we have understood the demand side. This chapter talks about the supply side of the commodity market.

Supply means that quantity of a particular commodity which a seller is ready to sell at a given price, at a particular place and during a particular period of time.

"Supply may be defined as a schedule that shows the various amounts of a product for which a particular seller is willing and is able to produce and make it available for sale in the market at each specific price in a set of possible prices during some given period."
—**Mcconnel**

"The supply of goods is the quantity offered for sale in a given market at a given time at various prices."
—**Thomas**

OVERVIEW

As the 'demand' of a commodity motivates the consumers to participate in economic activities to fulfill their requirements, in the same way the 'supply' of a commodity motivates the producers and suppliers to participate in productive activities to earn profits.

The interaction between the 'demand' and 'supply' actually maintains an equilibrium in the market. When price increases, the consumption (or say the demand for the item) decreases. This causes accumulation of stocks, if supply is maintained at the same level. Naturally, either supply is to be reduced or prices are to be decreased, so as to restore the equilibrium.

Like demand, supply is also affected at a particular price. The supply is different from stock which means the total quantity of a particular commodity is in the possession of a supplier.

Difference between Supply and Stock

Stock is that quantity of a commodity which is available with the sellers in the market at a specific time whereas supply is that quantity of commodity which a seller is ready to sell in the market on a definite price at a definite time. Thus stock is the amount of a produce stored up for future use. One must remember that supply and stock are the same for perishable goods like fruits, milk, etc. But for non-perishable commodities, stock is the potential supply.

DETERMINANTS OR FACTORS GOVERNING THE SUPPLY

Following are the major factors which govern the supply of a commodity:

Price of a Commodity: Other things remaining same, it is more profitable to sell a commodity at a higher price. Therefore, it is natural for the sellers to offer more of a commodity as the price ascends. In other words, the price of the commodity affects the quantity offered for sale. More quantities will be supplied at a higher price.

Prices of Related Commodities: Prices of related goods generally affect the relative profitability of a commodity, and thus exercise their influence on its supply. Let us say that the prices of nylon, rayon and silk clothes have risen, while the prices of cotton clothes do not alter. Obviously in the new situation, the relative profitability of cotton clothes has declined and as a result of it, their supply will be reduced.

Objectives of the Producers: In economic theory, it is often assumed that firms operate with a view to maximise their profits. But recently some empirical studies have revealed that sometimes firms wish to capture extensive markets for their products so as to maximise their sales. It is based on the principle that when the sales are increased, the ultimate profits also increase. If the firm is guided by the latter objective, it will offer relatively larger quantities for sale in various markets at different prices.

State of Technology: Technological developments result in an incessant increase in the supply of various products. Technological improvement, on the one hand, brings down the costs, and on the other hand raises the profits of the producers. This naturally provides incentives to them to increase the supply of their products. An example is the innovation and improvement in textile machinery which has considerably increased the production and supply of cotton textiles.

Prices of Factors of Production: When prices of either of the inputs (factors) of production increase, the cost of product also increases which discourages the producers-suppliers to increase the supply. On the other hand, when there is a decrease in the prices of inputs, the final product becomes cheaper and margin of profit increases, which ultimately results in an increased supply of the commodity to the market.

Natural Conditions: Natural conditions play a very important role in the supply of agricultural products. rain, frost, floods, dust-storms, pests, earthquakes, etc., adversely affect the agricultural production and thus, the supply of agricultural goods also varies with natural conditions.

Agreement among Producers: Supply is also influenced by the agreement among producers. They form a pool and enter into an agreement to restrict the supply of a commodity at some particular time. During this period, they create artificial scarcity. Consequently the supply is curtailed and they earn surplus profits. The motives behind such policy may be either economic or political. An example is the reduction in crude oil supplies, by oil producing countries during the period of conflicts.

Future Price Expectations: If the sellers expect a price reduction in future, they prefer to dispose off their stocks at the earliest as a result of which the supply of commodity increases. On the other hand, if any increase in price is expected, the suppliers will hold their stocks to earn higher profits in near future.

Number of Producers (Suppliers): When the number of producers or suppliers increases, the supply of a commodity will be more. With the decrease in number of producers or suppliers, the quantity supplied to market also decreases.

Monopolistic Policies: When there is only one producer or supplier of any particular commodity, this situation is known as monopoly. Such producer or supplier actually adopts monopolistic powers and deliberately changes either the supply of the commodity or prices, so as to earn maximum profit.

Economic and Political Conditions: If the political condition in a country is unstable, a kind of fear prevails among the common people and the business community. The net result is disturbance and dislocation in organised business and trade conditions which in turn, makes entire supply position abnormal.

In the same way, the economic crisis, strikes, lock-outs in factories and transport system cause a decline in the supply of the commodities in general. Even the setback in international trade often affects the normal manufacturing conditions and overall supply position is dislocated.

Taxes and Subsidies: The taxation and the subsidy policy of the government are other factors which regulate the supply of particular commodity. Indirect taxes (such as sales tax, excise duty, etc.) imposed by the government on a commodity are likely to increase its cost of production and, thereby, it may reduce its supply. On the contrary, a reduction in taxes may have the opposite effect.

Sometimes government pays subsidies on some commodities so as to assist the consumers to purchase the same and the producers to produce more of the commodities. Increase in subsidy increases both the consumption and the supply. On the contrary, decrease in subsidy increases the cost and reduces the supply. For example, the high import duty on some goods will restrict the import of those items from other countries and in turn, this policy will encourage the indigenous production of those particular commodities.

SUPPLY FUNCTION

A supply function is an algebraic expression showing the relationship between supply and the determinants of supply. A simple supply function can be stated as follows:

$$S_X = f(P_X, P_R, F, T, G)$$

Hence, *the supply function describes the functional relationship between supply of a commodity (say X) and other determinants of supply,* i.e., price of the commodity (P_X), price of a related commodity (P_R), price of the factors of production (F), technology (T), and goals or general objectives of the producer (G).

Each of these factors influences supply in a different way. To study the effect of each factor, we take other factors as constant, while considering the relationship between supply and one of the above variables. For example, if we want to study the relationship between price and supply of commodity X, we shall assume other factors like PR, F, T and G to remain constant or unchanged.

For a simple theory of price we want to know how the quantity supplied of a commodity varies with its own price. There is a functional relationship between price and quantity supplied of a commodity. The functional relationship can alternatively be written as:

$$\boxed{S_X = f(P_X)}$$

where, S_X is the supply of commodity X, f = function of and P_X = price of the commodity X.

SUPPLY SCHEDULE

The supply schedule is a type of tabulated representation of relationship between prices of the commodity and the quantity which the seller is ready to offer for sale. Similar to demand schedule, the supply schedule can be either 'Individual Supply Schedule' or 'Market Supply Schedule'.

INDIVIDUAL SUPPLY SCHEDULE

The *'Individual Supply Schedule'* represents the quantities of a commodity which any particular person is ready to offer for sale in the market against a series of prices (*i.e.*, at different prices) at a particular time. An imaginary individual supply schedule for Apples is illustrated in *Table 3.1.*

Table 3.1 : Individual Supply Schedule for Apples

Price per kg. (₹)	Quantity Supplied (kg.)
2	20
3	40
4	50
5	60

MARKET SUPPLY SCHEDULE

The *Market Supply Schedule* on the other hand, represents the total quantity of a commodity offered by all the suppliers (sellers) to the market, at different prices at a particular time. An imaginary market supply schedule for Apples is illustrated in *Table 3.2.*

Table 3.2 : Market Supply Schedule for Apples

Price per kg. (₹) (Col. 1)	Quantity Supplied (kg.) by Seller A (Col. 2)	Quantity Supplied (kg.) by Seller B (Col. 3)	Market Supplylitres (kg.) (Col. 2 + Col. 3)
2	20	40	60
3	40	50	90
4	50	60	110
5	60	70	130

Distinction between Individual Supply Schedule and Market Supply Schedule

Individual Supply Schedule	Market Supply Schedule
1. The individual supply schedule represents the quantities of a commodity which any particular individual seller is ready to offer for sale.	1. The market supply schedule represents the total quantity of commodity offered by all traders to the market at different prices, at a particular moment of time.
2. The individual supply curve can be used to graphically represent it for a particular commodity.	2. The market supply curve represents the market supply schedule for particular commodity.

Distinction between Demand Schedule and Supply Schedule

Demand Schedule	Supply Schedule
1. This represents different quantities which all the purchasers desire to purchase at different possible prices at a particular time.	1. This represents different quantities of a commodity that all the traders combined together are ready to supply to the market, at different possible prices.
2. The demand schedule reflects the reaction of consumers in respect of varying prices of a particular commodity.	2. The supply schedule reflects the behaviour and reaction of producers (or suppliers) with respect of varying prices.
3. The demand schedule obeys the law of demand.	3. The supply schedule follows the laws of supply.
4. It is assumed that all other factors (except the price) influencing the demand of particular item do not change.	4. It is assumed that all other factors which determine the supply of an item are unchanged, except its price.
5. It can be graphically represented by individual or market demand curves.	5. It can be graphically represented by individual or market supply curves.

SUPPLY CURVE

Supply curve is a graphic presentation of supply schedule indicating positive relationship between price of a commodity and its quantity supplied. The relationship between the quantities offered for sale in the market and the prices can be graphically illustrated. For this, the prices are plotted along y-axis and quantities along X-axis *(Fig. 3.1)*. The curve SS', obtained by joining various points is called as *Supply Curve*. This type of curves can be drawn to represent either the 'Market Supply' or the 'Individual Supply', for a particular commodity at any given instant or a period of time.

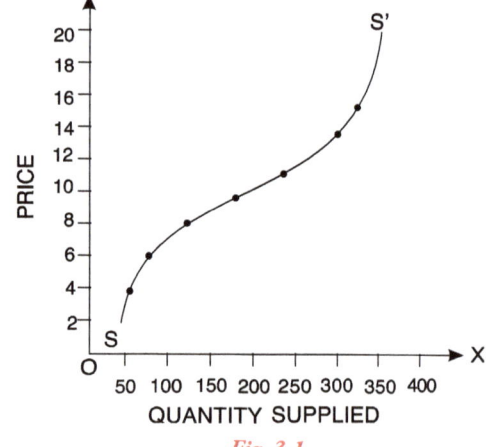

Fig. 3.1

The supply curve carries the same explanation and assumptions as a supply schedule. Like supply schedule, supply curve is also of two types:

1. Individual supply curve,
2. Market supply curve.

1. Individual Supply Curve: An individual supply curve is defined as the curve which shows various quantities of a given commodity which an individual producer is willing to supply at different prices during a given period of time, assuming no change in all other factors affecting supply. Individual supply schedule of *Table 3.1* is plotted graphically to derive an individual supply curve as shown in *Fig. 3.2* below.

Four points A, B, C, D corresponding to each price-quantity combination shown in *Table 3.1* are plotted in *Fig. 3.2* where we show price on Y-axis and quantity supplied on X-axis. By drawing a smooth curve through these four points, we get a curve SS, which is known as the supply curve. The positively sloping supply curve SS, shows the direct relationship between the price and the quantity supplied.

2. **Market Supply Curve:** Market supply curve is the curve which shows various quantities of a commodity which all the producers are willing to produce and sell at different prices during a given period of time. Market supply schedule of *Table 3.2* is plotted as market supply curve SS in *Fig. 3.3*.

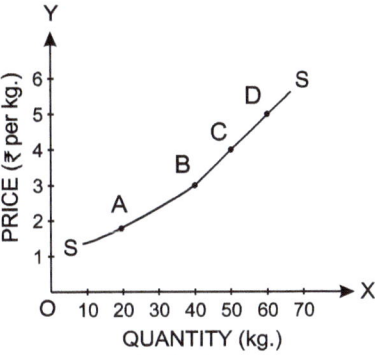

Fig. 3.2 : Individual Supply Curve

Here we have drawn market supply curve by directly plotting the market information about price of a commodity and the quantity supplied at each price. However, market supply curve can also be drawn as the horizontal summation of individual supply curves in the same way as we did in case of market demand curve in chapter 2. A market supply curve is upward (positive) sloping from left to right indicating a direct relation between price and supply. A market supply curve is sometimes called as industry's supply curve.

It is evident from *Table 3.1* and *3.2* as well as from *Fig. 3.2* and *3.3* that if price is less than ₹2 per kg, the sellers will not be prepared to sell any unit.

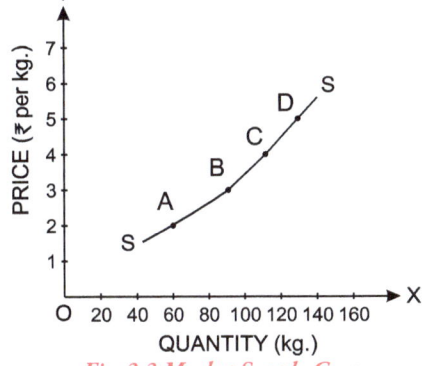

Fig. 3.3 Market Supply Curve

"*The price below which the sellers are not willing to sell their goods is called the reserve price.*"

A supply curve, like the demand curve, can be straight line or curve line. The typical supply curve slopes upward from left to right, *i.e.*, it has a positive slope. A positively sloping curve depicts the law of supply. Any particular supply curve is drawn on the basis of ceteris paribus, *i.e.*, other things remaining the same.

LAW OF SUPPLY

Now it must be clear that supply of a commodity is directly related to its price, *i.e.*, supply increases with increase in price and decreases with a reduction in price. Contrary to this, we have seen earlier that the relationship is just inverse in case of demand, *i.e.*, demand extends when price falls and *vice-versa*. On this basis, a general law of supply can also be concluded (similar to the Law of Demand) in the following words:

"*Other things remaining same, as the price of a commodity rises, the supply extends and as the price falls, the supply contracts.*"

At this stage, it is but natural to enquire as to why the supply extends at higher price and contracts at lower price? The answer is quite simple. The sellers will earn more profit at higher price other things being constant including cost of production, so they are motivated to sell more quantities of the commodities at higher price.

In the definition of *law of supply*, the qualifying condition, *i.e.*, other things remaining same, is very important condition. The 'other things' include the cost structure, fashion, financial position of seller, etc. If any of these vary, the quantities supplied will also be different and a deviation from the law of supply may be observed.

Assumptions of Law of Supply:
- There is no change in the goals of the firm.
- There is no change in the prices of related goods.
- The cost of all factors of production remains constant.
- The technology level remains constant.
- The future expectation regarding price does not change.
- The commodity is divisible.
- Law of supply states only a static situation.

WHY DOES THE SUPPLY CURVE SLOPES UPWARD TO THE RIGHT

The law of supply states that higher the price higher will be the quantity supplied and if the price is lower, the quantity supplied of the commodity will be lower. Hence, the price and the quantity supplied show the positive or direct relationship.

The very first reason between this positive relationship is the rising profit with rising price if other things remain constant. This motivates a firm to increase its supply of the commodity as well as attract other firms to enter the industry and supply the commodity.

Another reason is the substitution effect. The commodity whose price has gone up becomes more beneficial than its substitutes. So the suppliers withdraw the productive resources from the supply of substitutes and increase the production and supply of the commodity with rising price.

MOVEMENT ALONG THE SUPPLY CURVE AND SHIFT IN SUPPLY CURVE

Movement along supply curve refers to change in the quantity supplied of a commodity in response to change in the prices of the same commodity, other things remaining constant. It is expressed as extension or contraction of supply.

Whereas shift in supply curve means, increase or decrease in supply of a commodity at the existing price of the commodity due to change in determinants of supply other than the own price of the commodity. It refers to increase or decrease in supply.

MOVEMENT ALONG THE SUPPLY CURVE: VARIATIONS (EXTENSION OR CONTRACTION) OF SUPPLY

We have noticed from above that the quantity supplied of the commodity increases with a rise in its price and decreases when the price falls. The increase in quantity supplied is termed as extension while a decrease in it is called as contraction.

These variations can be represented in *Fig. 3.4*.

The point A on the supply curve SS' represents the quantity Q supplied at price P. When the price increases to P_1, the corresponding point on supply curve SS' is B, which represents the quantity supplied as Q_1. This is the extension of supply.

Similarly when the price decreases to P_2, the corresponding point on supply curve is C, which represents the quantity supplied as Q_2. It is the contraction of supply.

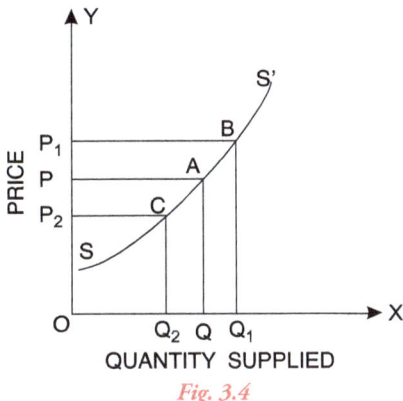

Fig. 3.4

SHIFT IN SUPPLY CURVES

When there is increase or decrease in supply of a commodity despite the price being same, this is known as shift in supply curve. This happens due to the change in certain conditions or factors (except the price of the commodity) on which supply depends. These conditions are assumed to be constant or given at a particular time. It is given by the phrase, 'other things being equal'. As long as these factors or conditions remain the same or remain constant, the supply schedule of the product will be almost the same. But when the assumptions change, the supply schedule (and the supply curve) will shift. When the assumptions change for the better, there will be a new supply curve but at a lower level (downward or rightward shift); if the assumptions change for the worse, there will be a new supply curve at a higher level (upward or leftward shift).

INCREASE IN SUPPLY: DOWNWARD OR RIGHTWARD SHIFT IN SUPPLY

Look at the given figures 3.5 (a) and 3.5 (b). The horizontal axis represents quantity supplied and vertical axis the price of the product. In both the figures, SS_1 stands for the original supply curve and S_2S_3 stands for the new supply curve after the assumptions have changed. In *fig. 3.5 (a)* the price is OP at which the producers initially supplied OQ quantity but are now willing to offer more, *i.e.*, OQ_1. This increase in supply is not due to rise in the price, for the price remains constant at OP, but it is because of change in the assumptions as for instance, fall in the cost of production, use of better techniques and processes of production, creation of more and larger firms, etc.

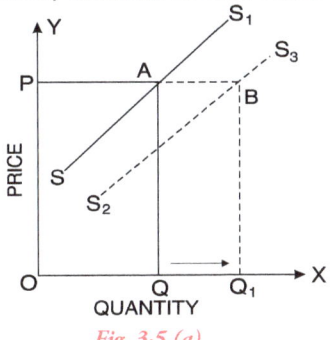
Fig. 3.5 (a)

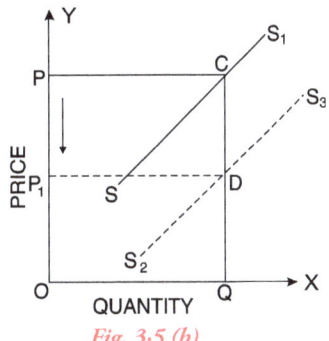
Fig. 3.5 (b)

In *fig. 3.5 (b)*, the same fact is illustrated, but in a different manner. In this figure, OQ quantity was supplied at OP price. But when the supply curve shifts downward, the same quantity OQ is supplied at a lower price, *viz.* OP_1. A lower supply curve represents the increase in supply which means:

(a) At a given price a larger quantity is supplied.

(b) A given quantity is supplied at a lower price.

DECREASE IN SUPPLY: UPWARD OR LEFTWARD SHIFT IN SUPPLY

A decrease in supply of a product is indicated by a higher supply curve, *fig. 3.6 (a)* and *3.6 (b)* represent the decrease in supply. In both the figures SS_1 refers to the original supply curve and S_2S_3 represents the supply curve under new circumstances, which may have occurred due to shortage of production on account of rise in cost, expectation for higher price in future, inferior technology, decrease in number of firms, etc. In *fig. 3.6 (b)*, suppliers are willing to supply the same quantity but only at a higher price. The decrease in supply will, therefore imply:

(a) At a given price, a smaller quantity will be supplied; and

(b) A given quantity will be offered at a higher price.

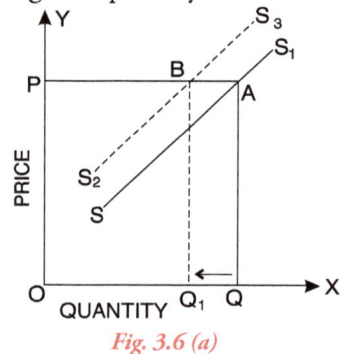

Fig. 3.6 (a)

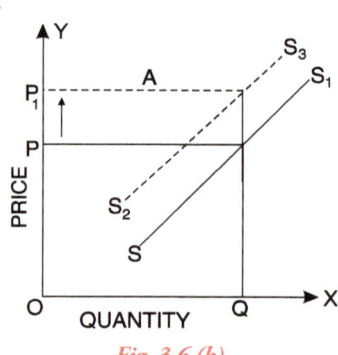

Fig. 3.6 (b)

We can repeat the fact that expansion and contraction of supply are due to the changes in price but increase and decrease in supply are due to the changes in the determinants of supply.

WHY THE SUPPLY CURVE SLOPES UPWARD?

The law of supply explains the relationship between price of a commodity and its supply. This law states that the supply of a commodity increases on increasing its price and decreases on a decrease in its price. Thus, there is a direct relationship between the price and the supply of a commodity. Supply curve slopes upward. But the question arises why does it happen and why does the supply curve slope upward? Main reasons for the operation of this law are as follows:

1. The price of a commodity serves as an incentive for producers and sellers. If the price of a commodity increases, it will motivate producers to produce more and sellers to sell more of that commodity in the expectation of more profits when other things including cost remain constant.

2. If the price of a commodity falls, producers and sellers would like to decrease the supply of that commodity because otherwise it will reduce their profit margin.

EXCEPTIONS TO THE LAW OF SUPPLY

Some of the exceptional conditions to the law of supply are described below:

- The law of supply does not apply to the rare articles like ancient coins, etc. Their supply being fixed, cannot be changed with change in price.

- Sellers will be forced to sell early in case of the perishable goods no matter whether the price is rising.
- The law of supply does not apply strictly to agricultural products whose supply is governed by natural factors.
- In case, if any seller is hard pressed for cash, he will like to sell his stocks at lower price. He may also reduce the price further, to attract the more purchasers.

LESSON AT A GLANCE

Supply: Supply of a commodity refers to the quantity which a seller is ready to sell at a given price, at a particular place and at a given time.

Determinants or Factors Governing the Supply: (i) Price of a commodity; (ii) Prices of related commodities; (iii) Objectives of the producers; (iv) State of technology; (v) Prices of factors of production; (vi) Natural conditions; (vii) Agreement among producers; (viii) Future price expectations; (ix) Number of producers (suppliers); (x) Monopolistic policies; (xi) Economic and political conditions; (xii) Taxes and subsidies.

Supply Function: A supply function is an algebraic expression showing the relationship between supply and the determinants of supply. A simple supply function can be stated as follows:

$$S_X = f(P_X, P_R, F, T, G)$$

Hence, the supply function describes the functional relationship between supply of a commodity (Say X) and other determinants of supply, *i.e.*, price of the commodity (P_X), price of a related commodity (P_R), price of the factors of production (F), technology (T), and goals or general objectives of the producers (G).

Supply Schedule: The supply schedule is a type of tabulated representation of relationship between prices of the commodity and the quantity which the seller is ready to offer for sale. Similar to demand schedule, the supply schedule can be either 'Individual Supply Schedule' or 'Market Supply Schedule'.

Individual Supply Schedule: The *'Individual supply schedule'* represents the quantities of a commodity which any particular person is ready to offer for sale in the market against a series of prices (*i.e.*, at different prices) at a particular time.

Market Supply Schedule: The *Market Supply Schedule* on the other hand, represents the total quantity of a commodity offered by all the suppliers (sellers) to the market, at different prices at a particular time.

Supply Curve: Supply curve shows the relationship between market prices and the amount which producers are prepared to bring to the market. Supply curve is also of two types : 1. Individual supply curve, 2. Market supply curve.

Law of Supply: The Law of supply expresses the relationship between the price of a commodity and its supply. When there is a rise in price, supply extends and when the price falls, supply contracts; other things being equal.

Movement along the Supply Curve: Variations (Extension or Contraction) of Supply: We have noticed that the supply of the commodity increases with a rise in its price and the supply decreases when the price falls. The increase in supply is termed as *extension* while a decrease in supply is called as *contraction*.

Shift in Supply Curves: Increase and Decrease in Supply: Increase or decrease in supply are due to changes in the determinants of supply. But the changes in assumptions can take place in long run only, though minor changes can take place in the short period as well.

Exceptions to the Law of Supply: Some of the exceptional conditions to the law of supply are: (i) The law of supply does not apply to the rare articles like ancient coins, etc. Their supply being fixed, cannot be changed with change in price; (ii) Sellers will be forced to sell in case of the perishable goods no matter whether the price is rising; (iii) The law of supply does not apply strictly to agricultural products whose supply is governed by natural factors; (iv) In case, if any seller is hard pressed for cash, he will like to sell his stock at lower price. He may also reduce the price further, to attract the more purchasers.

PROJECT WORK

Conduct a market survey daily for a period of one month and collect information about prices, quantities supplied and quantities purchased in regard to two vegetables, two fruits, common salt, wheat, rice, two pulses and milk.

On the basis of the above information, prepare a demand schedule, supply schedule and determine the market price for each day.

Calculate average equilibrium price (or normal price) of each commodity for the month. The average price should be treated as 'normal price' of the commodity and daily market prices be drawn on graph along with 'normal price'.

Classify the demands and supplies of each commodity as highly elastic, inelastic (or less elastic) as the case may be.

Justify the 'interaction between forces of demand and supply' on the basis of your work, giving suitable reasons.

QUESTIONS

A. Short Answer Type Questions:
1. What does the term 'supply' mean in Economics?
2. Explain clearly the difference between 'supply' and 'stock'.
3. Briefly explain any three factors on which supply depends.
4. What is a 'supply schedule'? Give one example.
5. State two factors that govern the supply of commodities.
6. State and explain the 'law of supply' with the help of diagram.
7. Write any four assumptions on which law of supply is based.
8. Why is the slope of supply curve different from that of the demand curve?
9. Explain equilibrium price with the help of demand and supply curves?
10. State two exceptions to 'law of supply'.

11. Differentiate between:
    (i) Extension in Supply and Increase in Supply.
    (ii) Contraction in Supply and Decrease in Supply.
12. How market supply responds to improvement in technology?
13. A farmer grows rice and wheat. How will an increase in the price of rice affect the supply of wheat?
14. If the government of India levies excise duty on sugar, in which direction will the supply curve of sugar shift.
15. Sometimes the supply curve of labour moves inward. Why? Explain with the help of a diagram.
16. Draw graph to depict the following : A change in the supply curve where the price remains constant but the quantity supplied decreases.
17. What effect does increased input prices have on the supply of a commodity? Draw a diagram to explain your answer.
18. Give two reasons for the positive slope of the supply curve.

Recent Year Questions:
1. There is an inverse relationship between quantity supplied and price of a commodity. This statement is True or False. [ICSE 2011]
2. Mention the impact of advanced technology on the supply of a commodity. [ICSE 2012]
3. State whether the following statement is true of false. Give reasons. "Supply and price are inversely proportional." [ICSE 2014]
4. State the law of supply. Explain it with the help of a diagram. [ICSE 2014]
   OR
   State the law of supply. [ICSE 2019]
5. State two assumptions of the law of supply. [ICSE 2015]
6. Construct an imaginary individual supply schedule. [ICSE 2016]

B. Long Answer Type Questions:
1. (i) What do you understand by the term 'supply'?
   (ii) State and explain the 'law of supply'.
   (iii) Draw a supply curve and explain why does supply curve slopes upward?
2. Mention the factors responsible for changes in the supply of a product. Explain five such factors giving suitable examples.
3. Explain the distinction between 'movement along a supply curve' and a 'shift in the supply curve'. Illustrate your answer with diagrams.
4. Prepare the market supply schedule from the individual supply schedules as indicated below:

Price (per unit) (₹)	Quantity supplied by individual		
	A (Units)	B (Units)	C (Units)
5	17	10	21
8	20	15	25
10	22	18	30
15	28	26	36

5. There are three firms A, B, C in the market. The supply schedule for the market and for firms A and B is given below. Prepare supply schedule for firm C.

Price	Firm A	Firm B	Firm C	Market Supply
10	0	25	-----	35
20	10	30	-----	60
30	20	35	-----	85
40	30	40	-----	110

6. The government imposes sales tax on a commodity. Indicate its impact on the supply curve.

Recent Year Questions:

1. Draw an individual supply curve based on an imaginary individual supply schedule. Distinguish between contraction in supply and increase in supply of a commodity. [ICSE 2007]
2. (i) Complete the following supply schedule and give a diagrammatic illustration of the same. [ICSE 2008]

Supply Schedule of Chocolates

Price (in ₹)	Supply (in units)
10.00	200
15.00	-----
20.00	-----
25.00	-----
30.00	-----
35.00	-----

   (ii) Briefly explain any two factors which determine the volume of supply in the market.
3. With the help of a diagram define decrease in supply. Discuss four factors, which determine this phenomenon. [ICSE 2010]
4. With the help of a hypothetical supply schedule draw a supply curve. State one exception to the law of supply. [ICSE 2011]
5. With the help of a diagram, state whether supply of a good is directly or inversely related to its price. Explain any four determinants of a supply. [ICSE 2013]
6. Explain how the following factors effect the supply of a commodity. [ICSE 2018]
    (i) State of technology
    (ii) Price of factors of production
    (iii) Goals of the firm.
    (iv) Future price expectations.
7. (i) Prepare on individual supply schedule.
    (ii) Draw a supply curve based on the schedule prepared above.
    (iii) State three assumptions of law of supply. [ICSE 2019]

04 Elasticity of Supply

The concept of elasticity of supply is a parallel concept to the concept of elasticity of demand. It may be defined as the responsiveness of the supply to change in the price of the commodity. It points out reactions of the sellers to a particular change in the price of the commodity. The supply of a commodity may increase or decrease consequent upon the change in price. The extent to which the quantity supplied of the commodity increases or decreases as a result of change in price is referred to as elasticity of supply. Elasticity of supply, thus, is the measure of change in supply due to change in price.

OVERVIEW

Price elasticity of supply is a measurement of percentage change in quantity supplied of a commodity in response to one percent change in its price. There are various degrees of elasticity of supply—perfectly elastic supply, perfectly inelastic supply, unitary elastic supply, relatively elastic supply and relatively inelastic supply. Elasticity of supply may be measured by Percentage or Proportional method. Elasticity of supply depends upon a number of factors.

DEFINITIONS OF ELASTICITY OF SUPPLY

"Elasticity of supply is the ratio of percentage change in quantity supplied over the percentage change in price." —**Prof. Lipsey**

"Elasticity of supply is defined as the percentage change in quantity supplied divided by percentage change in price." —**Prof. Bilas**

In simple words, elasticity of supply means the rate at which the supply of a commodity changes as a result of change in its price.

DEGREES OF ELASTICITY OF SUPPLY

There are five degrees of elasticity of supply:

1. Perfectly Elastic Supply
2. Perfectly Inelastic Supply
3. Unitary Elastic Supply
4. Relatively Elastic Supply
5. Relatively Inelastic Supply

Perfectly Elastic Supply: When without any change in price, supply changes to any extent, then the supply is perfectly elastic. Here, the supply curve will be horizontal and parallel to *x*-axis. It is illustrated in *Fig. 4.1.*

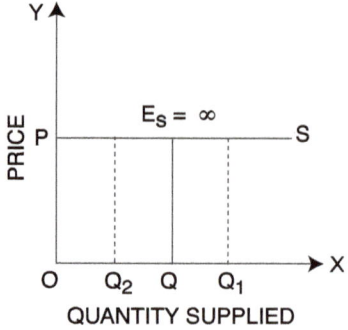

Fig. 4.1 Perfectly Elastic Supply

In this figure, PS is perfectly elastic supply curve. It is parallel to *x*-axis. At price OP supply may be OQ_1 or OQ_2. Symbolically, it can be said that $E_S = \infty$ or elasticity of supply is infinity.

Perfectly Inelastic Supply: Supply is perfectly inelastic when a change in the price causes no change in supply. In other words, price has no influence on supply. Here, the supply curve will be a vertical line parallel to *y*-axis. As shown in *Fig. 4.2*. QS is perfectly inelastic supply curve and is parallel to *y*-axis. It signifies that even if price changes to OP_1 or OP_2, supply remains unchanged *i.e.*, OQ. In this case, elasticity of supply is said to be zero (or $E_S = 0$). Supply of rare books, paintings, stamps and coins is of this type.

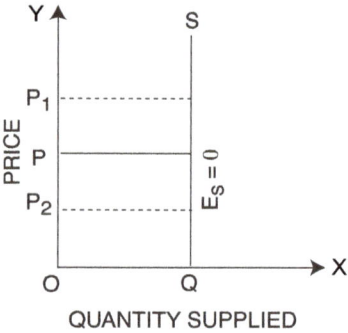

Fig. 4.2 Perfectly Inelastic Supply

Unitary Elastic Supply: Elasticity of supply is unitary when the change in the quantity supplied is in exact proportion to the change in price. The supply curve SS, which is a 45° line represents unitary elastic supply curve in *Fig. 4.3.* Herein a change in price PP_1 brings about an equal change in quantity supplied QQ_1. Symbolically, $E_S = 1$.

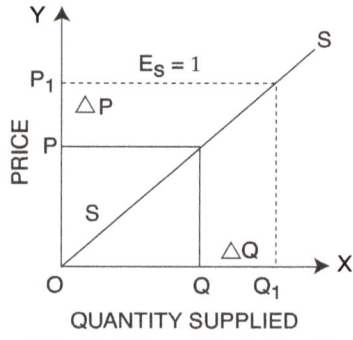

Fig. 4.3 Unitary Elastic Supply

Relatively Elastic Supply: Supply is said to be relatively elastic when a change in price brings about a larger change in quantity supplied. A rise in price leads to proportionately greater increase in quantity supplied and a fall in price brings about proportionately greater decrease in quantity supplied. Supply curve SS is more elastic supply curve in *Fig. 4.4.* It originates from the *y*-axis. Mathematically more elastic supply can be represented as Es > 1.

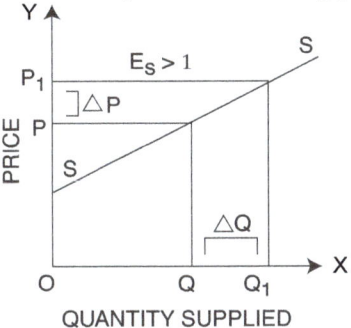

Fig. 4.4 Relatively Elastic Supply

Relatively Inelastic Supply: Supply is said to be less elastic when a change in price brings about proportionately smaller change in quantity supplied. A fall in price brings about proportionately smaller fall in quantity supplied and a rise in price brings proportionately smaller rise in quantity supplied. Supply curve SS in *Fig. 4.5* is less elastic. Symbolically, less elastic supply or inelastic supply is represented as $E_S < 1$.

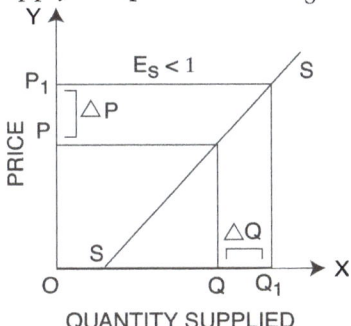

Fig. 4.5 Relatively Inelastic Supply

MEASUREMENT OF ELASTICITY OF SUPPLY

Percentage or Proportionate Method: Elasticity of supply can be measured with the help of the following formula:

$$\text{Elasticity of Supply } (E_S) = \frac{\text{Percentage Change in Quantity Supplied}}{\text{Percentage Change in Price}}$$

In mathematical symbols elasticity of supply can be expressed as:

$$\text{Elasticity of Supply } (E_S) = \frac{\Delta S}{\Delta P} \times \frac{P_0}{S_0}$$

Where S_0 is the original quantity supplied prior to change in price and P_0 is original price of the commodity and ΔS ($S_0 - S_1$) and ΔP ($P_0 - P_1$) represent the changes in quantity supplied and price. S_1 and P_1 are the new quantity supplied and new price respectively.

Now, since the price and quantity supplied generally move in the same direction, the coefficient of elasticity of supply viz., E_S, has a positive sign.

If the numerical result of this formula is equal to one, we say supply is unitary elastic. If it is more than one, supply is said to be relatively elastic and if it is less than one, supply is relatively inelastic.

The value of the coefficient of elasticity of supply varies between zero and infinity. The various results are tabulated below:

Table 4·1

Numerical Measure of Elasticity of Supply	Terminology	Description
1. $E_S = 0$	Perfectly Inelastic	Quantity supplied does not change as price changes.
2. $E_S < 1$	Relatively Inelastic	Quantity supplied changes by a smaller percentage than price change.
3. $E_S = 1$	Unitary Elastic	Quantity supplied changes in the same proportion as the price.
4. $E_S > 1$	Relatively Elastic	Quantity supplied changes by a large percentage than price change.
5. $E_S = \infty$	Perfectly Elastic	Supply changes are immeasurable.

Let us now use the formula to calculate price elasticity of supply by taking some examples.

SOLVED EXAMPLES:

1. Suppose the price of potatoes rise by 20%. As a result the quantity supplied increases by 30%, then calculate the elasticity of supply.

   Calculation:

   $$E_S = \frac{\% \text{ Change in Quantity Supplied}}{\% \text{ Change in Price}}$$

   $$= \frac{30}{20} = 1\cdot 5 \text{ (Relatively Elastic Supply)}$$

2. The price of a commodity increases from ₹20 to ₹30 while its quantity supplied increases from 100 units to 140 units. Calculate elasticity of supply.

   Calculation:

   $$E_S = \frac{\Delta S}{\Delta P} \times \frac{P_0}{S_0} \text{ or } \frac{\frac{\Delta S}{S_0}}{\frac{\Delta P}{P_0}}$$

$$= \frac{40}{10} \times \frac{20}{100} = 0.8 \text{ (Relatively Inelastic Supply)}$$

3. Price of a Java phone falls by ₹500 from ₹2,500 and its quantity supplied falls by 20 percent. Calculate the elasticity of supply.

   Calculation:
   $$E_S = \frac{\% \text{ Change in Quantity Demand}}{\% \text{ Change in Price}}$$

   $$\% \text{ Change in Price} = \frac{500}{2,500} \times 100 = 20\%$$

   Hence, $E_S = \frac{20}{20} = 1$ (Unitary Elastic Supply)

4. A firm's total revenue is ₹800 when the price of the commodity is ₹40. When the price increases to ₹50, its revenue becomes ₹1,200. Calculate the elasticity.

   Calculation:

Price (₹)	Total Revenue (₹)	Quantity Supplied (Units)
40	800	20
50	1,200	24

   $$E_S = \frac{\Delta S}{\Delta P} \times \frac{P_0}{S_0}$$

   $$= \frac{4}{10} \times \frac{40}{20} = 0.8 \text{ (Relatively Inelastic Supply)}$$

FACTORS AFFECTING ELASTICITY OF SUPPLY

Following are the main factors which affect the elasticity of supply of a commodity:

Nature of the Inputs Used: The elasticity of supply depends on the nature of inputs used for the production of commodity. If factors of production are those which are commonly used (and therefore easily available), supply of the commodity will be elastic. On the other hand, if specialised factors are used (which are not easily available), supply will be inelastic.

Natural Constraints: The elasticity of supply is also influenced by the natural constraints in the production of a commodity. If we wish to produce more teak wood, it will take years of plantation before it becomes usable. Supply of teak wood will therefore be inelastic.

Risk Taking: The elasticity of supply depends on the willingness of entrepreneurs to take risk. If entrepreneurs are willing to take risk, the supply will be more elastic. On the other hand, if entrepreneurs hesitate to take risk, the supply will be inelastic.

Nature of the Commodity: Perishable goods are relatively inelastic in supply than durable goods, because it is difficult to store the perishables goods.

Cost of Production: Elasticity of supply is also influenced by cost of production. If production is subject to law of increasing costs, then supply of such goods will be inelastic.

Time Factor : Longer the time period, greater will be the elasticity of supply. Because, over a long period of time, more and more factors are easily available and their inputs can be changed to increase (or decrease) output of the commodity.

Technique of Production: If the technique is complex and needs large stock of capital, then the supply of the commodity will be inelastic, because production cannot be easily increased. On the other hand, goods involving simple technique of production will have elastic supply.

LESSON AT A GLANCE

Elasticity of Supply: Prof. Lipsey has defined elasticity of supply in the following words, "Elasticity of supply is the ratio of percentage change in quantity supplied over the percentage change in price."

Degrees of Elasticity of Supply: (i) Perfectly elastic supply; (ii) Perfectly inelastic supply; (iii) Unitary elastic supply; (iv) Relatively elastic supply; and (v) Relatively inelastic supply.

Measurement of Elasticity of Supply: Percentage or proportionate method.

Factors Affecting Elasticity of Supply: (i) Nature of the inputs used; (ii) Natural constraints; (iii) Risk taking; (iv) Nature of the commodity; (v) Cost of production; (vi) Time factor; and (vii) Technique of production.

PROJECT WORK

Prepare a list of items of different categories like luxury goods, goods of comfort and goods of daily use. Conduct a survey of market in your town and prepare a list of price of these commodities over a period of six months. Mention any change that occurred in the supply of the items listed by you. Determine elasticity of supply on averages calculated from the information collected by you.

QUESTIONS

A. Short Answer Type Questions:
1. Define elasticity of supply.
2. What is perfectly elastic supply?
3. What do you mean by relatively elastic supply?
4. Name the method of measurement of elasticity of supply.
5. Mention any two factors affecting elasticity of supply.
6. What is meant by zero elastic supply?
7. Why does perishable goods have less elastic supply?

Recent Year Questions:
1. Price of a good rises by 2%. As a result its supply rises by 4%. Find out the price elasticity of supply.
   [ICSE 2011]

2. Draw and briefly explain a perfectly inelastic supply curve. [ICSE 2014]
3. The quantity of a commodity supplied increases by 25% when its price rises by 10%. Calculate price elasticity of supply. [ICSE 2014]
4. Indicate the degree of elasticity on the supply curves given below: [ICSE 2015]

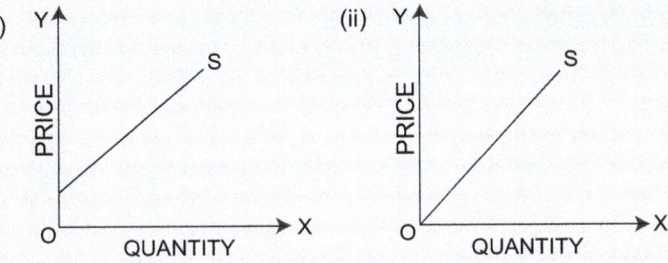

5. The price of a commodity rises from ₹20.00 to ₹40.00. Consequently its supply increases from 100 units to 400 units. Calculate the price elasticity of supply. [ICSE 2016]
6. Given below is the market supply schedule of a commodity. The individual supply schedules of firms B and C are given, prepare the individual schedule for Firm A: [ICSE 2018]

Price (₹)	No. of units supplied by Firm A	No. of units supplied by Firm B	No. of units supplied by Firm C	Total Supply
10		25	10	60
20		30	20	100
30		35	30	140
40		40	40	180

B. **Long Answer Type Questions:**
1. What do you mean by elasticity of supply? Give a proper definition of elasticity of supply.
2. Discuss the various degrees of elasticity of supply.
3. Explain the percentage method of measurement of elasticity of supply.
4. Explain any five factors affecting price elasticity of supply.
5. Price of a commodity increases from ₹10 to ₹12. As a result, its supply rises from 35 units to 42 units. Find out elasticity of supply.
6. The price of a commodity rises from ₹5 per unit to ₹6 per unit. Consequently its supply increases by 20%. Find out elasticity of supply.
7. As a result of increase in the price of milk from ₹20 per litre to ₹25 per litre, the supply of milk increases from 9,000 litres to 11,000 litres. Calculate the price elasticity of supply.

Recent Year Questions:
1. Define price elasticity of supply with the help of suitable diagrams explain the following degrees of elasticity:
   (a) Perfectly elastic supply
   (b) Perfectly inelastic supply. [ICSE 2012]
2. With the help of a formula calculate the elasticity of supply from the following table: [ICSE 2012]

Price (in ₹)	Quantity Supplied (units)
10	200
15	225

3. Define elasticity of supply. Explain any four of its determinants. [ICSE 2014]
4. (i) What is the impact of the behaviour of cost of production on elasticity of supply?
   (ii) Draw and explain the following degrees of elasticity of supply:
   (a) $E_p = \infty$ (b) $E_p = 0$ (c) $E_p > 1$ [ICSE 2016]
5. Identify and define the degree of price elasticity of supply from the diagram for the supply curves S_1, S_2, S_3, S_4. [ICSE 2018]

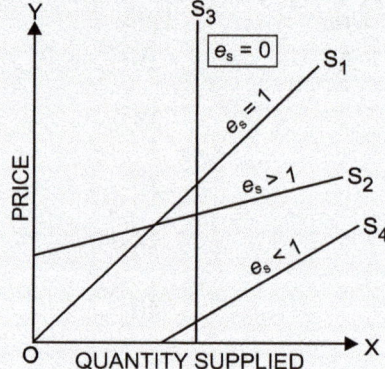

05 Factors of Production

'Production means production of material goods only'. —**Adam Smith**

This used to be the principal understanding regarding production. All the services, even though important for the prosperity and economic welfare of human beings (military, personnel, doctors, lawyers, teachers, domestic servants, etc.), usually, were not called production. **Adam Smith** observed that there was a fundamental difference between commodities and services as there is always a time gap between the production and consumption of commodities, while the production and consumption of services is always simultaneous. But **Adam Smith's** views were rejected by the later economists.

In modern Economics, the term production is used in wider meaning and applicability. Modern economists have defined production as a creation or an addition of economic utilities which are capable of satisfying human wants. In this context, economic utilities refer to the power of the goods and services, by which human wants are satisfied.

OVERVIEW

The study of Economics is mainly concerned with 'Production' and 'Consumption'. The 'Land', 'Labour', 'Capital' and 'Entrepreneur' are the basic Factors of Production.

The Land and Capital are passive factors whereas Labour and Entrepreneur are the active factors of production. However, the Entrepreneur is an active factor that is associated with risk factor. The Land includes not only land surface but also the mineral resources, oceans, fisheries, water bodies (lakes and rivers), weather elements, forests, etc., while capital refers to the man-made factor of production.

PRODUCTION IS TRANSFORMATION

In ordinary parlance, the term production is taken to be understood as the creation or making of any product. But when we consider it a little more deeply we find that nothing is created or made. We can only change or transform resources and, actually, this process of transformation is generally called the production process.

But in the modern context, production is related to value creation and it may be defined as follows:

"Production is a process of transformation which leads to creation or addition of value in a good or factor."

The production process can be shown as follows:

Input ⟶ Production Process (value addition) ⟶ Output

Since production is transformation, it can be done through the following changes:

Form Utility: When utility is created by changing the form of a matter or resource, it is called form utility. Conversion of cotton into cloth and sugarcane into sugar are some examples of form utility.

Place Utility: The utility created by removing an article from one place to another is known as place utility. Transportation of goods from the places where they are in abundance to the places where they are scarce or needed. For example, timber has greater utility in pulp factory or in carpenter's workshop than in jungle.

Time Utility: The utility which is created through the preservation or storage of a commodity over a period of time, is known as time utility. Fruits and vegetables are kept in cold storages to be sold for consumption in the off season.

Possession Utility: Possession utility is the utility which is created by transferring the possession of an article. For instance, books have greater utility with the reader rather with the publisher.

Service Utility: When utility is created by rendering of some services not embodied in a material object, is known as service utility. For example, a teacher who teaches to the students is an example of service utility. Similarly a doctor creates service utility by diagnosing a disease and providing medical prescription.

Knowledge Utility: The utility which is created through enhancing the people's knowledge is known as knowledge utility. A good example is an informative advertisement.

Hence, production means creation of utilities by any of the above method.

"Production may be defined as any activity (physical or mental) directed to the satisfaction of other people's want, through exchange." —**Prof. J. R. Hicks**

"Production can be defined as any activity that creates present and future utility." —**Peterson**

FACTORS OF PRODUCTION

Depending upon the availability of various items and the ultimate use of the product, numerous elements or agents, which in one way or the other help in. In simple words, various resources with the help of which the process of production is carried on are called factors of production. These factors are also called *Inputs*. Accordingly, anything which contributes to an Output can be conveniently called as *Input* or *Factor of Production*. Some of these factors are original (or natural) whereas some are man-made.

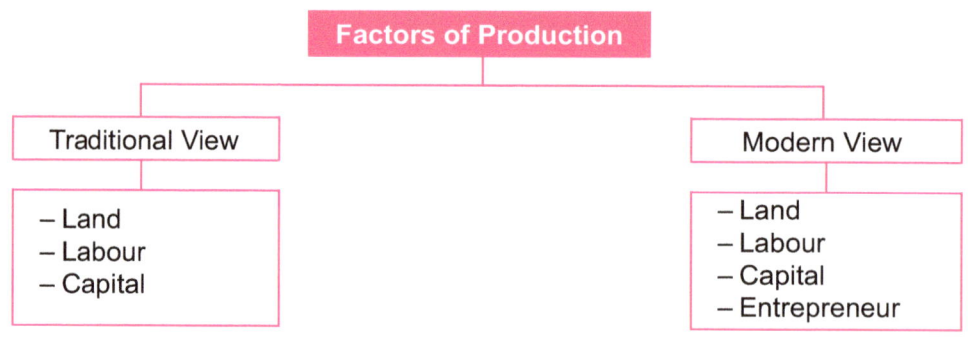

Traditional View: According to traditional view, following are the three main or basic factors of production.

    (1) Land,   (2) Labour,   (3) Capital.

However, the contribution of one factor or the other, to the production activities, may vary or to say that substitution may be possible between these factors to various degrees, but one thing is certain that the above factors are essential to carry out activities of production. For example, shoes can be manufactured either by using modern machines (employing more capital and less labour) or by using the old methods of large scale labour employment (*i.e.*, more labour with lesser or no machines at all).

Modern View: However, economists like **Benham** propounded that factors of production are not one or two, but they exist in millions. According to him, *"Anything which contributes to production is a factor of production"*.

Thus, every acre of land is a factor by itself and so is each individual worker. Indeed, the number is 'impossible to calculate exactly'. At the most, the similar items can be grouped together, *i.e.*, all similar acres of land can be grouped together and all similar workers into another group. However, even then, the number of each group shall also be very large. But, the modern economists disagree with the above classification. According to them, dissimilar items should not be grouped together. For example, their argument is that a work of mason and the work of clerk should not be put in the same group 'labour'. But both these views do not have practical significance.

But modern economists have agreed on the list of factors of production provided by **Dr. Alfred Marshall**. He included the fourth factor, *i.e.*, 'Organisation' to the above three basic factors of production. Thus, the four factors of production are:

    (1) Land,   (2) Labour,   (3) Capital,   (4) Entrepreneur or Organisation.

RELATIVE IMPORTANCE OF DIFFERENT FACTORS OF PRODUCTION

It is very difficult to say as to which factor of production is more important. Actually, all the factors are important and each has a special function to perform.

'Labour' is an active factor of production and sets the whole productive machinery in operation. *'Nature'*, *i.e. 'Land'* is a passive factor of production but is indispensable. Everything that people do, to convert natural opportunities in human satisfactions is not possible in vacuum, as everything we use can be ultimately traced to *'Nature'*. Even the human life itself is not possible without land. In spite of such importance, land cannot do anything of its own and man must work on *'land'* to achieve production.

'Capital' is also an important but passive factor. However, it has been derived from *'land'* and *'labour'* and it is sometimes called as *'stored-up labour'*. In the present circumstances, without the aid of tools and machinery, man cannot achieve production.

The *'Entrepreneur (Organiser)'* also plays an important role in modern times because it is the entrepreneur who takes up the risks and sets and directs the entire productive machinery into motion. It is under his leadership that production goes ahead and business prospers.

Therefore, it is right to conclude that all the factors of production are important. However, the degree of importance may be different under different circumstances.

LESSON AT A GLANCE

Production: Production is the process of creating various goods and services, which are consumed by the people of the country. Modern economists have defined production as a creation or an addition of economic utilities.

Production is Transformation: It is a process of transformation which leads to creation or addition of value in a good or factor. It can be done through the following changes: (i) Form utility; (ii) Place utility; (iii) Time utility; (iv) Possession utility; (v) Service utility; (vi) Knowledge utility.

Factors of Production: Depending upon the availability of various items and the ultimate use of the product, various resources, which in one way or the other help in accomplishing the production, are termed as factors of production. The following are the main factors of production: (i) Land; (ii) Labour; (iii) Capital; (iv) Entrepreneur.

Relative Importance of Different Factors of Production:

Land: It includes all the material and physical resources provided by nature as 'free-gifts'.

Labour: It includes all kinds of human efforts, *i.e.*, manual (physical) or mental, skilled or unskilled, scientific or artistic put-in by human beings in order to achieve monetary benefits.

Capital: It includes all man-made productive assets such as buildings, machinery, materials, fuels, etc.

Entrepreneur: The person who takes up the risk of productive activities.

PROJECT WORK

Visit a factory and a garden. Note down various items consumed in the factory for production, *i.e.*, labour and staff working there. Also note down such information related to the activities in garden in which fruits and vegetables are grown.

From the information given below prepare a list of:
(i) Items which can be classified as 'Land'.
(ii) Items which can be classified as 'Capital'.
(iii) Prepare a list of people who can be classified as 'Labour' and 'Entrepreneur' from the staff and people working in the factory.
(iv) Prepare a line diagram to show the relationship between different factors of production as listed above.
(v) Write a short note or summary as to how the factors are related to one another.

Compare the conclusions with respect to the factory and garden.

QUESTIONS

A. Short Answer Type Questions:
1. What is production?
2. How many factors of production are considered in modern economics?
3. Name the factors of production.
4. How is time and place utility created?

Recent Year Questions:
1. With the help of an example explain the process of creation of form utility. [ICSE 2009]
2. What is regarded as a factor of production and why? [ICSE 2010]
   - (i) Capital
   - (ii) Interest
   - (iii) Profit
   - (iv) Rent.
3. Mention two ways in which an entrepreneur is different from labour. [ICSE 2018]

B. Long Answer Type Questions:
1. Discuss the following:
   - (i) Land
   - (ii) Labour
   - (iii) Capital
   - (iv) Entrepreneur.
2. Discuss relative importance of each factor of production. Can productive activities be carried out in absence of one or two of the factors of production?

Recent Year Questions:
1. Explain an important characteristic of each of the following factors of production:
   - (i) Land
   - (ii) Labour
   - (iii) Capital
   - (iv) Entrepreneur. [ICSE 2012]

06 Land

For a layman, the term 'Land' generally refers to the surface of the earth. But in Economics, it includes all that, which is available free of cost from 'nature' as a gift to human beings.

"Land means the materials and the forces, which 'nature' gives freely for man's aid, in land and water, in air and light and heat."

—**Prof. A. Marshall**

"The modern definition is that land is a specific factor or that it is a specific element in a factor or again that it is specific aspect of a thing."

—**Prof. J. K. Mehta**

According to the old definition, land is a *free gift* whereas according to the modern definition, land has the feature of definiteness in character but there is no sacrifice involved in making it. Here '*no sacrifice*' means, it is a free gift.

Thus, the modern definition of land is almost the same as the old one.

OVERVIEW

Land includes all that is provided by nature as a free gift for use by mankind. It is something for which no cost is paid to get it. No productive operation is possible without land. It is the original source of all material wealth.

Different patches of land have different fertility. The productivity of land is greatly influenced by its fertility, proper use, its situation and the improvements done on it.

Since the availability of land is fixed, production per unit area must be improved to achieve more economic development. Therefore, proper use of available resources must be made to improve the productivity of land.

CHARACTERISTICS OF LAND

'Land' has specific characteristics, which distinguish it from other factors of production. The main characteristics of land are:

Free Gift of Nature: Basically, land is available from the *nature* as free of cost to the societies or human being as a whole. In the initial stages, man paid no price for the land acquired by him. However, to improve the usefulness or fertility of land or to make some improvements over land, some expenditure is to be incurred. But as such, it is available at no cost from nature.

Limited Supply of Land: Neither land can be stretched nor anything can be added to it to increase its availability. As such, the supply of land cannot be enhanced. However, only effective supply of land can be increased by making an intensive use of land. In the same manner, availability of sunlight, clean air and water, etc. are also limited.

Difference in Fertility: All lands are not equally fertile. Different patches of land have different degrees of fertility. Some locations are very fertile and have very good agricultural productivity, whereas some patches are totally barren and nothing can be grown there.

Similarly, the degree of richness of mineral wealth varies from place to place, making the land more useful or less useful from economic point of view.

Indestructibility of Land: Land is an indestructible factor of production. Man can change only the shape of a particular location and composition of its elements, but as such land cannot be destroyed. It can either be converted into a garden or to a forest or to an artificial lake. However, some parts of land get eroded due to natural factors, but that is immaterial because overall availability of land does not change.

Immobility: Unlike other factors, land is not physically mobile as a source. It is an immobile factor of production, as it cannot be shifted from one place to another. It lacks geographical mobility. Though some of the products of land may be transported like minerals and metals, etc. Some economists, however, describe land as a mobile factor on the argument, that it can be put to several uses.

Passive Factor of Production: Land is a passive factor of production, because it cannot produce anything of its own. Human element and capital inputs are required to be combined in an appropriate manner with land in order to obtain yields from it.

Effect of Laws of Returns: Since land is a fixed factor of production, the laws of returns are more effectively applicable on it. Increased use of capital and labour on a particular plot of land leads to an increase in crop production eventually at a diminishing rate.

Alternative Uses of land: Land is used for alternative purposes like cultivation, dairy or poultry farms, sheep rearing, building, etc. The use of land for any particular purpose depends not only on the return from that particular use, but also the returns from alternative uses. Other elements of land *i.e.,* water, sunlight, mineral and metals, herbs and other forest products, etc. can also be put to different uses.

Land is Heterogeneous: Land like other factors of production differs from another in respect of location, fertility, nature and productivity. Two pieces of land are not exactly the same.

FUNCTIONS OF LAND

Land is used for various purposes. In this sense, functions of land may be discussed as below:

Determines Agricultural Production: The supply of land resources in the country determines the level of agricultural production of the country. The fertility of the soil, however, determines the variation in the agricultural productivity.

Supply of Natural Resources: Availability of total land area also determine the availability of natural resources in a country. Proper utilisation of these resources help in raising the total output of the country.

Helping the Process of Industrialisation and Urbanisation: Land resources of a country also help in the process of industrialisation and urbanisation in the country because both of these processes require adequate land areas for their smooth progress.

Employment: In under-developed (Developing and Least Developed) countries nearly two-third of population is engaged in agriculture and other primary activities. Agriculture, forests, mines, etc., provide lot of employment opportunities to rising population.

Transport: the important modes of transport, *i.e.,* road and railways, water-ways and air-ways are mainly based on surface of the land, rivers, oceans and air; which are all constituents of land.

Trade: Products of land are traded within the country as well as form part of foreign trade. For example: food grains, minerals, timber, leather, hides and skins, wool, tea, jute, petroleum, milk, butter, etc.

Economic Growth: Land play an important role in the economic development of a country. Prosperity of gulf countries lies in the oil-wells situated there. Economic development of South Africa is mainly due to its fertile lands, irrigation and power facilities.

Life Base: We depend on land for our subsistence, residence and other necessities of life. Land provides food and healthy climate.

IMPORTANCE OF LAND

Fundamentally speaking, *Land* is the original source of all material wealth and it is of immense use to mankind. As such, it is an important factor of production inspite of it being a passive factor. An overall economic prosperity of a country is directly related to the richness of its natural resources.

Inspite of rich natural resources, a country may remain economically backward due to some unfavourable factors like technological backwardness or less capable human resources, etc., on account of which the natural sources are either under-utilised or not utilised. On the other hand, if a country does not have rich natural resources, it is comparatively much more difficult to make it prosperous.

The quality and the quantity of agricultural wealth of a country depends on soil, climate, rainfall and water resources. The industrial progress and prosperity of a nation depends on mineral resources. The presence of rich coal mines, waterfalls or petroleum wells directly help in the generation of electric power, which is a key factor for industrial development. The localisation of industries invariably depends on proximity of power and raw materials. All these basic elements are provided by nature.

In short, the importance of land is evident from the following points:
1. Land determines agricultural production.
2. The industrial progress and prosperity of a country depends on availability of mineral resources, *i.e.*, land.
3. Land influences total production of a country.
4. land influences the economic growth of a country.
5. land maintains ecological balance.
6. Land directly or indirectly fulfills the basic needs of the people.
7. Trade is influenced by land.

Therefore, all economic aspects, *i.e., agriculture, industry* and *trade* are influenced by natural resources, referred to by economists as '*Land*'.

FACTORS AFFECTING PRODUCTIVITY OF LAND

The factors affecting the productivity of land are discussed below:

Fertility of Land: The productivity of land is determined by its natural qualities and its fertility. A flat and levelled land is comparatively more productive than an undulating one. The rich soil is more fertile and productive. However, the agricultural productivity can be improved by proper and extensive use of manure and fertilizers along with adoption of mechanised farming.

Proper Use of Land: The productivity of 'Land' is directly related to its proper utilisation. For example, a piece of land situated in the heart of city is more suitable for construction of a house or a market place. If this piece of land is put for farming or agricultural use, its productivity will almost be negligible.

Location of Land : The location of 'Land' affects its productivity to a great extent. For example, the location of land near the market or bus station will result in economy of transportation charges and overall productivity from this point of view will naturally be higher. Similarly, for better agricultural productivity, its location near water resources is desirable.

Improvements on Land: The permanent improvements done on land, like construction of irrigation channels, hedging of fields or the construction of dams, etc., have positive effects on the productivity of land.

Ability of Organiser: Land is a passive factor of production and so it is essential to combine it with other active factors, in correct proportion, to achieve the optimum productivity. In order to accomplish it, an able organiser will successfully handle and combine the passive and the active factors in right proportions so as to achieve greater productivity. The competence and ability of an organiser will directly affect the overall productivity of land.

Land Ownership Laws: The 'Land Ownership Laws' prevailing in a country have a significant influence on the productivity of 'Land'. When a full ownership is conferred, the owner takes more interest in its development. For example, a cultivator possessing full ownership rights on land, does more hard work and the productivity automatically improves.

Availability of Efficient Labour: The productivity of land depends on the availability of efficient labour as land alone cannot produce anything without the efficient labour. If the labour is efficient, trained and capable to adopt modern techniques, only then she can make the proper use of land.

Irrigation Potentials: Productivity of land is considerably influenced by the availability of irrigation potentials. The land which has rich irrigation potential, will be more productive. Artificial means of irrigation, *i.e.*, wells, tubewells, canals, tanks, etc., help to maintain the adequate supply of water.

Availability of Capital: Capital is the fundamental factor that affects the productivity of land. The productivity of land can be improved a lot with the help of improved seeds, chemical fertilizers and machines. To fulfill all these requirements, sufficient capital should be available.

Government Policy: The productivity of land is affected by the government policy regarding agriculture. Agricultural productivity starts increasing when the government adopts a proper agricultural policy and provides required assistance to farmers. On the other hand, the State's negligence towards agriculture is regarded as one of the main causes of agricultural backwardness. This results in low agricultural productivity.

LESSON AT A GLANCE

Land: The term 'land' generally refers to the surface of land. But in Economics, it includes all that, which is available free of cost from nature as a 'gift to human beings'. In the words of **Marshall**, "Land means the materials and the forces, which 'nature' gives freely for man's aid, in land and water, in air and light and heat."

Characteristics of Land: (i) Free gift of nature; (ii) Limited supply of land; (iii) Difference in fertility; (iv) Indestructibility of land; (v) Immobility; (vi) Passive factor of production; (vii) Effect of laws of returns; (viii) Alternative uses of land; and (ix) Land is heterogeneous.

Functions of Land: (i) Determines agricultural production; (ii) Supply of natural resources; (iii) Helping the process of industrialisation and urbanisation; (iv) Employment; (v) Transport; (vi) Trade; (vii) Economic growth; (viii) Life base.

Importance of Land: In the production process, land is very important factor of production inspite of it being a passive factor. Overall economic prosperity of a country is directly related to the richness of its natural resources.

The main points of Importance of land are: (i) Land determines agricultural production; (ii) The industrial progress and prosperity of a country depends on land; (iii) Land influences total production of a country; (iv) Land influences the economic growth of a country; (v) Land maintains ecological balance; (vi) Land directly or indirectly fulfills the basic needs of the people; and (vii) Trade is influenced by land.

Factors Affecting Productivity of Land: (i) Fertility of land; (ii) Proper use of land; (iii) Location of land; (iv) Improvements done on land; (v) Ability of organisers; (vi) Land ownership laws; (vii) Availability of efficient labour; (viii) Irrigation potentials; (ix) Availability of capital; and (x) Government policy.

PROJECT WORK

1. Visit:
   (i) Your locality.
   (ii) Centre or main parts of your town.
   (iii) Some remote areas of your town and find out if some land is lying idle. Characterise each land on the basis of their fertility, location, use, availability of capital irrigation potential, etc. What are the various options for the best utilisation of each of these idle lying lands? The option could be construction of a house, bus stand, market place, etc. What efforts could you make in this regard?
2. Make a visit to your nearby village and enlist the name of atleast 20 farmers. collect information regarding their land and different crops they grow.

Prepare the list of: (a) Nature of land, (b) Items grown in Kharif and Rabi season, (c) Possession and availability of other natural resources.

Draw your conclusion with reasons and justification.

QUESTIONS

A. Short Answer Type Questions:
1. Define Land according to: (i) Marshall, and (ii) J. K. Mehta.
2. State the importance of land in brief.
3. Discuss one factor which increases productivity of land in India.
4. The area of cultivated land is more or less fixed in a country. Under such conditions, suggest two ways to increase the agricultural productivity of land.

[Hint: Improvements done on land, may be irrigation, better seeds, construction of dams, etc.]

Recent Year Questions:
1. Why is land considered a passive and an indestructible factor of production? [ICSE 2006]
2. Mention two factors affecting the productivity of land. [ICSE 2007]
3. State two characteristics of land as a factor of production. [ICSE 2008]
4. Explain two functions of land. [ICSE 2009]
5. Suggest two measures to enhance the productivity of land. [ICSE 2010]
6. Land is heterogeneous in nature. Explain. [ICSE 2019]

B. Long Answer Type Questions:
1. Land is a peculiar factor of production. Discuss.
2. Describe the main functions of land.
3. Discuss the importance of land as a factor of production. What are its chief characteristics?
4. Land is different from other agents of production. What are its peculiarities?
5. Discuss various factors which influence the productivity of land.

Recent Year Questions:
1. Define land and explain any three of its important characteristics. Suggest two measures to improve productivity of land. [ICSE 2011]
2. Define Production. Explain three factors which determine land productivity. [ICSE 2012]
3. Land is the original source of all material wealth. In this context, explain four determinants that influence the productivity of land. [ICSE 2013]
4. With reference to land as a factor of production:
    (i) Why is it considered a 'passive' and an 'indestructible' factor of production?
    (ii) Mention two ways in which land is different from capital.
    (iii) Discuss two important functions of land. [ICSE 2016]
5. Explain four reasons as to why land is considered to be an important factor of production. [ICSE 2019]

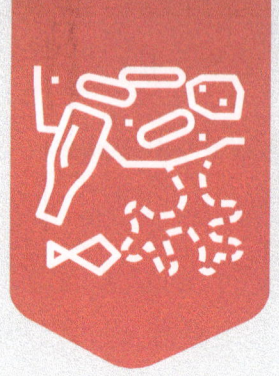

07
Destruction of Ecosystem

ECOSYSTEM AND LAND USE CHANGE

Oxford dictionary defines Ecosystem as "all the plants and living creatures in a particular area considered in relation to their physical environment". In other words, an ecosystem refers to a complex set of relationship among the living resources like humans, plants and other living organisms, and non-living resources like sunlight, water, minerals, soil and climate, etc., of an area. But changing global pattern of land use have had a significant negative effect on the ecosystem. Land use change is a complex dynamic process that links together natural and human systems. It has direct impact on natural resources: soil, water, atmosphere and thus directly relates to many environmental issues of global importance. The large-scale deforestation and subsequent transformations of agricultural land in many areas like housing, overgrazing, construction of new roads, highways and industries are examples of changing land use pattern to support human needs. Man has brought a substantial change in the ecosystem since the beginning of civilization. As per capita consumption of resources is increasing with the growing population, man tried to extract the maximum from the environment. The basic land use pattern that has changed around the world can be analysed as follows:

> **OVERVIEW**
> There is biotic balance in an ecosystem, which makes it possible to sustain the various inter dependent members (plant and animal life). Ecosystems maintain a very delicate balance. Various human activities threaten to disrupt this balance and destroy the world's ecosystem.
>
> There is destruction of natural ecosystem due to pressure on land and forest. Changing Pattern of Land Use, Migration, Industrialisation, Shifting Cultivation, Dwelling units, Mining, Urbanisation, Construction of Dams and Tourism are the major causes of destruction of ecosystem.

- The percentage of forest cover in the world has reduced.
- The amount of land for industries and housing has increased.
- The amount of land for roads and other transportation has also increased.
- The amount of wasteland has increased.

All such changes in the land use have been at the cost of destruction of natural ecosystem like forests, grassland, etc., for making available more land for agriculture and human settlement. Rural land has been converted into urban settlement and open spaces are vanishing. In the recent past, the world has lost approximately 500 million hectares of forest in building power and irrigational projects. This transformation has affected the functioning and balance of ecosystems at various places, which is responsible to sustain the various inter dependent members (plant and animal life) to maintain their individual group existence at a level.

The land use patterns have changed drastically in the past fifty years. The population is increasing, resources are depleting and pollution levels are increasing. In this chapter we will study the various causes of ecosystem destruction and how the land use patterns have changed over the years. The various causes for the destruction of ecosystems and changing pattern of land use are as follows:

INDUSTRIALISATION AND URBANISATION

Industrialisation is the process of manufacturing consumer goods and capital goods and of building infrastructure in order to provide goods and services to both individuals and businesses. It plays a major role in the economic development of underdeveloped countries like India to free themselves from the adverse effects of unemployment, poverty, fluctuations in the prices of primary products and deterioration in their terms of trade. Although, industrialisation is making rapid strides it is however, accompanied by growing negative impact on the environmental and social system.

Fig. 7.1 : Pressure of population on earth - Unhygienic Slums

The industries in and around the cities discharge their effluents, which are accumulated in the land system thus causing various health problems. The negative effects of industrialisation are worse than natural disasters in terms of life, injury and damage to properties. Well known examples are Bhopal gas tragedy (3rd December, 1984), Leakage of Chlorine gas from the Sewri industry (14th July, 2010) causing the destruction of both environment and human life. Green-house effect, Global warming and Acid precipitation are some of the impact of industrialisation on the environment. Industrialisation directly increases air and water pollution. This we can understand by the fact that the quality of air and river water has deteriorated around all the industrial cities of India which is being discussed by various reports on environmental degradation.

As a result of industrialisation, the process of urbanisation too is growing fast and this is having deep impact upon ecosystem. Urbanisation refers to general increase in urban population because of the movement of people from less industrialised region to more industrialised region in search of employment. The effect of urbanisation on environment is immense. One of the worst problems of urbanisation is unsystematic or unorganised growth of unhygienic slums around the industries and other areas; an overcrowded shabby living quarters. A slum is considered to be residential area where houses are unfit to live due to poor surroundings, unclean environment, dilapidated houses and poor sanitation, etc., which are detrimental for health. The person living in these slums are constantly exposed to all kinds of diseases because there is no ventilation, no drainage and no drinking water. It has also led to deterioration in the quality of city environments. Urbanisation also leads to deterioration of natural habitat like agricultural land, plants, plantation, forest areas, wetland, etc. This creates many other problems such as environmental degradation and loss of agricultural land.

Urbanisation has been taking pace significantly in numerous developing countries including India. By the last two decades the urban population of the developing world has grown by an average of 3 million per week and it will be more than double by the middle of 21st century. By 2050, Asia will host 63 percent of the global urban population, or 3.3 billion people. At the moment, India is among the countries of low level of urbanisation as compared to others. Number of population residing in urban areas has increased to 34.7 crores as per 2011 census. Only 28% of population was living in urban areas as per 2001 census. Now it has risen to 34.47% in 2019.

MIGRATION

Migration involves the movement of people from one place to another. Now-a-days, it is a common phenomenon, people are migrating from rural to urban areas. Low wages, poor facilities for education and health are forcing people to move out from rural areas. This results in concentration of population in a limited space, which further increases the stress on land by increasing number of squatter settlements, causing pollution. In this way migration affect ecosystem of rural and urban areas both. It causes air and water pollution also.

DWELLING UNITS

A dwelling unit is a single unit that provides complete and independent living facilities, including permanent provisions for living, sleeping, eating, cooking and sanitation. Because of the continuous migration of people into the industrial and commercial cities more and more space is required for housing or dwelling units. This has increased the demand for dwellings which are difficult to be made available at the pace of demand. Hence, people from rural areas start living in sheds, roads, slums and many such places. Housing in such places becomes a major health concern due to lack of proper sanitation, overcrowding and water supply. Today out of 3 billion people, nearly half of the world's population lives in cities and one-third of them are slum dwellers. The problem of slums has been faced by almost all the major cities throughout the developing world. To accommodate the migrating population, in many countries various public housing programs have been launched and slums have been cleared. Self-help housing scheme showed positive result in which poor people are allotted plots and building materials. This scheme was launched as 'Sites and Services' in India and many other countries. Such schemes improved the living conditions of urban areas. There are various housing scheme which is being implemented by the Government of India with an aim of providing shelter to the poor below poverty line and for the rehabilitation of slums. Some of them are:

- **Slum Rehabilitation Scheme:** Slum Rehabilitation Act 1995 was passed by Government of Maharashtra to protect the rights of slum dwellers and to upgrade these slums by providing employments, drinking water facility, electricity, toilet facility and proper drainage systems at their own locations.
- **Jawaharlal Nehru National Urban Renewal Mission (JNNURM):** Under this scheme, the Meghalaya government had initiated the construction of 600 dwelling units for the urban poor at Lumphira in Nongmynsong on the outskirts of the city.
- **Indira Aawas Yojana (IAY):** The objective of IAY is primarily to help construction of new dwelling units as well as conversion of unserviceable kutcha houses into pucca/

semi-pucca by members of SC/STs, freed bonded labourers and also non-SC/ST rural poor below the poverty line by extending them grant-in-aid.

- **Basic Minimum Services:** The objective of providing this scheme is to supplement the constitution of dwelling units for members of SC/ST, freed bonded labour and also non-SC/ST rural poor below the poverty line by providing them with grant.
- **National Agenda of Governance and Housing for All:** In the year 1998, the Indian government brought out a 'National Agenda for Governance' for ushering in a dynamic economic growth to bring in quality life for masses. This agenda included issues like Governance, Eradication of Unemployment, Housing for slum dwellers and shelter less.
- **Slum Environment Sanitation Initiative (SESI):** In November 2005, Slum Environment Sanitation Initiative (SESI) took a project to develop and demonstrate commodity led approaches for slum improvement focusing on water, sanitation and hygiene.
- **The Society for the Promotion of Area Resource Centres (SPARC):** It supports networks of slum dwellers across India, including the National Slum Dwellers Federation and Mahila Milan, together comprising two million poor slum dwellers in 72 cities. SPARC is managing high-profile resettlement projects in Mumbai and is using CLIFF to finance city-wide housing and sanitation projects benefiting around 790,000 people.

MINING

Mining is the process of extracting metals and minerals from the earth's crust. Gold, silver, diamond, iron, coal and uranium are just a few of the vast array of metals and minerals that are obtained by this process. Mining reaps huge profit for the companies that own them and provides employment to a large number of people. Despite its economic importance, the question that how does mining affect the environment is a pressing environmental issue. The harm caused to the environment by mining are as follows:

- It causes deforestation and removal of vegetation. In order to construct a mine large amount of land has to be cleared off trees and vegetation. This is bad for environment.
- The waste material remaining after the valuable minerals have been extracted is called tailing. These tailings are generally made up of hazardous material. Dust from these tailings causes air pollution.
- Mining also contaminate ground water because in the extraction of minerals, some toxins as cyanide and mercury are used that can permanently pollute water.
- Chemicals like arsenic and iron are very harmful. When it rains these chemicals find their way to ground water, surrounding water bodies and soil. This pollutes water bodies as well as affects agriculture.
- It requires vast amount of energy. Controlling the temperature of mines deep underground is very energy consuming as well.
- Mining has great effect on the quality of the air. Coal mines releases methane, which contributes to environmental issue because it is a green house gas.

On December 29, 2007, New Delhi-based Center for Science and Environment (CSE) in their report said mining is causing displacement, pollution, forest degradation and social unrest. The CSE report has made extensive analysis of environment degradation and pollution due to mining, wherein it has said, in 2005-06 alone 1·6 billion tons of waste and overburden from coal, iron ore, limestone and bauxite have added to environment pollution. On August 24, 2010 the Ministry of Environment and Forest (MoEF) has rejected permission for the Anil Agarwal promoted Vedanta mining project in Odisha. In a statement, the ministry has said that "the forest clearance for Vedanta stands rejected". Industries are ready and waiting for more eco-friendly method of mining.

CONSTRUCTION OF DAMS

Dams and reservoirs can be used to supply drinking water, generate hydroelectric power, increasing the water supply for irrigation and to improve certain aspects of the environment. However adverse environmental and sociological impacts have been identified during and after many reservoir constructions. The construction of large dams completely change the relationship of water and land, destroying the existing ecosystem balance which, in many cases, has taken thousands of years to create. Currently there are around 40,000 large dams which obstruct the world's river. Change in water flow following dam formation can alter river channel formation and impact the plants and animals that are able to live within the river system. Construction of dams changes a riverine habitat to a lake habitat, affecting the animal and plant communities living there. Water temperature downstream from a dam is often lower than it was prior to the dam's construction. Changes in water temperature can dramatically affect animal communities. Construction of dams also causes erosion of land. Most sediment is caught at the base of a dam, meaning the water that flows through the dams is much clear and holds fewer nutrient than prior to the dam's construction, fewer nutrients leads to destructing population of organism downstream from a dam. NASA Geophysicist Dr. Benjamin Fong Chao found evidence that large dams cause changes to the earth's rotation, because of the shift of water weight from ocean to reservoirs. Earth's daily rotation has apparently speed up by eight-millionths of a second since 1950.

Mega Projects (8 October, 2011): Bhutan ambitious plan to tap 10,000 MW of hydropower by 2020 may be following a clean and green path, but what has not been talked about is how it might affect or permanently destroy the country's pristine riverine ecosystem.

SHIFTING CULTIVATION

Shifting cultivation is also called Jhumming or Jhum Cultivation. It is a very old type of an agricultural practice in which plots of land are cultivated temporarily, and then abandoned. This system often involves clearing of a piece of land followed by several years of wood harvesting or farming, until the soil loses fertility. Once the land become inadequate for crop production, it is left to be reclaimed by natural vegetation or sometimes converted to a different long-term cyclical farming practice. The current practice of shifting cultivation in eastern and north eastern region of India is an extravagant and unscientific form of land use. Earlier the land was left for 10-15 years to be replenished but now the farmers start utilising land early. So the land does not get ready for cultivation.

States Showing Loss in Forest Cover (2005-2007)

States	Loss in Forest Cover w.r.t. 2005 Assessment (km²)	Main Reasons
Nagaland	−201	shifting cultivation
Andhra Pradesh	−129	departmental felling of eucalyptus plantations by APFDC
Arunachal Pradesh	−119	shifting cultivation, biotic pressure
Tripura	−100	shifting cultivation
Assam	−66	encroachment, shifting cultivation
Chhattisgarh	−59	mining, encroachment
Madhya Pradesh	−39	submergence
Maharashtra	−11	felling by FDCM
Haryana, Karnataka	−10	mining, encroachment
Goa, Dadra & Nagar Haveli	−5	mining, encroachment
Bihar, Jammu & Kashmir	−3	felling in TOF areas, biotic pressure after effects of tsunami
Andaman & Nicobar Islands	−1	after effects of tsunami

Slash and burn is a specific practice that may be a part of shifting cultivation. It is an agricultural procedure widely used in forested areas. Although it was practiced historically in temperate regions and today it is most widely associated with tropical agriculture.

The evil effect of shifting cultivation is divesting and far reaching in degrading the environment and ecology of these regions. It has a great negative impact on the environment. Slash and burn method involves burning down of trees, which releases harmful gases into the atmosphere and causes air pollution. These harmful gases affect the health of people living in surrounding area. Shifting cultivation can also kill many species of flora and fauna in the process so it is a major cause of loss of biodiversity. This has also resulted in large scale deforestation, soil and nutrient loss and invasion by weeds and other species.

LESSON AT A GLANCE

Ecosystem: The living community (Flora and Fauna of the Habitat), and the physical environment functioning together as an independent, and relatively stable systematic environment.

Changing Pattern of Land Use: This changing pattern of land use took place as human society changed from agricultural society to an industrial and urbanised one. Due to growing population, increasing need for resources and economic development, ecosystem started deteriorating.

Industrialisation and Urbanisation: The industries in and around the cities discharge their effluents, which are accumulated in the land system, which has negative impact on the environment. Due to industrialisation the density of population in urban areas increases because of the migration of people from less industrialised regions to more industrialised regions.

Migration: Movement of people from one place to another, results in concentration of population in a limited space, causes deforestation, pollution, etc.

Dwelling Units: To accommodate the migrating population, more dwelling units are developed, in such places which lack proper sanitation conditions and water supply. The lack of safe drinking water facilitates the spread of water borne diseases.

Mining: Process of extracting minerals from the earth's crust. It causes soil erosion, landslides and land degradation.

Construction of Dams: Dams can be used to supply drinking water, generate hydroelectric power, increasing the water supply for irrigation, etc. It changes a riverine habitat to a lake habitat, affecting the animal and plant communities living there.

Shifting Cultivation: An agricultural system in which plots of land are cultivated temporarily and then abandoned. It involves burning down of trees, which releases harmful gases into the atmosphere and causes air pollution.

PROJECT WORK

1. Visit to two slums areas of your city and collect the information on the provision of basic services and infrastructure in slums, including energy, housing, transport, sanitation, water, health and education. And suggest the measures which can be taken either by individuals or by modifying schemes of the government for improving the living conditions of slum dwellers.
2. Visit to two chemical industries of your city and make a chart showing the negative effects of chemicals and the discharge effluent on environment, land and water bodies. And suggest some measures which can be taken by the government to control its hazards.

QUESTIONS

A. Short Answer Type Questions:
1. What is ecosystem destruction?
2. What are the factors affecting ecosystem destruction?
3. Define the term land use.
4. How do changes occur in land use?
5. How the changing pattern of land use affect ecosystem?
6. What is the effect of industries on global warming?
7. Name the two industrial disasters.
8. What do you mean by urbanisation?
9. What do you mean by dwelling units?
10. How will you define a slum?
11. How does mining affect the environment?
12. What is required to generate hydro-power?
13. Give the name of Geophysicist who found evidence that large dams cause changes to the earth's rotation.
14. What do you understand by shifting cultivation?
15. What are slash and burn cultivation?

Recent Year Questions:
1. Briefly explain the impact of constructing dams on the ecosystem. [ICSE 2013]
2. How does the practice of shifting cultivation affect the environment adversely? [ICSE 2014]

OR

Briefly explain any two impacts of shifting cultivation on ecosystem. [ICSE 2018]
3. State an adverse impact of urbanisation on the ecosystem. [ICSE 2014]
4. State whether the following statement is true or false. Give one reason for your answer.
Construction of dams can have negative impacts on the ecosystem. [ICSE 2016]
5. Mining operations can destroy ecosystem. Give two reasons to support the statement. [ICSE 2019]

B. Long Answer Type Questions:
1. List the various purposes for which land is used.
2. Why do people migrate and what are the effects of migration?
3. What is the negative impact of industrialisation and urbanisation on the eco-system?
4. Discuss the various schemes for upgradation of dwelling units.
5. Discuss the various drawbacks of dams.
6. About 45 percent of India's land is degraded, air pollution is increasing in all its cities, it is losing its rare plants and animals more rapidly than before and about one-third of its urban population now lives in slums, says the State of Environment Report India 2009 brought out by the government. The prime causes of land degradation are deforestation, industrialisation, shifting cultivation, mining

and excessive ground water extraction. The report points out that while India contributes only about five percent of the world's greenhouse gas emissions that are leading to climate change, about 700 million Indians directly face the threat of global warming today, as it affects farming, makes droughts, floods and storms more frequent and more severe and is raising the sea level. In the section on urbanisation, the report points out that 20 to 40 percent of people living in cities are in slums.

(i) Define destruction of ecosystem.
(ii) What is the effect of shifting cultivation on ecosystem?
(iii) Explain the destruction of ecosystem due to:
   (a) Dwelling units.
   (b) Urbanisation.

Recent Year Questions:

1. What is meant by ecosystem? Explain three adverse effects of mining on the ecosystem. [ICSE 2013]
2. What is meant by industrialisation? Explain four impacts of industrialisation on the environment. [ICSE 2014]
3. What is meant by migration? Explain three ways by which migration impacts the ecosystem. [ICSE 2015]
4. Define Ecosystem. Explain any two impacts of each of the following on the ecosystem:
   (i) Industrialisation
   (ii) Automobiles
   (iii) Dwelling houses. [ICSE 2016]

08 Labour

In an ordinary sense, the term 'Labour' means the manual work done by a worker, *i.e.*, work requiring a lot of physical effort or exertion. In other words, by 'Labour', we generally mean a sense of 'hard work' or 'difficult work'. However, in economics; the word 'Labour' is used in a much wider sense and it indicates all kinds of efforts—'Physical' and/or 'Mental'—made to earn a living.

"Any exertion of mind or body undergone partly or wholly with a view to some good other than the pleasure derived directly from the work, is called Labour."
—**Prof. A. Marshall**

"Labour consists of all human efforts of body or of mind which are undertaken in the expectation of reward." —**S. E. Thomas**

Thus, 'labour' includes only those efforts of men—'physical' or 'mental'—which are basically made to earn a living.

In other words, by 'Labour' we mean only human effort, *i.e.*, the work done by a person. The work done by machines or animals is not 'labour'. Labour is a basic factor of production without which nothing can be produced.

Labour always indicates some kind of 'mental' or 'physical' exertion undertaken with a motive to earn money. Any effort or exertion undertaken for the sake of pleasure or social service is not considered as labour.

Both physical and mental efforts are required to complete a work. However, in some kinds of work, more physical labour is involved as compared to mental exertion. Whereas in some other cases, more mental exertion is required than physical labour. As such, one cannot clearly classify any work as purely physical labour or mental labour.

OVERVIEW

Labour is an active factor of production. It includes all human efforts (physical as well as mental) made for the sake of monetary gain. The mobility of labour is usually low, while the efficiency of labourer differs from person to person.

The division (specialisation) of labour is the modern concept and it is a system adopted in large-scale industries and big business organisations. The division of labour is advantageous to producers as goods or commodities of uniform quality can be produced economically. It is beneficial to workers also as their efficiency and living standards are improved and the mental and physical strains also are reduced. The society and the nations are also benefitted due to systematic and rapid economic development.

The efficiency of worker is the production capacity of worker. The lower efficiency of workers in India is mainly attributed to climatic conditions, socio-religious factors, general working conditions and to a certain extent, due to outdated technology and worn-out equipments besides their education and experience.

If a student plays a game (cricket or hockey) vigorously, with great exertion of body and mind for pleasure only or a mother looks after her child out of affection or a man works in a garden for pleasure/hobby; then these exertions are not considered by economists as 'labour' because they have not done their physical and mental work with an objective of earning money. But, when a cricket coach or a football coach teaches the players to improve their game or a nurse attends to a child in hospital, or a man works in a garden, in order to get monetary remuneration, economists call such efforts or exertions—'physical' or 'mental'—as 'labour'. But if the work has, at any time, been done for the sake of pleasure, recreation or for satisfying any kind of religious, patriotic or social feelings, then it will not be treated as 'labour'.

In modern times, the factory workers, engineers, supervisors, office clerks, teachers, doctors, traders, managers, etc., who undergo any kind of mental or physical exertions in order to get a monetary reward, are called 'Labour'.

CHARACTERISTICS OF LABOUR

Labour is an active factor of production, which makes it distinctly different from other factors of production. Moreover, labour is not only a 'means of production' but also an 'end of production'.

The following are some of the important characteristics of labour, which make it different from other factors of production.

The Labourer (Worker) and his Labour are Inseparable: The efforts of a worker cannot be separated from him. A labourer's work has to be delivered in person. But this is not the case with other factors of production. For example, a farmer has to be present in the field to plough the field, but the owner of the field does not need to be present at the time of the cultivation unless and until he himself is the farmer. Hence, it can be said that a labourer has to carry his labour-power with him.

The Labourer Sells his Services (Labour) Only: A labourer (worker) sells his services only and not himself. When a worker sells his services (labour), he himself remains quite independent and retains his identity. A labourer may or may not agree to do a work. The 'labour' factor comes into consideration when he agrees to offer his services on certain terms and conditions.

Labour is an Active Factor of Production: Land and capital are inactive factors of production because they cannot produce anything on their own, but labour is an active factor. This is because the labourer is a living entity. A labourer (worker) can think, act and move in different ways and manner and thus, can function according to his need or circumstances. A worker can perform his services without co-operation from land and capital, but land and capital cannot be put to any use for productive purpose unless and until efforts from labourer are made available.

Labour is Highly Perishable: If a labourer does not work for a day, his one day's work will be lost forever. As such the labourer (worker) agrees to work, even at a low wage, when he feels that his labour is likely to be wasted. Because of this peculiarity, the labourer does not have the same bargaining power similar to his employer.

Labour has Weaker Bargaining Power: As compared to the employer, the bargaining power of the worker is low. *Firstly*, labour is perishable. Therefore, worker opts to accept the low wages offered by the employer rather than go without work. *Secondly*, the economic position of the employer is stronger than that of the worker because he has money power and the power to hire many units of labour while a labourer has only one unit of labour, he himself. *Thirdly*, due to illiteracy and other reasons, the workers are unorganised.

Labour has Typical Nature of Supply: Individual labour supply is not similar to the supply of any other factor. As price of any factor rises the supply of it also rises, but that is not the case with labour. As wage rate rises, a labourer becomes willing to supply more labour, thus labour supply also rises. But as wage rate increases further the labourer may wish to enjoy more leisure than to work for longer hours, as his living standard has improved. Hence, the supply of labour falls.

Supply of Labour Changes Slowly: The supply of labour cannot be increased or decreased quickly, as the supply of labour is related with the population of the country. If at any time, the demand for unskilled workers increases, it cannot be supplemented quickly *"by just making orders or indents"* as it can be possibly done in case of other commodities. For more supply of labour, we have to wait for the growth of population, which may take a long period of about 15-20 years. Similarly, if the demand for engineers or doctors increases, then also it will take many years to arrange the required number of such professionals for which there will be a need of establishing more educational institutions (Engineering and Medical Colleges).

Similarly, when the demand of workers decreases, it will not be possible to reduce it quickly, because any method involved to kill the people or forced emigration cannot be resorted to reduce the population (or the supply of labour) of a country. Thus, it is very clear that the supply of labour changes quite slowly.

Human Factor: Labour is human factor. Hence several human considerations are to be kept in mind while dealing with the labour, such as, moral considerations, ethical considerations, devotion, motivation (including incentives), family background, etc.

Labour is Less Mobile: The goods of various kinds can be moved from one locality to another in a very convenient manner. The capital too can be transferred and moved in a very convenient way within the country. The flow of capital from one country to another is also easy, if there are chances of more profit and there is no risk to the invested capital. But, the mobility of labour is not so easy. Even the most remunerative employment opportunities do not attract many trained personnel from other countries. This is due to the labourers' sentimental attachments to his home and surroundings. The problems of language, differences in living habits and social customs, etc., are some other important factors affecting mobility of labour.

Labourers Differ in Efficiency: The manufactured goods, commodities, tools and machines are mostly symmetrical and can be inter-changed conveniently. For example, if a particular type of tool is broken, or requires replacement due to wear and tear, it can be easily replaced by another one of a similar type and the work can be managed in the same manner. But this is not possible in case of labourer, because the efficiency of each individual worker is different. Therefore, if a trained and an experienced worker falls sick or resigns, it is very difficult to get a worker of the same skill and the same efficiency. This is the main reason as to why different workers or different categories of workers get different wages.

Quality of Workers can be Improved: The quality of labour can be improved to a great extent by proper education and practical training, with establishment of schools, colleges, technical training institutions, workshops, etc. It has been observed that countries with better training facilities for their human resource can produce efficient and competent labour force.

It has been observed that the countries having better training facilities for their human force, have produced efficient and competent doctors, engineers, architects, etc. Thus, it is very clear that quality of labour can be improved by developing proper training infrastructure.

Labour has Alternative Uses: It is possible for any labourer to engage himself in different fields of work, for example, an unskilled worker can work as a rickshaw-puller or hawker or porter, etc.

Distinction between Land and Labour

Land	Labour
1. Land is a passive factor of production.	1. Labour (including entrepreneur) is an active factor of production.
2. Land is not mobile.	2. Labour is mobile.
3. Land has a different identity from its owner. The land owner need not be present at the site when land is being used as a factor of production.	3. Labour cannot be separated from labourer, *i.e.*, the labourer has to present himself for using his labour power.
4. The landowner can accumulate any amount of land. land does not get wasted, if not used same day. it can be kept as it is (undamaged) for any period of time. Thus, land is not perishable.	4. The labour power cannot be accumulated. it is wasted if not used same time. Thus, labour is perishable.
5. The land as factor of production does not possess an element of judgement because it is a passive factor of production.	5. The human labour possesses an element of judgement, as it is an active factor of production.
6. The total quantity of land remains fixed for short as well as long duration. However, the quantity of potentially usable land can be increased by reclamation over a short period.	6. The supply of labour is fixed for a very short period, but with the growth of population, the supply of labour increases over a long period.
7. The land is the ultimate source of all factors of production, as the man requires land to survive and carry on various activities.	7. Labour is the active factor, which puts efforts on land to produce goods. A land without labour cannot have any economic activity.

LABOUR: AN IMPORTANT FACTOR OF PRODUCTION

If we examine the contribution of various factors of production (land, labour, capital and entrepreneur or organiser), we find that labour is a very significant factor of production. A nation having plenty of rich land but no labour force, cannot attain any economic development or prosperity. Agriculture, industries, mining, transport system, trade activities, etc., all require sufficient and efficient workers for proper functioning.

Labour is an active factor of production. The land and capital do not play any active role in production. These factors become productive only with the co-operation of labour. Capital itself has no identity, but actually it is the result of human efforts exerted on land. For example, a steel tool or an implement is a capital good, but earlier it was only iron ore. It has been converted to steel tool by the efforts of labour. Thus, it is very clear that all capital things or commodities have been produced by the workers.

ENTREPRENEUR–SPECIAL TYPE OF LABOUR

Even though the organiser and entrepreneur have been regarded as separate factors of production, yet in fact these are special types of workers, who have some special abilities and special functions to perform. An organiser, for example, has ability to organise an industry and that capability is acquired after having special kind of training. Otherwise, an entrepreneur is also like an ordinary labour. The only difference between him and an ordinary worker is that the former has to do a lot of mental work and has to implement his decisions regarding planning, co-operation, execution and motivation to achieve desired production targets whereas the latter has to only carry out mental or physical work entrusted to him by the former (employer or entrepreneur).

Due to special abilities and experience, the entrepreneur is able to take decisions. He also possesses ability to direct his workers in respect of plans made by him so that the production units may earn maximum profits and may develop and keep the goodwill. The ordinary worker, however, only performs the duties as planned and assigned by the entrepreneur.

Thus, in fact the *Organisers* and *Entrepreneurs* are also labourers but possessing some special capabilities. So when *organisers* and *entrepreneurs* are included in the term labour, it becomes the only active factor of production.

LABOUR AND ECONOMIC ACTIVITIES

All kinds of trade and economic activities—National (internal) or International depend upon labour force.

In case of labour strikes or lockouts, the production of mills and factories declines which adversely affects the National and International trade as well as the economy as a whole. Similarly, the trading activities of a nation suffer a set-back, when the workers engaged in transport and communication suspend the work or adopt go-slow tactics.

According to socialists, the contribution of other factors in the process of production is quite insignificant and they believe that all the wealth in the society is due to labourers only. Therefore, they propose that labourers are entitled to get a good share out of the total profit of the productive concern. **Karl Marx** pleaded very strongly in favour of labourers. In his opinion, the surplus available with the capitalist is due to efforts of labour and this surplus with the capitalist is created because the labourers are paid less. Thus, surplus accumulated with the capitalists is nothing but robbery and exploitation.

In modern times, various governments make plans for different national programmes and frame different national policies, keeping in view the labour force of the country. *Labour welfare programmes, labour utilisation schemes, programmes of technical or vocational education, programmes for self-employment, etc.,* are a few such programmes. Now-a-days, the governments have come to realise that the problem of labour force is one of the most important problems in underdeveloped nations as well as in developing nations.

In India, the rapidly growing population (from which we get the country's labour force) is a serious problem and proper utilisation of increasing labour force is very essential for achieving economic development.

DIVISION (SPECIALISATION) OF LABOUR

Adam Smith in his book *"The Wealth of Nations"* was the first to put forward the idea of division of labour. He suggested a division of manufacturing process into uncomplicated and simple operations which are to be performed by different units.

With the invention of machines and the large-scale production of goods, the specialisation or the division of labour has become necessary and important. Earlier, when the production was on a small-scale and there were no machines, the people were doing most of the jobs themselves to fulfill their needs. For example, the farmer besides cultivating his land used to grow vegetables and fruits, tamed cows and buffaloes for milk and butter and also worked as a carpenter for building and repairing his articles of work and household furniture.

Now-a-days, with the help of machines and the universal use of *'money'* and *'currency'*; the commodities are being produced on large-scale. As such one worker is usually required to produce only one or some specific type of item(s) for which he has capability and aptitude. Other items or services can be procured by paying money, which he earns by doing his specific job.

The division of labour has become all the more important and essential now because of increasing complexity of working processes. To accomplish the work successfully, the complicated work is divided into smaller simple segments and accordingly the labour is engaged to perform the task relating to each segment. Thus, a worker is required to perform only one specific type of work and its regular repetition improves his skill and efficiency.

"The system of distributing a particular type of job(s) to a particular type of worker, is known as specialisation or division of labour."

"Division of labour is defined as a system wherein the operations necessary to make a finished product are so minutely divided that each worker performs only one or at most only a few simple operations."
— **A. H. Smith**

"The specialisation of workers in particular parts of a production process is called the division of labour."
— **Penguin dictionary of economics**

The effect of division of labour is clearly visible these days, in every industry. In automobile plants initially a bare chassis is put on the conveyor belt which passes through the different units of the plant where, section wise, different units are installed on it one after another. At the other end it comes out of the plant as a finished product. It is not only in the manufacturing plants, but in other fields also where there is economic activity like, Hospitals, Hotels, Educational Institutions, etc., where division of labour is a common phenomena.

Here, it must be clearly understood that the division of labour is concerned not only with the people, but also for the whole region. Some examples of regional specialisation of labour are those of West Bengal (for jute and jute goods), Switzerland (watch-making), Denmark (dairy products), etc.

Thus, specialisation or division of labour means that every person or region specialises in production of one particular commodity or service in full or in parts.

TYPES OF DIVISION OF LABOUR

Division of labour may be simple, complex and territorial depending upon various factors involved. The division of labour can be classified as below:

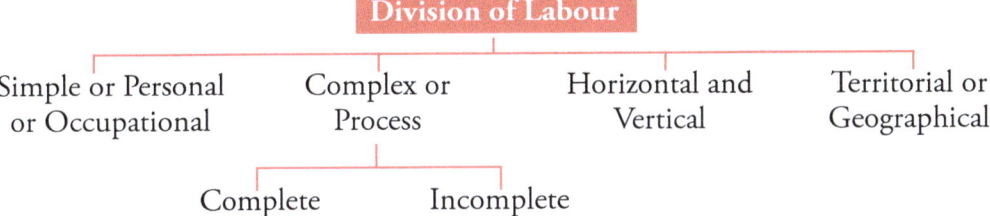

1. Simple (Personal or Occupational) Division of Labour

The people around us can be divided into farmers, traders, doctors, teachers, weavers, etc., according to their respective occupations. This type of division is called simple or occupational division of labour in which people are specialised in one type of occupation. In case of more complex works further divisions are made. A specialisation in the medical field is a very good example of occupational division of labour. There are specialists of skin disease, heart, eye, dentists, etc. This type of division is also known as personal division of labour because each individual takes up only one specific job depending on his ability and aptitude. In simple words, simple division of labour or occupational division of labour refers to when one person performs a particular occupation only like blacksmith, dentist, etc.

2. Complex or Process Division of Labour

In this system the total work is divided into many small steps or processes. Each specialised function is undertaken by an individual or a group of individuals leading to the final product. This type of division of labour is further classified in following two categories:

Complete Process of Complex Division of Labour: In this system the total work is divided into parts or processes and sub-parts or sub-processes in such a manner so that the product of each part or process is able to yield a commodity in a complete form for the next process. For example, consider the jobs done in a cotton mill, where spinning, weaving, sizing, bleaching, etc., are done by different processes and by different workers in such a way that completely finished cloth is finally made for use.

Incomplete Process of Complex Division of Labour: In this system the work is divided into different processes and sub-processes in such a way that only a part or a component of a commodity is produced. Since the part produced in one process is not directly passed on to the next process in a complete form, this system is known as incomplete process of complex division of labour. For example, the different parts of an automobile are incomplete parts unless and until they are assembled together to produce the complete car.

3. Horizontal and Vertical Division of Labour

Horizontal Division of Labour: When the process of production is divided between different parts in such a way that the different parts of the process can run simultaneously, then it is called horizontal division of labour. The different parts of an automobile can be manufactured simultaneously and assembled together at the end. Hence, the workers engaged in producing different parts of an automobile is an example of horizontal division of labour.

Vertical Division of Labour: On the other hand, vertical division of labour is related to the successive stages of production of a commodity. For example, in order to produce cotton textile, raw cotton has to be transformed into yarn by spinning. Only then the yarn can be woven into cloth. Spinning and weaving cannot be done simultaneously on the same bag of raw cotton. Hence, the division of labour of the workers in the cotton textile industry is an example of vertical division of labour.

4. Territorial or Geographical Division of Labour

It is a fact that certain areas or regions have some special geographical conditions, e.g., availability of power resources, sufficient raw materials, suitable climate, etc., which help in the establishment and development of a particular type of industry there. These peculiar circumstances result in geographical or territorial division of labour. The examples are development of cotton textile mills in Mumbai (Bombay) and Ahmedabad, on account of abundant availability of raw cotton and the favourable climatic conditions in Maharashtra and Gujarat. The concentration of jute industry in Hoogly region of West Bengal and Iron and Steel industry in Jamshedpur and Bhillai are some of the other examples. It is also called National division of labour.

Such kind of geographical specialisation may also take place at the international level where countries endowed with certain products may export them to other countries and import the necessary commodities in which other countries are endowed in rich manner. For example, the gulf countries are rich in mineral oil which they export; while Japan is deficient in Iron and Steel which it imports from other countries. Such specialisation is called International specialisation or division of labour.

The process division and territorial division of labour are growing rapidly these days. Personal or occupational division of labour is declining gradually because of the widespread use of machines and large-scale production under the factory system. In fact, the overall economic advantages gained in industrial developments are due to division (specialisation) of labour.

ADVANTAGES OF DIVISION OF LABOUR

The advantages of division of labour can be studied under four categories: (i) Advantages to producers, (ii) Advantages to workers, (iii) Advantages to consumers and (iv) Advantages to the society. The division of labour has been advantageous to society as a whole, *i.e.*, to producers, to workers, to consumers and to society, as will be clear from the following:

1. ADVANTAGES TO THE PRODUCERS

The division (specialisation) of labour helps the producers in their productive activities to earn more monetary benefits in the following ways:

Increase in Production: With the specialisation (division) of labour, the workers become more skilled and efficient. They acquire higher speed in work output, which ultimately results in more production, quantitatively as well as qualitatively. This directly enables the producers to earn greater amount of profit.

Reduction in Cost of Production: The specialised (expert) worker with the help of machines, produces more quantity of goods in less time and with minimum wastage. This reduces the cost of production thereby resulting in more profit to producer.

Improvement in Quality: As the worker acquires greater skill in performing the work, the quality of the commodity produced is better. The good quality product becomes more and more popular and acceptable to the consumer. This increases the overall turnover thereby enhancing the profit of the producer.

Scope for Mechanisation: By the division of labour, a worker is required to work only for the simple process or sub-process. For such segments of work, machines can be introduced easily. The use of machines, by the skilled (specialised) worker helps in standardisation of the product as well as in achieving a higher production, thereby providing more earnings to the producer.

Economy in use of Tools and Implements: With the division of labour, the use of tools and implements becomes comparatively economical. This is because of the fact that a particular worker requires one machine or a few tools, which he uses more frequently, speedily, accurately and carefully (skillfully). This ultimately adds to the earnings of the producer.

Economy of Large-scale Production: With the help of the division of labour, the commodities are being produced on large-scale, and in an efficient and quick way. This results in all kinds of internal and external economies for the production units. As such the cost of production is reduced and simultaneously the quality of manufactured goods is improved. This ultimately yields more profit to the producer. Other advantages—more employment, geographical advantages, scope for inventions and innovations, etc.

2. ADVANTAGES TO THE WORKERS

Besides being beneficial to the producer, the division of labour is also beneficial to the workers. Benefits to the workers accrue in the following ways:

Right Man at Right Place: Under this division of labour, the individual worker is assigned a job for which he is best suited. This helps the work to be completed in the most appropriate way, besides providing a feeling of job satisfaction to the worker because a worker feels a kind of pleasure when he performs the job of his taste, capability and aptitude.

Improvement in Efficiency: The worker is assigned one type of work, according to his aptitude and skill so that he attends the work with zeal and devotion which naturally improves the efficiency of the worker. Practice makes him perfect and so gradually he becomes an expert of that job. The improvement in efficiency makes him an expert of the job and directly increases his remuneration whereby the worker gets some benefit.

Saving of Time: Due to the fact that a worker has to carry out only one type of job, he is not required to move frequently from one job to another. Also he needs not to change the tool or machine now and then. Thus, he can work continuously without any loss of time and gives more output.

Less Training Period: Under the division of labour, only a part of job is required to be attended by the worker for which he can be imparted necessary training in a very short duration.

Reduction in Physical and Mental Strain: By continuously performing a small part of the total work, the worker becomes fully trained which reduces mental and physical strain. With the aid of machines, his work becomes still easier.

Increased Employment Opportunities: Due to the division of labour, the number and variety of jobs have increased. This has paved the way for the setting up of large number of large-scale and small-scale industries and the subsidiary units. This rapid industrialisation creates more employment opportunities for the workers. Even less skilled or unskilled workers get a chance for some kind of job.

3. ADVANTAGES TO THE CONSUMERS

Since the division (specialisation) of labour ultimately results in an overall improvement in the quality of product and reduction in costs, the consumers are also benefitted.

Availability of Goods at Cheaper Rates: Large-scale manufacturing of almost all types of commodities is possible now, because of the specialisation of labour. The large-scale production improves the external as well as internal economies in the production process, thereby resulting in a lower cost of production. The lower cost of production makes it possible for wholesalers and retailers to sell goods at cheaper rates.

Large Varieties of goods: Besides the reduction in cost of production, large varieties of each type of commodities are also readily available on account of simplification and division of complex processes of production. The division (specialisation) of labour has made it possible to manufacture at cheaper rates, the products requiring higher skill. For example, car is now being conveniently produced by making the appropriate division of labour, in which many simplified jobs are being done by less skilled or unskilled labour at cheaper rates. As there was no division of labour in the past, many of the commodities were available at very high price due to the complex process of production. Only the rich people could afford those goods.

Improvement in the Standard of Living: Due to the availability of a variety of goods at cheaper rates, the consumers have a better choice for purchasing the goods of their choice and standard. Consumption pattern of the society reflects its standard of living. The coming up of new manufacturing units, has resulted in a situation, where every now and then, some new variety of product appears in the market. This has provided a greater opportunity of selection and choice of goods to the consumers.

4. ADVANTAGES TO THE SOCIETY

There are some advantages of specialisation of labour to the society as well.

Rapid Economic Development: Through division of work, all the other resources are utilised to maximum extent. Consequently more employment opportunities are generated leading to increased economic growth and economic development. Society benefits from rapid economic development.

Increased Number of Organisers (Entrepreneurs): Possibility of better quality products, low cost of production and higher profits due to division of labour attract the people of entrepreneurial flair to start new production ventures. This is beneficial for the entrepreneurs, labourers and society as a whole.

DISADVANTAGES OF DIVISION OF LABOUR

We have discussed the advantages of the division of labour, which have benefitted the various groups and sections of the society. But there are certain inherent demerits in such system, which are as follows:

Monotony of Work: Under the division of labour, the worker is required to perform the same type of job again and again. The job becomes monotonous and the worker gradually loses interest in it. This zeal and initiative to learn and do something new gets diminished, if he continues same job for months together and this causes a kind of mental fatigue. Ultimately, it becomes harmful, both to the employer as well as to the worker, because under the condition of mental fatigue, the quality of work deteriorates. To overcome this situation, the assignment of some new type of work must be planned, which may provide a kind of freshness to the mental status of the worker.

Retards Development of Personality: Since the worker does only the same type of job, over and over again, either by using his hands or legs or both; his muscles and mind remain active only in that particular direction repeatedly. This hampers his mental and physical development in other directions. Consequently, his mental outlook becomes narrow and it restricts the development of his overall personality.

Lack of Skill and Craftsmanship: Lately, it has been observed that mastery of ancient craftsmanship and artistic skill is disappearing gradually, as the worker is required to perform only a part of total work. For example, a worker in a shoe factory knows either making of sole or simply finishing the job of the shoe. Thus, division of labour is resulting in a disappearance of artistic skill among the workers, because his contribution in completion of a commodity is not so significant.

Excessive Interdependence: Due to specialisation (division) of labour, the inter-dependence between workers increases manifold. Since every worker produces only a small part of the complete commodity, they depend on each other for the final product. In case a unit of workers decides to remain absent the whole of the production line is affected.

Danger of Overproduction: The commodities and goods are produced cheaply in large-scale these days. This sometimes leads to the situation of production of more goods than the demand. This is called *'overproduction'* or *'boom'*. Under such circumstances, the producers suffer great losses and have no option but to produce less till the situation becomes normal. This situation is known as *'depression'* or *'underproduction'*. Thus, the specialisation (division) of labour generates a kind of economic cycle of *'boom and depression'*; which is very harmful for steady economic developments and due to this, the society suffers as a whole.

Defects of Factory System: The division of labour has resulted in a large-scale production under factory system, where thousands of workers are employed and, the work is done by utilising different types of machines. Since the factory system has certain inherent defects, the society as a whole suffers due to these defects. Most important defects of the factory system are:

- Concentration of wealth in few hands,
- Overcrowding of population in industrial region,
- Water and air pollution,
- Unhygienic environment around industrial units,
- Exploitation of women and children, who are employed as workers, and
- Moral degradation.

Imbalance in Territorial Development: On account of territorial division of labour, some areas become more developed and advanced as compared to others. This creates a regional imbalance. The regions around Kolkata (Calcutta), Mumbai (Bombay), Kanpur, Jamshedpur, etc., are economically more advanced, whereas many parts in Rajasthan, Madhya Pradesh, Odisha and North-eastern states are highly backward.

However, these regional imbalances can be removed to some extent, by the government, by making proper planning for the development of backward areas.

NECESSARY CONDITIONS FOR THE DIVISION OF LABOUR

Some of the conditions, which are necessary for the elaborate specialisation (division) of labour are discussed below:

Attitude of Workers: The co-operative attitude and adjustability amongst the workers is the most important factor for the success of the division of labour. The people of society must be ready to work and live together and only then economic development can be accomplished.

Use of Money Economy: The use of money in society is a must, *i.e.*, the society must be in an advanced stage of economy, where the money is a medium of exchange and a measure value of goods and services. Without the use of money, the distribution of wages, salaries, purchase of raw materials, machines, and sale of products, etc., cannot be fulfilled. These conditions are very essential for the division of labour.

Adequate Supply of Labour and Capital: Division of labour is possible only when labour and capital goods are available in plenty. The division of labour is neither possible nor feasible without adequate labour and capital goods (plants, machinery, etc.).

Exact Standards of Measures and Weights: A uniform and rationalised standards of weights, length, area, etc., should be adopted throughout the country. This helps in the expansion of market for the commodity and makes way for large-scale production, which is a very essential condition for the proper division of labour.

Scope of Division in Complete and Incomplete Processes: The division of labour is useful and possible, only if the production process can be divided into smaller parts or sub-parts. Thus, the possibilities of splitting up of a process, determines the division of labour.

Technological Progress: Improvements in technological progress, transport and communication, manufacturing and inventing different types of goods, machines tools, food processing and preservation, etc., are very essential for the development of trade and industries. These in turn, affect the division of labour and its success.

Competent Organisers: The division of labour encourages the establishment and development of large-scale factories, which employ large number of workers on different jobs. For successful functioning of such large industries and factories, highly capable and competent organisers or entrepreneurs are required who only can successfully handle the complex situations of work, can suitably assign the work to different workers and can properly direct them to perform their duties for achieving the objectives of the business.

EFFICIENCY OF LABOUR

The productive capacity of a worker is termed as 'Efficiency of Labour'. In simple words, efficiency of labour refers to the quality and quantity of goods and services which can be produced by a labourer during a given period under certain prevailing conditions. For determining the efficiency of labour, following four aspects are kept in view:

- The quantity (or amount) produced by a worker,
- The quality of the item produced by a worker,
- The time spent by a worker in producing that product.
- Production under prevailing conditions.

Efficiency of labour can be defined as under:

"By efficiency of labour is meant the ability of labour by virtue of which it is productive."
—**J. K. Mehta**

"By efficiency of labour we mean the amount of work which a labourer can do within a given time."
—**D. R. Saxena**

To sum up, the efficiency of that worker will be more who, under certain given circumstances; produces more quantity of a better quality product in comparatively less time. To understand it more clearly, study the data given in the *Table 8·1:*

Table : 8·1

Name of the worker	Number of baskets made	Time taken	Quality of the products
A	10	7 Hrs.	
B	9	7 Hrs.	As per requirements (Good)
C	9	7 Hrs.	
D	8	7 Hrs.	

From the data given in the *Table 8·1*, it is clear that during the same duration of 7 hours, the worker named A has made 10 baskets. Under similar conditions, other workers named B, C and D have completed the making of 9, 9 and 8 baskets respectively. In other words, we can say that the worker named A is more efficient than others. It should, however, be clearly understood that *efficiency is a relative term*. It is not an absolute entity.

However, when the conditions of work or quality of product are different, simple comparison, as done above, may not be correct. For instance, examine the data given in *Table 8·2:*

Table : 8·2

Name of the worker	Number of baskets made	Time taken	Quality of the product
E	10	7 Hrs.	Poor
F	10	7 Hrs.	Good
G	10	7 Hrs.	Good
H	10	7 Hrs.	Very Good

It will be clear from the above table that the quantitative output (*i.e.*, number of baskets made) is the same but the quality of work done differs. The qualitative efficiency of worker 'H' is highest, and that of 'E' is the lowest.

Thus, the 'efficiency of labour' is the relative term and it is measured by comparing the productive capacities—both quantitatively and qualitatively—of all the workers or all the categories of workers employed for specified job.

The efficiency of workers depend on several factors because the workers are human beings and they have different feelings, abilities, choice and attitudes. The factors affecting the efficiency of workers can be classified in two categories:

(a) General factors: (i) Racial characteristics, (ii) Climatic condition.

(b) Specific factors: (i) General and technical education, (ii) Personal quality and character, (iii) Experience, (iv) Proper and prompt wages, (v) Machinery, (vi) Duration of work.

CAUSES OF LOW EFFICIENCY OF LABOUR IN INDIA

The efficiency of Indian labour is comparatively low as compared to that of developed countries like U.S.A., U.K., Canada, Japan and Germany and accordingly the productivity is also low in India. There are several causes for low efficiency and some are discussed below:

Hot and Enervating Climate: India is a sub-tropical country and its climate is hot and enervating. It reduces the workers' capacity for hard and continuous work for long hours. This is the most important natural cause of low efficiency of labour in India.

Low Wages: If higher efficiency leads to higher income, then only the workers have the incentive to become more efficient. But generally the wages of labour in India are low and so is the standard of living. As such, the workers are not in a position to keep themselves physically and mentally fit and in sound health, and they have little leisure time for recreation. This is also a cause of low efficiency.

Inadequacy of Machinery, Equipments and Raw Materials: The availability of equipments and the supply of raw materials is not adequate. In general, the machines are either outdated and of poor standard or these are usually in worn out conditions. Besides this, the frequent breakdowns of machines and shortage of electricity cause the downfall in the productive capacity (or efficiency) of workers.

Uncongenial Factory Environment: Many factories in India have poor and unhygienic working conditions. The facilities of canteen (*i.e.*, low-cost meals), recreation and relaxation are not provided. This creates an uncongenial environment and affects the productivity of workers.

Workers' Habits and Socio-religious Factors: The cultural and religious inclinations towards spiritualism in preference to materialism and blind faith and superstitions amongst the labourers, causes reduction in their productivity. Moreover, a large number of workers are alcoholic and gamblers. This altogether alters the attitude of workers towards hard work and in turn lowers their efficiency.

Migratory Character: A very high proportion of workers usually come to work in factories from villages when their agricultural activities are minimum. During the period when the agricultural activities start, these workers take leave or remain absent from work. This type of migratory behaviour lowers the efficiency of workers and productivity of industrial units.

Education and Training: The workers, in general, do not have proper education and practical training about the work. To overcome this, the government is doing a lot for workers, so that they get the required practical training and necessary education.

Inefficient Management: The managers and organisers usually lack in originality, initiation, planning and creative thinking. Moreover, they are not interested in understanding the industrial psychology, but they are more interested in the exploitation of workers. This attitude ultimately leads to the reduction in overall productivity of the workers.

Absence of Adequate Social Security Schemes: In India, social security schemes used to hardly exist—particularly in unorganised sectors of the Indian economy, such as, agriculture and tiny industrial establishments. But now the situation has been changing.

SUGGESTIONS FOR IMPROVING THE EFFICIENCY OF INDIAN WORKERS

The Government of India is seriously interested in the overall economic development of the country and every possible step is being taken. However, following are some suggestions, which may definitely help in improving the efficiency of workers.

- The payment of wages should be fair and prompt. The government has however enacted the Minimum Wages Act for this purpose, so that each category of worker is paid according to the job he performs.
- A part of profit, earned by the concern must be paid to workers as an incentive.
- Working conditions in the factories should be improved. Even though the Factory Act has clearly mentioned about the working conditions, the proper implementation and enforcement of same is needed.
- The total period of work per day should not be more than eight hours. In this regard also, proper enforcement of law is necessary. Also other facilities like holidays, leaves, etc., should be given to workers.
- Social security network should be built up to protect the workers against illness, factory accidents, old age problems and unemployment in form of insurance, medical aid, etc.

- Effective steps should be taken to create awareness amongst the workers regarding evil effects of activities like gambling, drinking, etc.
- General and technical education and training facilities should be extended.
- Other fringe benefits like housing facilities, medical aid, group insurance, etc., should be provided to workers.
- Besides all these measures (to be taken either by the employer or the government), it is essential that workers should not resort to practice of strikes and conflicts with the employer. They should also be co-operative which will ultimately benefit both the worker and the employer.
- The labour unions should also motivate the workers to adopt constructive and positive approach, rather than instigating them to create disputes and conflicts.

The government has passed and enacted several legislations to improve the working conditions of workers. The enforcement of these laws is not satisfactory although the working environment has been found to be greatly improved since independence.

LESSON AT A GLANCE

Labour: By labour we mean only human effort, *i.e.*, the work done by a person. Labour always indicates some kind of mental or physical exertion undertaken with a motive to earn money.

Characteristics of Labour: (i) The labourer and his labour are inseparable; (ii) The labourer sells his services only; (iii) Labour is an active factor of production; (iv) Labour is highly perishable; (v) Labour has weaker bargaining power; (vi) Labour has typical nature of supply; (vii) Supply of labour changes slowly; (viii) Human factor; (ix) Labour is less mobile; (x) Labourers differ in efficiency; (xi) Quality of workers can be improved by investing capital, and (xii) Labour has alternative uses.

Importance of Labour: Labour is a very significant factor of production. The natural resources of a country cannot be utilised in the absence of labour.

Division of Labour: By division of labour, we mean distributing a particular type of job to particular type of worker.

Types of Division of Labour: Simple (Personal or occupational) division of labour; Complex or process division of labour; Horizontal and Vertical division of labour; and Territorial or geographical division of labour.

Advantages of Division of Labour: Division of labour is beneficial to producers, workers, consumers and society in different ways.

(A) Advantages to the Producers: (i) Increase in production; (ii) Reduction in cost of production; (iii) Improvement in quality; (iv) Scope for mechanisation; (v) Economy in use of tools, and implements; (vi) Economy of large-scale production.

(B) Advantages to the Workers: (i) Right man at right place; (ii) Improvement in efficiency; (iii) Saving of time; (iv) Less training period; (v) Reduction in physical and mental strain; (vi) Increased employment opportunities.

(C) Advantages to the Consumers: (i) Availability of goods at cheaper rates; (ii) Large varieties of goods; (iii) Improvement in the standard of living.

(D) Advantages to the Society: (i) Rapid economic development; (ii) Increased number of organisers (entrepreneurs).

Disadvantages of Division of Labour: (i) Monotony of work; (ii) Retards development of personality; (iii) Lack of skills and craftsmanship; (iv) Excessive interdependence; (v) Danger of over production; (vi) Defects of factory system; (vii) Imbalance in territorial development.

Necessary Conditions for the Division of Labour: (i) Attitude of workers; (ii) Use of money economy; (iii) Adequate supply of labour and capital; (iv) Exact standards of measures and weights; (v) Scope of division in complete and incomplete processes; (vi) Technological progress; and (vii) Competent organisers.

Efficiency of Labour: Efficiency of labour is the relative term and it is measured by comparing the productive capacities both quantitatively and qualitatively of all the workers or all the categories of workers.

Causes of Low Efficiency of Labour in India: (i) Hot and enervating climate; (ii) Low wages; (iii) Inadequacy of machinery, equipments and raw materials; (iv) Uncongenial factory environment; (v) Workers' habits and socio-religious factors; (vi) Migratory character; (vii) Education and training; (viii) Inefficient management; and (ix) Absence of adequate social security schemes.

Suggestions for Improving the Efficiency of Indian Workers: (i) Payment of wages should be fair and prompt; (ii) Workers should get incentive; (iii) Working condition of factories should be improved; (iv) There should be proper enforcement of labour-laws; (v) Social security; and (vi) General education should be extended.

PROJECT WORK

Make a case study of particular institution, *i.e.*, industrial unit, and select a group of persons and study about the quantity of some commodities produced. Make an assessment report on the efficiency of different persons working in a group. (This study requires cautious and confidential recording of data).

Note : *The case study in respect of labour involves several types of data, information, etc., hence the students are advised to take regular guidance of their teacher.*

QUESTIONS

A. Short Answer Type Questions:
1. Define Labour and give one characteristic of labour.
2. Which of the following is considered as 'labour' in Economics?
    (i) The work of teacher in a classroom.
    (ii) Participation in annual Athletic Meet of your school.
    (iii) Repairing his own furniture by a carpenter.
    (iv) Washing of children's clothes by mother.
3. Discuss entrepreneur as a special type of labour.
4. How is division of labour limited to the extent of market?
5. Explain any two conditions on which the division of labour depends.
6. State two ways by which a worker benefits from his increased efficiency.

7. State four factors which determine the efficiency of labour.
8. Distinguish between simple and complex division of labour. Explain three conditions which favour division of labour.
9. Define the term mobility of labour. Discuss its importance with reference to the economic progress of a country.

Recent Year Questions:
1. Mention two factors which have increased mobility of labour in recent times from rural to urban area. [ICSE 2007]
2. Which of the following will be treated as labour in Economics? Give a reason for each:
    (i) Preparation of food by housewife,
    (ii) Singing for one's own pleasure,
    (iii) Driving his master's car by a driver.
    (iv) Playing cricket by Mahendra Singh Dhoni. [ICSE 2009]
3. Suggest two measures to improve efficiency of labour in the unorganised sector in India. [ICSE 2010]
4. Briefly explain the impact of division of labour on cost of production by a firm. [ICSE 2011]
5. The extent of division of labour depends on the size of market. Briefly explain. [ICSE 2011]
6. Briefly explain why labour is considered to be the means and end of production. [ICSE 2013]
7. State whether the following statement is true or false. "Slow growth rate in Indian agriculture has increased mobility of labour from rural to urban areas." [ICSE 2013]
8. State whether the following statement is true or false. Give reasons. "Efficiency of labour is influenced by working conditions." [ICSE 2014]
9. Suggest two measures to improve the efficiency of labour in India. [ICSE 2014]
10. What is meant by labour in economics? [ICSE 2016]
11. Explain any one disadvantage of division of labour. [ICSE 2016]
12. What is the impact of division of labour on cost of production? [ICSE 2016]
13. State whether the following statement is true or false. Give one reason for your answer.
    Labour is the beginning and end of production. [ICSE 2016]
14. List any two causes for the low efficiency of labour in India. [ICSE 2018]
15. Which of the following is considered as labour in Economics? [ICSE 2019]
    (i) Acting done by film star.
    (ii) The judgement given by a judge in the court.
    (iii) Washing of clothes by a washerman.
    (iv) Preparation of tea by housewife.

B. Long Answer Type Questions:
1. Explain with the help of examples, the meaning of labour in Economics.
2. Describe the characteristic peculiarities of labour as an important factor of production.

3. Explain the importance of labour in modern economic system. What are the special characteristics of labour in India?
4. Labour is a unique factor of production. Discuss giving four points.
5. What do you understand by 'division of labour' (or specialisation)? With the help of examples, describe various types of division of labour.
6. Describe the various forms of division of labour. Explain, why the division of labour is adopted?
7. Discuss the merits and demerits of division of labour. Also explain the conditions which favour the division of labour.
8. Explain by giving examples as to how division of labour increases the output and efficiency of firms.
9. Suggest various measures that can be adopted to improve the efficiency of Indian labour.
10. Explain two benefits of division of labour on producers and consumers.
11. (i) Define efficiency of labour.
    (ii) Explain two ways in which labour is different from capital.
    (iii) What happens to supply of labour at very high wages?
12. India is ranked 126th among 177 nations in the human resource development index. State any two causes of low efficiency of Indian labour. Give three suggestions to improve the quality of labour in India.
13. (i) Explain four factors on which efficiency of labour depends.
    (ii) Give two causes of inefficiency of Indian labour.

Recent Year Questions:
1. Differentiate between physical and mental labour. State four ways in which division of labour will influence production in an economy. [ICSE 2010]
2. Define efficiency of labour and explain any three of its benefits. Briefly explain two causes of the low efficiency of labour in India. [ICSE 2011]
3. Explain with the help of an example the Horizontal and Vertical division of labour. Mention any three merits of division of labour. [ICSE 2012]
4. 'Efficient labour force is an important economic ingredient.' In this context, define efficiency of labour. Explain three factors that determine the efficiency of labour. [ICSE 2013]
5. Define labour as a factor of production. Explain in brief three characteristics of labour. [ICSE 2014]
6. What do you understand by division of labour? Explain three ways by which division of labour is beneficial to producers. [ICSE 2015]
7. What do you understand by efficiency of labour? Discuss any two causes of low efficiency of labour and suggest one measure to improve it. [ICSE 2016]
8. (i) Name any two industries where division of labour is possible.
   (ii) Explain any three demerits of division of labour. [ICSE 2018]
9. Why is labour an important factor of production? Explain the following characteristics of labour. [ICSE 2019]
    (i) Labour cannot be seperated from the labourer.
    (ii) Labour can improve its efficiency.
    (iii) Labour is perishable.

09 Capital and Capital Formation

CAPITAL

Another important factor of production is 'Capital' and the study of this chapter relates to its various aspects, like different forms of capital, different ways and means of capital formation and importance of capital formation. But before commencing a detailed study of these aspects, it is important to know and understand the meaning of capital. Capital is defined as :

"All those man-made goods which are used in further production of goods."

Thus, capital is a man-made resource or factor of production. Machines, tools and equipments of all kinds, buildings, railways and all means of transport and communication, raw materials, etc., are included in capital. As such "all capital is wealth but all wealth is not capital".

Before exactly defining the 'Capital', we shall examine some of the definitions given by different Economists:

> **OVERVIEW**
>
> *Capital is an important factor of production. The capital formation implies the creation of real assets, which are the results of human efforts made on land (natural resources) with an aim of getting some income from these items for future production. Actually it can be called as 'produced means of production'. It must be borne in mind that any money lying idle is not classified as capital. It is an important and indispensable factor of production, resulting out of savings.*
>
> *Some of the important characteristics of capital are that it is man-made, mobile, elastic and subject to depreciation.*

"Capital consists of all those goods, existing at present time which can be used in anyway, so as to satisfy wants during the subsequent years."
—**J. R. Hicks**

According to this, all those things, which satisfy human wants are capital goods. It means that both, consumer goods as well as producer goods should be included in 'capital', as both satisfy human wants in one way or the other. But as a matter of fact, the consumer goods are not included in 'capital' because the consumer goods will be consumed in a single use only and will not be utilised for further production of wealth.

"Capital is the produced means of production."
—**Bohm Bawerk**

According to this definition, only those producer goods are included in capital, which have been produced by human efforts.

"Capital goods are the products (tools) of the past labour (efforts) used for further production."
—**VAN Sickle and Roger**

Thus, capital is productive in the sense that it enables a worker to produce more goods or services, during the physical life of the product.

"Capital goods are produced goods that can be used as factor inputs for further production."
—**Prof. Samuelson**

"Capital consists of those kinds of wealth other than free gift of nature, which yield income."
—**Prof. A. Marshall**

Thus, several economists have defined 'capital' differently. However, from the above definitions, following facts about 'capital' can be concluded :

'Capital' includes all those goods (items or commodities) which are used for further production of more goods, *e.g.*, machines, tools, factory buildings, transport equipments, etc.

'Capital' is the result of human efforts made, on natural resources, in the past. As suggested by *Cairncross*, stocks, shares, government bonds, securities, etc., are also included in 'capital', because all these yield income to the investors.

TYPES OF CAPITAL

Capital has been classified in different ways depending upon its use (or purpose) and its actual physical status (nature).

Trade Capital and Social Capital: **Prof. Marshall** defined these as below:

Trade Capital includes all such items, which an individual uses for his trade or occupation. The tools, raw materials, ploughs, wells, etc., are few such items.

Social Capital includes all those kinds of items, which yield commodities and services for the society as a whole. It means the social facilities on which community has the collective ownership are known as social capital. Government hospitals, schools, power plants, dams, mines, roads, bridges, railways, public enterprises, etc., are some examples. From this classification, it will be clear that social capital has a much wider coverage than the trade capital.

Fixed Capital and Working Capital:

Fixed Capital refers to the producer goods having long life which can be used again and again in productive processes. Their utility does not get exhausted in a single use. Machinery, plants and factory buildings, transport equipments, etc., are some of such components.

Working Capital includes all those items, which can be used for a specific purpose only once. It is directly absorbed into the finished products. Cotton and paper are such examples, which are used only once in productive processes of making cloth and printing of books respectively. Other examples are photographic films (film industry), printing ink (printing press), wheat (flour mills), petrol and diesel (transport industry).

Sunk Capital and Floating Capital:

Sunk Capital is that category of capital, which can be used to produce only one type of commodity or service and it cannot be shifted to any other use. It always remains at the place where it is fixed. For example, an ice factory and an oil mill use capital only to produce ice and oil respectively and no other commodity.

Floating Capital includes all such items, which can be put to alternate uses. The use of such commodities is not restricted for any specific purpose. In other words floating capital is the capital which can be used for several purposes or by several industries. Leather can be used for making different types of goods like shoes, belts, toys, etc. The important examples are electricity, money, fuels, workshop machines, etc.

Concrete Capital, Money Capital and Debt Capital: *Cairncross* has classified and defined these forms of capital as below:

Concrete Capital includes all that property, which is in the hands of both producers and has money value. This is also called real capital. Some examples are furniture, buildings, cars, trucks, industrial units, household goods, books, etc.

Money Capital is utilised by the producers for the purchase of tools, machines, buildings, transport, etc. Money itself does not have any value, but it actually helps in purchasing and procuring things, which are utilised for producing different kinds of goods. It should, however be kept in mind that the money lying idle with a person cannot be termed as money capital, because it is not being used for arranging any kind of productive goods or activities.

Debt Capital represents the invested funds which yield income. All investments made in shares, stocks, government securities, etc., which help the investors to earn income. These are also considered productive and so these are called debt capital.

Internal Capital and External Capital:

Internal Capital is the capital of a country which is used within its territory.

External Capital is the capital which is obtained from foreign countries and used in our country.

National Capital and International Capital:

National Capital includes all the private and public capital in a country. The buildings of all the factories, *i.e.*, private or public are the examples of national capital.

International Capital is owned by two or more than two countries. For example, Kosi Project is a joint project of India and Nepal. International Monetary Fund, World Bank, etc., cover international capital.

Consumption Capital and Production Capital:

Consumption Capital is that capital which is invested for the direct satisfaction of human wants, *e.g.*, capital spent on food, clothing, health, education, etc.

Production Capital is the capital which directly helps in the production of goods, *e.g.*, machines, tools, factories, etc.

Private Capital and Public Capital:

Private Capital is the capital which is invested in private sector or by private people. For example, Industries belonging to Tatas and Birlas.

Public Capital means the capital which is invested by the government in public sector, is called public capital. For example, Bhilai and Durgapur Steel Plants.

Remunerative Capital and Auxiliary Capital:

Remunetrative Capital is that capital which is given to workers in the form of wages is known as remunerative capital. For example, wages given to a bricklayer.

Auxiliary Capital helps a labourer to produce goods. A hammer, a pair of pliers, wood, etc., are auxiliary capital for a carpenter. Therefore, machines, raw material, electricity, etc., are the examples of auxiliary capital.

CHARACTERISTICS OF CAPITAL

Important characteristics of 'Capital' are as follows:

Capital is the Result of Past Labour: Capital is a produced factor of production. When human efforts are combined with natural resources with the objective of developing producer goods like tools, machinery, etc., then the emergence of capital takes place.

Capital is Result of Savings: Capital is man-made and is born out of savings done by man. Its supply is increased or diminished by the efforts of man. Thus, capital is a man-made factor of production.

Capital not an Indispensable Factor: Capital is not an indispensable factor of production. Production can be possible even without capital, whereas, land and labour are the original and indispensable factors of production.

A Mobile Factor: Capital has the highest mobility amongst all the factors of production. The land is immobile, labour has low mobility, whereas 'capital' has both 'place mobility' and 'occupational mobility'.

Its Supply is Elastic: The supply of capital is elastic and can be adjusted easily and quickly according to demand. On the other hand, the supply of land is fixed and the supply of labour can neither be increased nor decreased quickly.

Not a Permanent Factor: Capital depreciates gradually, if capital is used again and again. For example, if any machine is used for a considerable period, then it may not be suitable for any further use due to depreciation (*i.e.*, wear and tear).

Risk of Returns in the Use of Capital: There is considerable amount of risk involved in the use of capital.

To be Replenished or Reproduced: Capital is temporary, as it has to be reproduced and replenished from time to time.

Not a Free Gift: Production of capital involves some cost as it is not a natural gift. It is earned with hard labour and sacrifice.

Capital is Prospective: Capital is considered much prospective, as the accumulation of capital yields an income.

IS LAND CAPITAL?

Both capital and land are factors of production. Land is nature's free gift to man. It is not a produced means of production. It is limited in area, and is of infinite variety. On the other hand, capital is man-made and can be increased at will. Land lacks mobility, whereas capital is fairly mobile. Supply of land does not depend on the price for its use (*i.e.*, rent). If, therefore, rent falls, its supply cannot be withdrawn. But the supply of capital varies with its price. For all such reasons, land can be distinguished from capital and is not regarded as capital.

Distinction between Land and Capital

Land	Capital
1. Land is natural gift.	1. Capital is produced by the human being, and used as a means of production.
2. The total supply of land is limited in each country.	2. The supply of capital is variable.

3. Land is not mobile.	3. The capital is mobile to a great extent.
4. The life of land is permanent.	4. The life of capital is not permanent.
5. Land involves no production cost as it is a free gift of nature.	5. Capital involves production cost as it is man-made.

DIFFERENCE BETWEEN CAPITAL AND OTHER RELATED CONCEPTS

WEALTH AND CAPITAL

Wealth refers to all economic goods which are relatively scarce and bear some price. The chief characteristics of wealth are : (i) It has utility and transferability, (ii) It is relatively scarce and marketable. All goods and services possessing such characteristics are considered as wealth. Examples are house, jewellery, machines, factory, furniture, etc. Hence, wealth includes both the consumer goods as well as producer goods.

Capital implies producer goods only, *i.e.*, machines, factory, buildings, tools, raw materials, etc. All such capital goods possess the characteristics of wealth and therefore, it may be called that *all capital is wealth, but all wealth is not capital.*

However, *all wealth cannot be considered as capital* because only that part of wealth which is used in the process of production, is regarded as capital.

Thus, wealth consisting of producers goods or real capital is called capital, like textile machine. However, wealth used for consumption is not capital, like car is just a wealth. Income-yielding wealth is also regarded as capital, because wealth by itself does not yield any income and when it is used in the process of production, it yields income. Therefore, when car is run as a taxi, it is a capital. Wealth which satisfies one's desire directly, is however, just wealth and not capital.

MONEY AND CAPITAL

Money used for starting any business by purchasing machineries, tools, raw materials, etc., is regarded as capital and therefore, it is termed as 'liquid capital' or 'money capital'. But in economic sense, money cannot be considered as capital because money itself cannot produce any kind of goods. In brief, money cannot be considered as a distinct factor of production, but only as a means by which other factor units and particularly capital goods can be acquired. Thus, money is only a part of capital.

FUNCTIONS OF CAPITAL

The important functions of capital are described below:

Provision for Subsistence: Capital provides food, cloth and shelter to the workers engaged in production, because in actual practice, production is a long drawn out affair and has to pass through many stages before it reaches the market and brings income to manufacturer. But the workers have to subsist during this period, for which the wages are paid from the capital money (capital fund). Subsequently, when money from consumers reaches the producer, it is again accumulated as capital money.

Provision for Appliances: Capital is used to provide tools and implements for use by the workers, when they are needed. It is clear that these things are essential for production, without their aid, large-scale production is impossible.

Provision for Raw Materials: A part of the capital is used for arrangement of raw materials for production purposes. Every concern must have, on hand, a sufficient supply of raw materials of good quality.

Provision for Marketing and Sales Promotion: The producer of goods has to arrange for the sale of the goods produced by him. For this, the goods produced are to be transported to the market. Simultaneously, the publicity and advertisements about his products has to be made. All these activities are met out of the capital fund (capital money).

Economic Development: The most important function of the capital is to promote the economic development of the country. For a satisfactory development of the country, adequate funds are very essential. The progress of many developing and underdeveloped countries gets retarded, because of the paucity of funds.

Expands Employment Opportunities: Since capital expands production, it also expands employment. Thus, if we are to reduce the volume of unemployment in a country, we must pay attention to capital formation in the country.

CAPITAL FORMATION

The 'capital formation' actually signifies a very important aspect of economic development. In simple words, capital formation means creation of capital. This means making and increasing of more capital goods, such as machines, tools, factories, buildings, etc., which are to be used in producing more goods. It should, however, be very clearly understood that capital formation does not mean increase in money-capital, but it actually refers to increase in physical capital, *i.e.*, machinery, factories, transport equipments, bridges, power projects, dams, irrigation systems, etc. To sum up, capital formation implies the creation of real assets.

"Formation of capital implies that society uses its present production not only for the satisfaction of its consumption but also uses a part of it on capital goods, that is making machines, transport facilities or other production equipments." —**Nurkse**

"In circumstances of restrained economic growth and industrialisation, capital formation should be understood to be limited to machinery, instruments and inventories which are directly capable of being used in work." —**Prof. Kuznets**

"The amount of wealth, a country adds to its capital during a period, is known as the capital formation during that period." —**Benham**

Capital formation takes place in three stages:

(1) Creation of Savings: Depends on (a) ability to save, (b) desire to save and (c) opportunity to save. Developed countries with high per capita income have higher saving power than the less developed countries.

(2) Mobilisation of Savings: This involves the mobilisation of the savings of various households and individuals for investment. This is mainly done by institutions like banks, insurance corporations and finance corporations.

(3) Investment of Savings: The savings of the people need to be invested by businessmen and entrepreneurs in different productive system like agriculture, industry, transport and communication, etc.

FACTORS INFLUENCING OR AFFECTING CAPITAL FORMATION

The following are the factors affecting the formation of capital in a country:

Volume of Saving: The accumulation of capital directly depends upon saving. Saving means the difference between income and consumption. The difference can be utilised for capital formation.

"Larger the volume of savings, larger the size of capital, smaller the volume of saving, smaller is the size of capital."
— **Prof. A. Marshall**

The amount saved as money is mobilised and then converted to capital assets.

Ability to Save: It directly depends upon the income of the individuals and the taxation policy of the government. Higher income and low taxation leads to higher rate of capital formation.

Willingness to Save: It depends upon many personal, family and national considerations like family affection, desire to start a business, old age consideration and unforeseen emergencies.

Profit of Public Sector Enterprises: Public sector enterprise is a very important form of business organisation. Since these are owned by the government rather than by individuals, all the profits of this enterprise can be used for capital formation by the government.

Trade Conditions: The prosperity encourages and enhances the saving but depression reduces the saving of people. Capital formation is greatly affected by market conditions of boom and depression.

Facilities of Investment: When the people are provided with more facilities to mobilise the savings, the people save more and invest more. The commercial banks, post offices, stock markets, etc., encourage the people to save more. More saving leads to more capital formation.

Assistance to Investors: Finally, the government may try to increase capital formation by providing assistance to potential investors in various ways. (For instance, by giving tax benefits to newly set-up production unit; by providing proper infrastructure, etc.) These steps are particularly useful when investment is constrained, not by the policy of saving, but by the unwillingness of the producers to invest the savings that are available in the economy.

Monetary Policy: The monetary policy pursued by the government also constitute an important factor affecting capital formation in the country. While this policy, by itself, does not act as sources of capital formation, it acts as factors affecting the sources. Higher interest rate on savings is very important for raising savings.

Income Tax Policies: To raise the rate of capital formation in the country by raising interest rates can succeed only when the cause of low investment is due to low savings. One popular method is to grant income tax benefits to people who wish to save (for instance, by exempting from income tax that part of income which is saved).

Commodity Taxation: Commodity taxation can also be used to raise the rate of savings. If items of consumption—especially items of luxury consumption are subjected to high rates of sales taxes, this will raise the prices of the consumption goods (because the sales taxes are added to the prices of the goods). This will reduce consumption in the country. Naturally, savings will increase if income remains unchanged.

Deficit Budget: There are other fiscal measures also that can be adopted for the purpose of increasing capital formation in the country. The government often comes forward to establish large public sector projects. These increase the capital formation by creating social overhead capital. The costs of establishing these projects are often covered by budget deficits. To cover the budget deficits government may resort to public borrowings from the savings of the people.

Inflation: The financing of a budget deficit by printing new money often leads to inflation. It should be noted, however, that inflation itself is one of the ways in which savings can be promoted.

LESSON AT A GLANCE

Capital: All those man-made goods which are used in further production of wealth are referred as capital. Thus, capital is a man-made resource or factor of production.

Types of Capital: (i) Trade capital and Social capital; (ii) Fixed capital and Working capital; (iii) Sunk capital and Floating capital; (iv) Concrete capital, Money capital and Debt capital; (v) Internal capital and External capital; (vi) National capital and International capital; (vii) Consumption capital and Production capital; (viii) Private capital and Public capital; (ix) Remunerative capital and Auxiliary capital.

Characteristics of Capital: (i) Capital is the result of past labour; (ii) Capital is result of savings; (iii) Capital not an indispensable factor; (iv) A mobile factor; (v) Its supply is elastic; (vi) Not a permanent factor; (vii) Risk of returns in the use of capital; (viii) To be replenished or reproduced; (ix) Not a free gift; and (x) Capital is prospective.

Functions of Capital: (i) Provision of subsistence; (ii) Provision for appliances; (iii) Pro-vision for raw materials; (iv) Provision for marketing and sales promotion; (v) Economic development; and (vi) expands employment opportunities.

Capital Formation: According to Benham, "The amount of wealth, a country adds to its capital during a period, is known as the capital formation during that period."

Factors Influencing Or Affecting Capital Formation: (i) Volume of saving; (ii) Ability to save; (iii) Willingness to save; (iv) Profit of public sector enterprises; (v) Trade conditions; (vi) Facilities of investment; (vii) Assistance to investors; (viii) Monetary policy; (ix) Income tax policies; (x) Commodity taxation; (xi) Deficit budget; and (xii) Inflation.

PROJECT WORK

1. Visit an industrial unit and also a hydropower generation unit. Prepare a list of various items being used for producing different commodities. Classify the items so listed under different categories of capital. Prepare a separate list of items which cannot be classified as capital. Mention reasons also.

   Using the list of various items used above, prepare a summary explaining how each of the items is utilised for further production of goods and how these items and activities contribute towards formation of capital.

In case you conclude from your observations that capital formation is not adequate, what more capital items you suggest to be added for particular institution, *i.e.*, industry and power generation unit. Also mention the probable benefits you envisage from the addition of items suggested by you.

2. Visit a nearby town also and find out if any kind of development schemes are in progress. If yes, what type of capital formation is likely to occur there? How are the funds being mobilised and invested?

   Draw your conclusion about the expected economic development from the above schemes of capital formation.

3. Visit an agricultural farm and a manufacturing firm near your residence or your school. For each of these two production units:

   Prepare a list of various inputs (other than land and labour) used in the production process; For each of these inputs, explain whether and why you consider it to be capital; Mention under which category of capital each of these inputs falls (for instance, whether it is fixed capital or circulating capital, sunk capital or floating capital, etc.); Find out how much capital has been invested in the firm; How much capital has been obtained from different sources (own savings, loans from banks, loans from other sources, etc.); the opinion of the owner(s) of the firm (and also give your own opinion) regarding how additional capital can be obtained and what steps should be taken by the government for capital formation in industries. Prepare a brief report and give your opinions.

QUESTIONS

A. Short Answer Type Questions:

1. What is 'Capital'?
2. What are the characteristics of capital?
3. Explain the importance of capital in modern economy.
4. How would you distinguish land from capital?
5. Are the following capital? Write 'yes' or 'no'.
   (i) Pen of a student.
   (ii) Utensils at home.
   (iii) Goodwill of a business.
   (iv) A house on rent.
   (v) Furniture in a house.
6. Which form of capital, money capital or real capital has a greater impact on the national output? Give reasons to justify your answer.
7. What is capital formation?
8. Describe briefly, the important stages of capital formation.
9. What is the difference between 'Capital' and 'Wealth'?

   Or

   "All capital is wealth, but all wealth is not capital". Explain.
10. Explain three factors on which the capital formation of a country depends.

11. State the factors which determine the creation of savings in a country.
12. Define the role of capital in production.
13. Distinguish between:
    (i) Trade capital and Social capital.
    (ii) Money capital and Concrete capital.
14. 'Saving is essential for capital formation'. Explain.
15. Why is capital considered an important factor of production in the modern world? Give two reasons in support of your answer.

Recent Year Questions:
1. Capital is the result of past labour. Briefly explain. [ICSE 2012]
2. Explain in brief the Sunk Capital. [ICSE 2012]
3. Distinguish between Fixed and Circulating Capital. [ICSE 2012]
4. State two reasons for low capital formation in a developing economy. [ICSE 2013]
5. Classify the following capital goods:
    (i) Machines,
    (ii) Cotton yarn,
    (iii) Oil mill,
    (iv) Bridge. [ICSE 2013]
6. State two characteristics of capital as a factor of production. [ICSE 2014]
7. Why is capital called a 'produced means of production'? [ICSE 2015]
8. Differentiate between floating and sunk capital. Give an example for each. [ICSE 2015]

OR

Distinguish between sunk capital and floating capital. [ICSE 2019]
9. Define real capital. Give two examples. [ICSE 2016]
10. Out of the following capital used in cotton textile industry, classify the following as fixed or circulating capital. [ICSE 2018]
    (i) Cotton yarns,
    (ii) Dyes,
    (iii) Power,
    (iv) Weaving machines.
11. Capital is a passive factor of production justify the statement. [ICSE 2018]
12. Differentiate between capital and capital formation. [ICSE 2019]

B. Long Answer Type Questions:
1. What do you mean by fixed and circulating capital. Give reasons in each case. Which of the following is fixed and which is circulating capital:
    (i) Stock of raw cotton in a textile mill.
    (ii) A pair of bullocks used for ploughing.
    (iii) A motorcar owned by a doctor.
    (iv) Water stored in an irrigation dam.
2. Explain the meaning of 'capital formation'. Explain three important factors, which affect the rate of capital formation?
3. Explain clearly the factors, which affect the creation of savings in a country?

4. Read the extract given below and answer the questions that follow:
   ### The Times of India, New Delhi
   Today's youths are in no mood to wait especially when it comes to investments. Investors in the age group of 24 to 30 want to stay invested only for one or two years rather than having their money blocked for 10-20 years.
   (i) Define capital formation.
   (ii) Explain four ways of increasing investment in India.

Recent Year Questions:
1. State one important function of capital.
   Differentiate between:
   (i) Capital and wealth.
   (ii) Capital and land. [ICSE 2009]
2. Define capital formation. Explain any four causes of low capital formation in a developing country. [ICSE 2010]
3. Explain in brief the first stage of capital formation. [ICSE 2011]
4. Define capital and explain three important functions of capital. [ICSE 2013]
5. (i) What is capital formation?
   (ii) What are the three stages of capital formation?
   (iii) Explain three reasons for the low rate of capital formation in India. [ICSE 2015]
6. (i) What is considered as capital in economics?
   (ii) Discuss any three characteristics of capital. [ICSE 2018]

10
Entrepreneur

When the factors of production are to be combined in order to produce something, a fourth factor is required. Goods and services do not produce themselves but need some conscious thought process in order to plan and implement manufacture. This thought process is often called entrepreneurship. Bill Gates, the founder of 'Microsoft' the successful software company, is an entrepreneur. It is hard to say what makes Bill Gates more financially successful than say the local seller of computers.

OVERVIEW

The entrepreneur is an active factor of production. It is a type of special labour, which actually bears the risk of business and combines all the remaining factors (land, labour and capital) properly, so as to achieve the business objectives most economically and efficiently.

An entrepreneur is a person who starts an enterprise. He searches for change and responds to it.

The economists view him as a fourth factor of production along-with land, labour and capital. It is an active factor of production. Labour is another one.

The sociologists feel that certain communities and cultures promote entrepreneurship more successfully. For example in India, we say that Gujaratis and Sindhis are very enterprising.

Still others feel that entrepreneurs are innovators who come up with new ideas for products, markets or techniques.

To put it very simply an entrepreneur is someone who perceives opportunity, organises resources needed for exploiting that opportunity and exploits it. Computers, mobile phones, washing machines, ATMs, Credit Cards, Courier Service, and Ready to Eat Foods are all examples of entrepreneurial ideas that got converted into products or services.

Some definitions of an entrepreneur are listed below.

It is originated from the French word 'entrependure' which means one who undertakes or one who is a 'go-between'.

"An entrepreneur is a person who pays a certain price for a product to resell it at an uncertain price, thereby making decisions about obtaining and using the resources while consequently admitting the risk of enterprise."
—**Richard Cantillon**

"An entrepreneur is an economic agent who unites all means of production-land of one, the labour of another and the capital of yet another and thus produces a product. By selling the product in the market he pays rent of land, wages to labour, interest on capital and what remains is his profit. He shifts economic resources out of an area of lower and into an area of higher productivity and greater yield."
—**J. B. Say**

"Entrepreneurs are innovators who use a process of shattering the status quo of the existing products and services, to set up new products, new services." —**Schumpeter**

After studying the above definitions which are given by other experts, we conclude that *"entrepreneur is an individual (or group of individuals) who establishes, organises, operates and assumes the risk for new business enterprise."*

FUNCTIONS OF AN ENTREPRENEUR

An entrepreneur frequently has to wear many hats. He has to perceive opportunity, plan, organise resources, and oversee production, marketing, and liaison with officials. Most importantly, he has to innovate and bear the risk. The main functions of an entrepreneur are as follows:

Innovation: Innovation is one of the most important functions of an entrepreneur according to **Schumpeter**. An entrepreneur uses information, knowledge and intuition to come up with new products, new methods of reducing costs of a product, improvement in design or function of a product, discovering new markets or new ways of organisation of industry. Through innovation, an entrepreneur converts a material into a resource or combines existing resources into new and more productive configurations. It is the creativity of an entrepreneur that results in invention (discovery of something new) and innovation (application of knowledge to create new products, services or processes).

Systematic innovation means monitoring the following for innovative opportunity:

- The unexpected success or failure or any unexpected outside event, (*e.g.* when the IT bubble burst the ITES sector started growing).
- Innovation based on process need (*e.g.* plate based cameras, film based cameras, digital cameras).
- Changes in industry and market structure (*e.g.* video cassette VCD, DVD, Blue ray disc).
- Demographics changes (*e.g.* increasing number of working women and nuclear families in most metropolitan cities).
- New knowledge (*e.g.* Pentium chip).

Risk and Uncertainty Bearing: According to **Hozelist** "an entrepreneur performs the function of risk and uncertainty bearing." Every decision pertaining to development of new products, adapting new technologies, opening up new markets involves risk. Decision-making in an environment of uncertainty requires anticipation of risk. Profit is said to be the reward for anticipating and taking such risks. However it is pertinent to mention that the entrepreneur is not a gambler, he only takes calculated risks. An entrepreneur develops the art of decision-making under conditions of uncertainty as a matter of survival.

Organisation Building: An entrepreneur has to organise men, material and other resources. He has to perform the functions of planning, co-ordination and control. He has to use his leadership qualities to build a team, generate resources and solve problems. With his organisational skills, an entrepreneur builds an enterprise from scratch, nurtures it and makes it grow. His vision sows the seeds for a sound and vibrant organisation and synergies are built in the enterprise.

According to **Kilby** in a developing country even the imitator entrepreneurs are very important and the entrepreneurial role encompasses the following:

- Perception of market opportunities.
- Gaining command over scarce resources.
- Purchasing inputs.
- Marketing the products.
- Dealing with bureaucrats.
- Managing human relations within the firm.
- Managing customer and supplier relations.
- Managing finance.
- Managing production.
- Acquiring and overseeing assembly of the factory.
- Industrial engineering.
- Upgrading process and product.
- Introducing new production techniques and products.

DISTINCTION BETWEEN LABOUR AND ENTREPRENEUR AND CAPITALIST AND ENTREPRENEUR

Entrepreneur and Labour

Following are the factors which make distinction between the entrepreneur and labour:

Nature of Risk: Labourers are not involved to bear risk in the business. They receive the reward for their labour in the form of wages. On the contrary, an entrepreneur has to bear all the risks in the business.

Nature of Work and Reward: Labourers get the wages for their work in certain period which are fixed while an entrepreneur receives profit in return of work which are uncertain.

Nature of Activities: The labourer has to perform only fixed activities while the entrepreneur performs all jobs concerned with the business.

Mobility: A labourer is more mobile than the entrepreneur.

Entrepreneur or Organiser and Capitalist

The differences that exist between the entrepreneur and the capitalist are:

Nature of Work: A capitalist provides capital on loan. He is only a creditor, whereas the entrepreneur's job is to set-up the business.

Nature of Risk: An entrepreneur bears loss or gain of the business, while the capitalist has no link with the profit and loss. He gets the fixed amount in the form of interest for his capital after a fixed time.

QUALITIES TO BE A SUCCESSFUL ENTREPRENEUR

Visionary: The very first quality to be an entrepreneur is to have a vision. This vision must be associated with organisation's contribution towards society. The meaningful existence of an organisation is not possible until and unless it provides some kind of value in terms of goods and services to the society, directly or indirectly. Ratan Tata developed a vision to provide a cost effective car to the society where people with lesser resources might also travel with their families. The result was "Nano". Dhirubhai Ambani developed a vision to provide a communication facility which was cheaper than a postcard. The result was "Reliance Communication".

Innovator: An entrepreneur needs to be innovative. He must develop new product ideas, new uses of product, new markets, new location, new production methodology, new features of a product or new business models, etc., which may either increase the value of the products and services or reduce their cost.

Risk Taker: An entrepreneur must be a risk taker. This is not at all necessary that whatever venture he starts proves to be a success. The customer may not accept the product or service which he offers. In real world thousands of new businesses start and close each day. This may result in the losses. So he must be ready to bear the risks associated with the business like financial risk, social risk and morale risk, etc.

Analytical: An entrepreneur needs to be very analytical. He must evaluate the cost and benefit aspect of every decision. He must take every decision by keeping all the possible factors in mind. If he feels difficulty in making any decision, he must take help of business consultants who are experts in their respective areas.

Good Interpersonal Skills: Entrepreneur and labour are the only active factors of production. Labour in itself cannot make decisions without the entrepreneur's permission. So it is entrepreneur who directs labour to properly utilise other resources in an appropriate manner. This interaction between entrepreneur and labour needs an entrepreneur to be good in interpersonal skills so that he may direct the labour in the cordial manner and get the work done through labour properly. Failure in good interpersonal skills on the part of entrepreneur may result in the terms of labour unrest which is not beneficial for any business.

Good Communication Skills: An entrepreneur must have good communication skills to deal with the labour, customers, government officials and suppliers, etc. It is communication only through which he will be able to share his thoughts with other people and get business deals in his favour by making his point of view clear to other people. If he is not good in communication skills, his success is entirely doubtful.

ROLE OF ENTREPRENEURS IN ECONOMIC DEVELOPMENT

Performs the Role of an Administrator: The modern economic development is due to the emergence of dynamic, intelligent and enterprising entrepreneurs. An entrepreneur shoulders the responsibility right from the planning the whole business and expanding it from foundation to full development. For this, he assumes the responsibility for the quantity, quality and nature of the product. He arranges for the purchase of raw materials and sale of the finished product. Also he has to administer discipline, control, and remuneration to the labour, working under him as per his direction. In other words, he has to take care of the organisation, *i.e.*, its property, working and achievements.

Performs the Role of a Coordinator: In coordinating and guiding different factors of production, the entrepreneur makes use of land for constructing a building for the organisation or industry. He invests his money capital in building, machinery, equipments, tools and raw materials. Simultaneously, he organises the labour and directs them as per the requirements of different tasks. For better results, it becomes necessary that he must utilise most up-to-date machines and make appropriate provisions for their repairs and replacements, as the case may be. For this, proper supervision should be introduced in the working system.

Proper Utilisation of Labour Force: The utilisation of skilled, semi-skilled and unskilled workers in right proportion is another important function, in which correct and equitable allocation of duties is done by the entrepreneur (sometimes this task is performed by manager as per the direction and policies made by the entrepreneur). The direction of labour involves encouragement of savings in energy, improvement in skills and minimisation (or elimination) of wastage of materials and the manpower.

Proper Marketing of the Finished Products: The entrepreneur has to make arrangements for the marketing and sale of the finished product. This involves the employment of sales personnel (sales manager and sales representatives), arrangement for publicity and advertisement, the execution of orders and dispatch of goods.

Undertakes the Responsibility to Distribute due Remuneration to Each Factor of Production: The entrepreneur undertakes the responsibility to distribute proper remuneration to each factor of production. He has to pay rent to the landlord (for rented building), interest to capitalist and wages to labourers. To manage all these aspects, he requires higher degree of moral qualities of leadership, courage and confidence. He should be capable of motivating and inspiring others in times of difficulties and business crisis. Actually, the task of coordinating the various interests and channelising them in proper manner to achieve desired results is a task of complicated intricacy and sizeable magnitude and all this is not within the capacity of everybody. But only a few talented persons possess that capacity and skill to manage an enterprise.

An Entrepreneur is both Foresighted and Farsighted: The most important pre-requisite of a successful entrepreneur is that he should have both foresightedness and farsightedness. The ability of proper judgement about market fluctuations, correct estimation of future demands and a wide knowledge of market and its conditions are some special qualities, which an entrepreneur must possess in order to gain desired success in the business.

Plays the Crucial Role of an Innovator: The entrepreneur's role has long been recognised as an innovator. An entrepreneur discovers and develops new ideas, new techniques, new products, new markets, new sources of supply of raw-material, new opportunities, new methods of production and new combinations.

Miscellaneous: (i) Generates new employment opportunities, (ii) Role in balanced regional development, (iii) Provides economic leadership, (iv) Complements and supplements economic growth from a backward economy to developed economy, and (v) Assists in bringing social stability, etc.

LESSON AT A GLANCE

Entrepreneurship: An entrepreneur is the fourth factor of production. In the earlier stages of economic development it had no separate identity, but it was a part of labour. In the words of **Prof. Benham**, "The term entrepreneur means the person or a group of persons controlling the policy of a firm".

Functions of an Entrepreneur: (i) Innovation; (ii) Risk and uncertainty bearing; (iii) Organisation building.

Qualities to be a Successful Entrepreneur: (i) Visionary; (ii) Innovator; (iii) Risk taker; (iv) Analytical; (v) Good interpersonal skills; (vi) Good communication skills.

Role of Entrepreneurs in Economic Development: (i) Performs the role of an administrator; (ii) Performs the role of a coordinator; (iii) Proper utilisation of labour force; (iv) Proper marketing of the finished products; (v) Undertakes responsibility to distribute due remuneration to each factor of production; (vi) An entrepreneur is both foresighted and farsighted; (vii) Plays the crucial role of an innovator; and (viii) Miscellaneous.

PROJECT WORK

1. Visit a factory owned by one single person and another by a group of persons. Make a list of owner(s) and various types of jobs he (they) is (are) required to do. Classify his (their) jobs under different types of functions and mention the risk involved in each of his (their) functions and decisions.

   Make a note of your observation in the form of a brief essay, and mention the importance of the person(s) in the context of economic development of that organisation by making a reference to the enterprises you have visited.

2. Visit a firm, talk to the persons who are overall incharge. Prepare list of the various functions performed by them. Determine whether these persons are entrepreneurs or merely organisers. If they are entrepreneurs, state your opinion regarding whether they are good entrepreneurs or not.

QUESTIONS

A. Short Answer Type Questions:
1. Who is an entrepreneur? Explain the importance of an entrepreneur.
2. State three most important functions of an entrepreneur.
3. Explain the meaning of an enterprise or organisation.
4. Explain in brief, three functions of an organiser.
5. Explain risk bearing in business by an entrepreneur.
6. Distinguish between:
   (a) Entrepreneur and Capitalist.
   (b) Entrepreneur and Labour.

Entrepreneur

Recent Year Questions:
1. "An entrepreneur is an organiser but an organiser need not be an entrepreneur." Explain. [ICSE 2009]
2. "Entrepreneurs are innovators" said Schumpeter. Briefly explain. [ICSE 2011]
   OR
   "Entrepreneurs are innovators." Briefly explain. [ICSE 2019]
3. Differentiate between an entrepreneur and labour on the basis of :
   (i) Nature of work.   (ii) Nature of risk involved. [ICSE 2013]
4. State two 'active' factors of production. Give reasons to support your answer. [ICSE 2015]
5. State two qualities of a successful entrepreneur [ICSE 2016]

B. **Long Answer Type Questions:**
1. What do you mean by an entrepreneur? State the qualities of an entrepreneur.
   OR
   "Entrepreneur is moderate and dynamic." In the light of this opinion, discuss the qualities of an entrepreneur.
2. The entrepreneur is called the 'Captain of Industry'. Explain with reasons.
3. Examine the role and functions of an entrepreneur in capitalist economy.
4. Describe the important functions of an entrepreneur. How are his activities, as a factor of production different from that of an organiser?
5. "There is positive coordination between entrepreneurship and economic develop-ment." Give five arguments in support of your answer.
6. What are the differences between entrepreneurship and other factors of production?
7. Why an entrepreneur is important in modern world of business?
8. "Entrepreneurship is not labour even though there are human factors associated with the same business." Explain.

Recent Year Questions:
1. Most of the functions of an entrepreneur are performed by paid professionals. With suitable examples explain the following functions performed by an entrepreneur:
   (i) Risk bearing   (ii) Uncertainty bearing   (iii) Innovations
   (iv) Decision making. [ICSE 2008]
2. State one difference between an entrepreneur and other factors of production. Explain any four qualities in an individual to be a successful entrepreneur. [ICSE 2014]
3. Who is an entrepreneur? Explain any three functions of an entrepreneur. [ICSE 2015]
4. Explain four ways by which an entrepreneur can promote economic develop-ment. [ICSE 2016]
   OR
   Explain four ways in which an entrepreneur contribute to economic development. [ICSE 2019]

11
Alternative Market Structures: Basic Concepts

For a layman, market is a place where buyers and sellers gather in order to buy and sell a particular commodity. In economics, however, the word market is used in a wider sense. It is not confined to a particular place. In economics, a market means a system or setup or a facility in which the buyers and sellers of a commodity meet and strike a deal (transaction) about the price and quantity to be bought and sold. A mall, vegetable mandi, grain mandi, e-commerce and share market, etc., are examples of different markets.

OVERVIEW

Market is a place where goods are bought and sold. In economics, market means whole of the network in which buyers and sellers of a commodity keep in touch with one another. Market has been defined by various economists in different ways. Market may be classified on the basis of the competition.

The term market has been defined as under:

"Economists understand by the term market, not any particular market place in which things are bought and sold, but the whole of any region in which buyers and sellers are in such free intercourse with one another that the prices of the same goods tends to equality easily and quickly."
—**Cournot**

"By a market, economists mean any organisation whereby buyers and sellers of goods are kept in close touch with each other."
—**Stonier and Hague**

"The term market refers not necessarily to a place but always to a commodity and the buyers and sellers who are in direct competition with one another."
—**Chapman**

CHARACTERISTICS OF MARKET

Market is a Facility or System and not a Place: Market does not mean a particular place or locality. It means a facility or system which helps buyers and sellers of a commodity to interact to decide about the quantity and price of the commodity.

Presence of Buyers and Sellers: There must be both the buyers and sellers in a market. However, the number of buyers and sellers may be large or small depending upon many factors.

A Single Commodity: The term market means the market for a single commodity alone. There may be different markets for different commodities.

FACTORS DETERMINING FORMS OF MARKET

There are certain factors which affect the type of market for a commodity or on the basis of which we can differentiate between market structures:

Number of Buyers and Sellers for a Commodity: Number of sellers influence the market according to the amount of share that each firm has in total supply and in-effect influences the price and the number of buyers affect the extent of influence a buyer has on the market. If there is single buyer he would exercise larger control on market, whereas when the number of buyers are more, they would exercise less control.

Nature of the Product or Commodity: This is an important factor by which one market form can be distinguished from another and this also governs the amount of competition in the market which in turn depends on how similar are the goods produced by different firms.

Knowledge of the Market: Forms of market are differentiated on the basis of amount of knowledge buyers and sellers have about a product that includes:

- Market conditions.
- The competitive price (*i.e.*, price at which a product is sold by other sellers).
- Nature and quality of the product. The difference in the knowledge one has determines whether there is uniform price or difference in price of a commodity prevailing in the market.

Freedom of Entry or Exit of the Firms: Markets are differentiated from each other in a way how a firm enters and exits the industry. Whether entry or exit is free that is without any stringent rules and restrictions or the entry and exit is restricted.

Degree of Influence on Price: Markets differ from each other on the basis of what kind of and how much influence does a firm has on the determination of price of a commodity. It decides whether the firms are 'price takers' or 'price makers'.

(i) **Price Taker:** This is the market where firms cannot have any influence on the market price. They have to accept the price, whatsoever set by the industry.

(ii) **Price Maker:** This is the market where firms have a great influence on price determination.

MARKET STRUCTURES

Really speaking, no two markets are exactly the same. They differ widely thus, there are different forms or structures of market. Market structure refers to the types of market in which the producers or firms operate and transact business. The economists from time to time classified the various market structures as under:

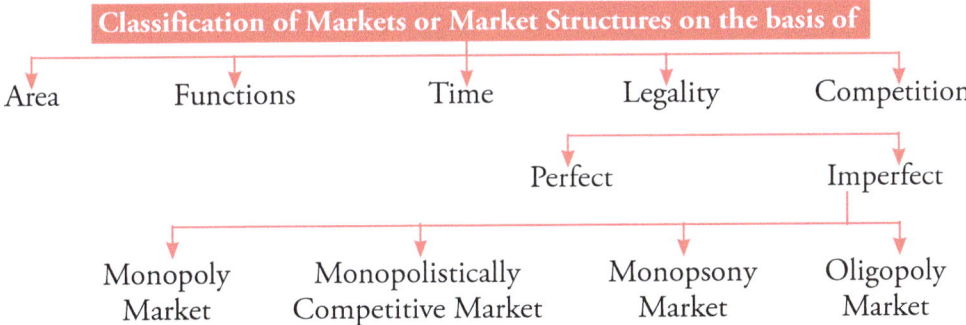

On the Basis of Competition

There are two types of competitions:

(I) Perfect Competition Or Perfectly Competitive Market

Perfectly Competitive Market or Perfect competition is an ideal state of economic affairs which does not exist in any industry in its complete entirety but exists in similar form like stock market, wholesale markets for vegetable and grains, etc. A perfectly competitive industry has multiple firms selling the homogeneous products as well as large number of buyers. The number of firms and buyers is large so that no single firm or buyer can influence price and the products are so similar that the consumer has no reason to choose one for another. Two factors that are necessary in perfect competition are perfect knowledge and perfect mobility. There is free entry and exit of firm in the industry.

Features of Perfectly Competitive Market or Perfect Competition: Following are the main features of perfectly competitive market or perfect competition:

Large Number of Buyers and Sellers: There are many buyers and sellers each with an insignificant share of the market. This means that each firm is too small relative to the overall market to affect price by changing its own supply. So a single firm's decision has no impact on market price. Each individual firm must accept the market price. So each individual firm is assumed to be a price taker. Similarly, each individual buyer is too insignificant to influence the market price by changing his/her quantity of demand.

Thus, a policy of uniform price exists in the perfectly competitive market.

Homogeneous Product: An identical output is produced by each firm - in other words, the market supplies homogeneous or standardised products that are perfect substitutes for each other. Consumers perceive the products to be identical. As a result, all the sellers have to sell their products at a uniform price. If any of the sellers tries to sell his product at a higher price, his product will be out of market.

Perfect Knowledge of Market: Both the sellers and the buyers have perfect knowledge of market conditions which includes demand, supply and prices. If some firms decide to charge a price higher than the ruling market price, there will be a large substitution effect away from this firm.

Free Entry and Exit of Firms: There is no restriction upon the entry of a new firm in the market or the exit of an existing firm. This means that the market is open to competition from new suppliers. Due to this characteristic, all the firms can get only normal profit in long run.

Perfect Mobility of Factors of Production: Factors of production are perfectly mobile under perfect competition. In other words, factors of production can freely enter or quit from one industry to another.

All firms (industry participants and new entrants) are assumed to have equal access to resources (technology, other factor inputs) and improvements in production technologies achieved by one firm can spill-over to all the other suppliers in the market.

Absence of Selling and Transportation Cost: Perfect competition assumes that all the producers and the purchasers of a commodity are sufficiently close to each other and as a result, there are no selling and distribution costs.

Pure Vs Perfect Competition

Pure competition and perfect competition are different from each other in terms of degree. Pure competition has all the features of perfect competition except perfect knowledge and perfect mobility of factors.

Pure or perfect competition is rare in the real world but the model is important because it helps to analyse industries or markets.

(II) Imperfect Competition

Imperfect competition is a competitive situation in any market where the conditions necessary for the perfect competition are not satisfied. In other words, it is a market structure that does not meet the conditions of perfect competition.

Imperfect Market: The market structures in which imperfect competition exist are called imperfect markets. This refers to that when any of the characteristic features of perfect competition does not exist like if there is:

- Restricted flow of information on cost and prices.
- Excessive power of some suppliers.
- Differences among sellers to keep the prices high.
- Discrimination by sellers among buyers on the basis of their buying power.

On the basis of degree of imperfection, there may be of the following forms:

1. Monopoly Market or Monopoly

According to some economists, monopoly is that market structure which is characterised by a single producer of a commodity and where there are no close substitutes for that commodity. It is very rigorous description of a monopoly situation because it is almost impossible to find a firm which produces a distinct product which has no substitute at all. It is a known fact that goods have substitutes though they may not be close substitutes. Examples of a monopoly can be found in local public utilities like railway and electricity, etc.

Main Features of Monopoly Market:

- There is a single seller or producer of a particular commodity. Thus, it may be called a single firm industry.
- There is no close substitute of the commodity. Thus, cross elasticity of demand for the commodity is almost zero.
- No new firm can enter the market easily.
- The producer has substantial control over the price of the commodity.

Price Discrimination

When a firm is able to sell same product or service to two different categories of consumers at different prices then it is known as Price Discrimination. Generally a Monopoly firm is able to practice price discrimination successfully. For example, an electricity company sells same electricity to domestic and commercial consumers at different prices.

Distinction between Perfect Competition and Monopoly

Basis of Difference	Perfect Competition	Monopoly
1. Number of sellers or producers	A large number of sellers or producers.	A single seller or producer.

2.	Entry and Exit of firms	New firms can easily enter into the market and existing firms can leave the market.	New firms cannot enter into the market and existing firms cannot leave the market.
3.	Substitute of commodity	There are many substitutes of commodity available in the market.	No close substitute of commodity is available in the market.
4.	Knowledge of market	Buyers have perfect knowledge of market.	Buyers do not have perfect knowledge of market.

2. Monopolistically Competitive Market or Monopolistic competition

Monopolistic Competition is a market structure which contains the features of both Perfect Competition and Monopoly. This structure is very near to reality and large number of firms and commodities belonging to his structure can be found.

This is a market structure which is characterised by a large number of small firms, similar but not identical products sold by all firms, relative freedom of entry into and exit out of the industry, and extensive marketing and selling expenses, etc.

Main Features of Monopolistically Competitive Market:

Large Number of Buyers and Sellers: A monopolistically competitive industry contains a large number of firms, each of which is relatively small compared to the overall size of the market. This ensures that all firms are relatively competitive. In particular, each firm has hundreds or even thousands of potential competitors.

Free Entry and Exit: Monopolistically competitive firms are relatively free to enter and exit an industry at any time.

Imperfect Knowledge of Market: In monopolistic competition, buyers do not know everything, but they have relatively complete information about alternative prices. They also have relatively complete information about product differences, brand names, etc. Each seller also has relatively complete information about production techniques and the prices charged by their competitors.

Individual Price Policy of the Firms: Under monopolistic competition every firm may have its own price policy.

Non-Price Competition: Another important feature of monopolistic competition is the non-price competition. All the firms try to capture the market through various methods of competition other than price cutting. These methods may be the guarantee of free repairs, after sale service, gift scheme with a particular purchase, special discount on a particular purchase, etc.

Product Differentiation: The goods produced by firms operating in a monopolistically competitive market are subject to product differentiation. The goods are essentially the same, but they have slight differences in packaging, brand names, etc.

The goods sold by the firms are close substitutes for one another, just not perfect substitutes. Most important, each good satisfies the same basic want or need. The goods might have subtle but actual physical differences or they might only be perceived different by the buyers.

For example, Colgate, Pepsodent, Close-up, Babool, Anchor are all toothpastes, but are still different from each other. Similar is the case of tea. There are brands like Taj Mahal, Brooke Bond, Tata, Lipton, etc., are all producers of tea, but still different from each other. Restaurant industry is an industry which is a good example of monopolistic competition. Restaurant industry contains large number of firms selling differentiated products (same dish of two firms will not taste same) which are close substitute of each other.

Product differentiation is usually achieved in one of three ways: (1) Physical differences, (2) Perceived differences, and (3) Support services.

1. **Physical Differences:** In some cases the product of one firm is physically different from the product of other firms. One good is chocolate, the other is vanilla, one good uses plastic, the other aluminium, etc.
2. **Perceived Differences:** In other cases goods are only perceived to be different by the buyers, even though no physical differences exist. Such differences are often created by brand names, where the only difference is the packaging.
3. **Support Services:** In still other cases, products that are physically identical and perceived to be identical are differentiated by support services. Even though the products purchased are identical, one retail store might offer "service with a smile", while another provides express checkout.

Role of Advertising in Monopolistically Competitive Market

Advertising is information provided by a company about its product or operation, usually through media such as television, radio, newspapers, magazines, and the internet, to promote or maintain sales, revenue, and/or profit.

It is commonly used by firms operating under monopolistic competition as a way to create product differentiation and thus to acquire some degree of market control and thus charge a higher price.

It affects to the extent that a firm can inform buyers about physical differences or create the perception of such differences then product differentiation increases, and also if advertising convinces buyers that a good is different (and better) than comparable products, then a firm can charge a higher price.

The real world is widely populated by monopolistic competition. Perhaps half of the economy's total production comes from monopolistically competitive firms. The best examples of monopolistic competition come from retail trade, including restaurants, clothing stores and convenience stores.

Toothpaste and toilet paper manufacturers often engage in monopolistic competition practices. Rather than change the products themselves, producers change the packaging, the design, or simply claim through advertising that their product is best.

The restaurant industry is another example of monopolistic competition, especially in the fast food industry in which all services are basically the same, but are marketed differently, and there exists a perception that some fast food restaurants must be better than others.

Examples of Monopolistic Competition are Banks, Radio Stations, Clothing, Computers, Frozen Foods, Canned Goods, Sporting Goods, Fish and Seafood, Jewellery, Health spas, Apparel Stores, Convenience Stores.

It could be said, to name an example of monopolistic competition, firms who control oil production or gas production are monopolistic. They produce identical products except for branding, but due to a relatively less number of firms who control the vast amount of the product, can control the price to an extent by decreasing supply slightly.

Monopolistically Competitive Market is a Blend of both Perfectly Competitive and Monopoly Market

In effect, monopolistic competition is something of a hybrid between perfect competition and monopoly.

Features of Perfectly Competitive Market

1. Large number of firms.
2. No barriers to entry or exit.

Features of Monopoly Market

1. Each firm makes a product that is slightly different from the products of competing firms.
2. Close substitutes but no perfect substitutes.
3. An attempt to increase price normally results in a lower volume sold.

Distinction between Perfect Competition and Monopolistic Competition

Basis of Difference	Perfect Competition	Monopolistic Competition
1. Product	Products of all the sellers and producers are homogeneous.	Products are different but substitute to one another.
2. Price policy	All the sellers and producers follow uniform price policy.	All the producers and sellers follow individual price policy.
3. Knowledge of market	Buyers and sellers have perfect knowledge of market.	Buyers and sellers are not fully conversant with product differentiation.

Distinction between Monopoly and Monopolistic Competition

Basis of Difference	Monopoly	Monopolistic Competition
1. Number of sellers	There is only one producer or seller of a commodity.	There is a large number of buyers and sellers of a commodity.
2. Product differentiation	There is no question of product differentiation.	Product of each seller is slightly different from that of others.
3. Entry of new firms	New firms cannot enter into the market.	There is free entry and exit of firms.

4. Competition	There is no question of competition.	There is non-price competition among the sellers.
5. Price policy	Monopolist may adopt uniform price policy or price differentiation policy for different consumers.	All the firms follow individual price policy.
6. Substitutes of products	There is no close substitute of the commodity.	There are many close substitutes of the commodities.

3. Monopsony Market

Monopsony is a word drawn from Greek language. It is a combination of two parts *i.e.* MONO stands for single and PSONY stands for buyers or one who demands goods and services. Some economists consider monopsony market a sub-part of imperfect market. According to **John Solman**—"Monopsony is a market with a single buyer or employer." Generally monopsony is applicable to factor market.

Mr. Joan Robinson used the term monopsony to refer the market in which there is a single buyer. The older phrase was 'monopoly buyer', but this term literally meant 'single seller buyer' which was illogical and absurd. Monopsony is a single buyer or a purchasing agency which buys the whole or nearly whole of a commodity or service produced. It is important to remember that monopsony refers to the single buyer in the market, e.g., Railways buying wagons and rail engines, Electricity board is the single buyer of power, etc., while on the seller side, there may be single seller, or a few sellers or a large number of sellers.

Main Features of Monopsony Market:

There is a single buyer or consumer.

There may be single seller or few sellers or large number of sellers.

The monopsonist is able to influence the market price of the product or a factor of production.

Distinction between Monopsony Market and Monopoly Market

Monopsony Market	Monopoly Market
1. It represents a specific form of buyer's market.	1. It represents a specific form of seller's market.
2. In this market, only single buyer exists for one particular product or factor service.	2. In this market, there is only one seller for particular product or factor service.
3. There are many sellers of the factor service or a particular commodity as against a single purchaser.	3. There are many purchasers of factor service or a particular commodity as against a single seller or manufacturer of that commodity.

4. The buyer can bring down the price of the factor service or product by reducing the quantity of purchases.	4. The seller can increase the price of factor service or product by either curtailing the supply or the production.
5. In case monopsonist wants to purchase more quantities of an item or factor service, he has to pay additional price for it, because the suppliers may not like to spare additional quantities.	5. In case monopolist wants to supply more of its product or factors service, he has to allow some concessions in the form of cash or kind, so that purchasers are motivated or encouraged to avail the advantages.
6. In monopsony, the purchaser controls the market affairs.	6. In monopoly, the producer/supplier controls the market trends.

EXTENT OF MARKET

Extent of market means the size and area of a market. Market of one commodity may be local, confined to a particular village or area whereas the market of other commodities may be national or even international.

LESSON AT A GLANCE

Meaning of Market: In economics, a market means a system or setup or a facility in which the buyers and sellers of a commodity meet and strike a deal (transaction) about the price and quantity to be bought and sold.

Characteristics of Market: (i) Market is a facility or system and not a place; (ii) Presence of buyers and sellers; (iii) A single commodity.

Factors Determining Forms of Market: (i) Number of buyers and sellers of a commodity; (ii) Nature of the product or commodity; (iii) Knowledge of the market; (iv) Freedom of entry or exit of the firms; (v) Degree of influence on price.

MARKET STRUCTURES:

On the Basis of Competition

1. Perfectly Competitive Market:

Perfect competition is a state of market in which there is a large number of buyers and sellers and a homogeneous product.

Main Features: (i) Large number of buyers and sellers; (ii) Homogeneous product; (iii) Perfect knowledge of market; (iv) Free entry and exit of firms; (v) Perfect mobility of factors of production; (vi) Absence of selling and transportation cost.

2. Imperfect Competition Market:

Monopoly Market: Monopoly is that market situation which is characterised by a single producer of a commodity and where there are no close substitutes for that commodity.

Main Features: (i) Single seller or producer; (ii) No close substitute of the commodity; (iii) Closed entry; (iv) Substantial control over the price.

Monopolistically Competitive Market: In case of monopolistic competition, a firm has some control over the price of the commodity because there are many sellers of the commodity.

Main Features: (i) Large number of buyers and sellers; (ii) Free entry and exit; (iii) Extensive knowledge of market; (iv) Individual price policy of the firms; (v) Non-price competition; (vi) Product differentiation.

Monopsony Market: Monopsony is a market situation where there is single buyer or a purchasing agency which purchases whole or nearly whole of a commodity or service produced.

PROJECT WORK

Select a place where goods are bought and sold. Prepare a list of main characteristics of this market. With the help of this list, identify type of this market.

(a) Select any product such as toothpaste, tooth brush, toilet soap, TV, refrigerator, cooler, ready-made cotton shirt, washing machine, etc.
(b) Try to identify the number of firms producing and selling that product.
(c) Nature of market structure.
(d) Locate the nature of advertisement done by the concerned company.
(e) Comments of consumers.

Prepare your project report taking into consideration the above factors.

QUESTIONS

A. Short Answer Type Questions:
1. Define market.
2. State any three features of market.
3. Explain the term monopoly.
4. What is monopolistic market?
5. Give any three main features of monopolistic market.
6. State any two differences between perfect competition and monopoly.
7. Distinguish between pure competition and perfect competition.
8. Explain term monopsony market.
9. Why is advertising and market research an important component of the monopolistically competitive market?
10. State any two factors affecting the type of market for a commodity.
11. Give two examples of monopolist markets in India.
12. What is the implication of freedom of entry and exit of firms under perfect competition?
13. Under which market form is the product homogeneous.

14. Identify the market forms of the following:
    (i) The Government of India is the sole buyer of fighter aircrafts.
    (ii) Goods sold are homogeneous.
    (iii) Motorcar market in India.
    (iv) Market for toilet soaps in India.
15. Identify the market forms for the following :
    (i) Railways in India
    (ii) Textile Industry in India
    (iii) Perfectly elastic demand
    (iv) Telecom Industry in India
16. Define the term market.
17. State two important characteristics of monopoly.

Recent Year Questions:
1. Mention one feature each of a monopoly market and of a perfect market present in a monopolistically competitive market. [ICSE 2010]
2. Why are selling costs not required in a perfectly competitive market? [ICSE 2010]
3. What is product differentiation? To which market is it relevant? [ICSE 2010]
4. Producers in a perfect market are price takers. [ICSE 2011]
5. Why do producers incur high selling costs in an imperfect market? [ICSE 2011]
6. State one similarity between monopolistic competition and monopoly. [ICSE 2011]
7. Citing reasons state the advantage of monopolistic competition over monopoly. [ICSE 2012]
8. Producers in a Monopoly market are price makers. Briefly explain. [ICSE 2012]
9. There are no substitute goods in a monopoly market. Give a reason to support your answer. [ICSE 2013]
10. State one difference between monopsony and monopolistic competition. [ICSE 2013]
11. State whether the following statement is true or false. Give reasons:
    "The price level in a perfectly competitive market is determined by an individual seller." [ICSE 2014]
12. In which form of market do producers and consumers have perfect knowledge about the market conditions? [ICSE 2014]
13. Mention two features of monopoly. [ICSE 2014]
14. What is meant by product differentiation? [ICSE 2014]
    OR
    What is meant by product differentiation? In which market from it is prevalent? [ICSE 2019]
15. What is meant by monopsony? Give an example. [ICSE 2015]
16. State the market form of the following commodities:
    (i) Railways
    (ii) Automobiles

(iii) Shampoos
(iv) Fighter Aircrafts. [ICSE 2015]
17. Give a reason for the following statement:
Selling costs are higher in Monopolistic competition. [ICSE 2015]
18. Identify the market forms for the items given below: [ICSE 2016]
   (i) A single seller
   (ii) Homogeneous goods
   (iii) Product differentiation
   (iv) A single buyer
19. State whether the following statement is true or false. Give one reason for your answer.
"A monopolist can sell the same product at different prices to different customers." [ICSE 2016]
20. State any two differences between monopolistic competition and perfect competition. [ICSE 2018]
21. Highlight the importance of selling costs in a monopolistically competitive market. [ICSE 2019]

B. Long Answer Type Questions:

1. What is market? Explain its salient features.
2. What do you mean by perfect competition? Enumerate its main features.
3. What is monopolistic competition? What are essentials of monopolistic competition?
4. Write two similarities and two dissimilarities between perfectly competitive market and monopolistically competitive market.
5. Define the term market. Differentiate between monopoly and monopolistically competitive markets on the basis of number of sellers, product differentiation, entry of new firms, price policy and importance of advertising expenses.
6. Compare monopolistic competition and perfect competition on the basis of any four characteristics.
7. Define a perfectly competitive market. Discuss three differences between a perfectly competitive market and a monopoly. Explain any four factors that lead to monopoly.
8. What is meant by a monopoly market? Discuss any four differences between monopoly and monopolistic competition.

Recent Year Questions:

1. The given statement is correct or incorrect. Give reason to support your answer: Uniform price is a key feature of perfectly competitive market. [ICSE 2009]
2. Monopolistic competition is perfect blending of monopoly and perfect competition. Explain. [ICSE 2009]
3. Explain two similarities and two dissimilarities between a perfect market and an imperfect market. [ICSE 2011]
4. Under which type of a market are producers 'price-takers'? Explain three of its characteristics. [ICSE 2013]

5. With the help of an example explain the meaning of price discrimination. To which market is it relevant? Explain any two similarities between a perfect market and a monopolistically competitive market. [ICSE 2014]
6. What is perfect competition? Describe any three characteristics of perfect competition. [ICSE 2015]
7. (i) Define a monopolistically competitive market. Give two examples of this market structure.
   (ii) Explain two important features of this type of market. State one similarity and one difference between monopolistic competition and perfect competition.
[ICSE 2016]
8. (i) Why can a monopolist charge different prices in different market.
   (ii) Explain any three features of monopoly. [ICSE 2018]
9. Point out the differences between perfect competition and monopoly on the basis of: [ICSE 2019]
   (i) Number of sellers
   (ii) Market place
   (iii) Entry of firms
   (iv) Types of products produced

12 The State and Economic Development

The role of state has undergone a sea change since the evolution of state system of administration from time immemorial. In the olden times, the states used to be the military states and the main focus of the rulers was on the internal and external security and foreign relations. But as the staunch monarchies have reduced and there came the system of democratically elected governments, the role of state has undergone a tremendous change. Now the military states have changed to welfare states with very wide focus on welfare and developmental activities along with the security and foreign relations.

The extent of the role of the State in respect of welfare and economic decisions depends on the nature of an economy. In a predominantly capitalistic economy, the State provides, regulates and maintains the economic framework and the economic decisions are taken by the buyers and sellers in the market operations within the framework. In a predominantly socialistic economy, the State is the main decision maker in respect of the production and pricing.

India is a mixed economy which contains the feature of both *i.e.*, the capitalist economy and socialist economy. Hence, in this system both the private and public sector exist side by side. Public sector is owned by the government. One of the significant factors of public sector in India is that, this sector does not work with profit motive as the main objective rather it's prime objective is the upliftment of the masses of the country.

The Indian Constitution also embodies the goals of socialistic pattern of society which provide necessary guidelines to the government for working in relation to the economy. These guidelines determine the extent of government's responsibility in supervising, directing and controlling the economy.

OVERVIEW

The most important responsibility of the Government of a country is 'well-being' of its people for which the State adopts several measures to achieve socio-economic objectives.

Improving the living standard of people and providing full employment are the most important functions besides attaining social security, reducing inequalities of income and wealth, and creating better conditions of work.

In brief, the State exists to achieve overall improvements in the status of its people. In order to achieve this goal, the State plays a very significant and positive role, so that the economic progress of the nation is accelerated. The State, therefore, takes appropriate steps to develop sound monetary and banking network. It also controls monopolistic attitudes so as to attain price stability within reasonable limits.

Economic development implies the development of economy of an underdeveloped country. The concept of this refers to that process by which per capita income and economic welfare of an underdeveloped country increases.

"The raising of income levels in poor countries is called economic development."

—**A. Maddison**

"Economic development is simply an increase in economic welfare." —**Colin Clark**

Economic development is a process whereby the real per capita income in a country continues to grow in the long run. Economic development and structural changes in the economy go hand-in-hand. By structural changes, we mean a shift in the relative significance of the various sectors of the economy. For example, in a underdeveloped economy, agriculture is the main source of income but as the economy develops the significance of industries and services increases. State plays a very-very significant role in the economic development of a country as it depends on the policies enacted by the states.

Therefore, the power of the government must be used for general welfare of the people. The guidelines for the working of the economy are provided through the *Directive Principles of State Policy* in our Constitution.

THE ROLE OF STATE IN PROMOTING ECONOMIC DEVELOPMENT
OR
FUNCTIONS OF THE STATE IN PROMOTING ECONOMIC DEVELOPMENT

Now-a-days, the state plays a vital role in promotion of economic development of a country, particularly of an under-developed country. The under-developed countries lack even the basic necessities of life, such as, food, cloth, housing, healthcare, education, etc. They suffer from a number of problems like high incidence of poverty, chronic problem of unemployment and widespread inequality in the distribution of income and wealth. All these factors have necessitated active participation of the state in the task of promoting economic development. The state can promote economic development in the following ways:

Promoting Capital Formation: Capital is the life blood of all economic activities. Government is required to play an important role in capital formation. It has to use fiscal and monetary resources to generate necessary resources for capital formation.

Development of Economic Infrastructure: Another important role of state in promoting economic development is the development of economic infrastructure. It includes the development of transport systems (road, air and sea), raw-material, irrigation works, gas, power and electricity, bridges, communication network, technical know-how, provision of adequate water, housing, etc. The absence of economic infrastructure can retard economic development. The availability of adequate economic infrastructure promotes agricultural and industrial development.

Improvement in the Standard of Living: The economic policy of the government should be directed towards providing better food, better clothing, better housing, etc., to its people or to say, the living standard should be better and improved. The living standard of the people will be better only when the per capita income increases. Generally, in developing and underdeveloped countries, the per capita income is low, which can only be increased by economic development. Various measures and policies may be adopted for development of different economic sectors, like agriculture, industry, trade, transport, commerce and infrastructure.

Though standard of living in advanced countries like USA, UK and Canada is already quite high yet people living there are having desire for a still higher standard of living and the government in those countries directs its policies and activities in maintaining and further improving the living standard.

Full Employment: Unemployment is a kind of wastage of manpower. Moreover, under-employment or disguised unemployment has similar evil effects on the society. If the unemployed workers are put to work, they will produce goods or services that will benefit the worker himself as well as the nation. Thus, the government makes sincere efforts to provide enough and adequate employment opportunities. This is one of the most important duties of the government.

Hence, the objective of every government is the achievement of full employment. This refers to the full utilisation of all the factors of production including labour. Full employment has been defined as:

"As a situation where involuntary unemployment is reduced to minimum possible level."

—**Keynes**

Modern economists feel that full employment can be achieved by increasing the capital investment:

- to start new industries,
- to build up public works, and
- for miscellaneous other schemes which lead to employment generation for the citizens.

The governments of all the countries, whether developed or underdeveloped; have accepted the policy of securing full employment in principle. For underdeveloped countries, the role of the government becomes more important because of higher unemployment existing there.

Thus, for well-being and welfare of its citizens, the government's policies and activities should be aimed at providing full employment, so that per capita income increases.

Social Security: A person having low income develops a feeling of financial insecurity. Moreover, if any mishappening like sickness or accident or unemployment occurs, he cannot earn during such a situation and his sufferings increase. A rich person can tide over such situation from his savings but generally the poor does not have the savings to overcome such eventualities.

So, it's become imperative on the part of the state to develop social security infrastructure. This social security infrastructure must include free or heavily subsidised healthcare facilities and provision of unemployment allowance or employment opportunities for a person in the phase of unemployment.

India has developed such social security measures *i.e.*, Mahatma Gandhi National Rural Employment Guarantee Scheme (MGNREGS), Pradhan Mantri Jeevan Jyoti Bima Yojna, Pradhan Mantri Suraksha Bima Yojna and Rashtriya Swasthya Bima Yojna, etc., at the national level.

Rapid Industrialisation: The participation and support of the state affects the process of industrialisation in less developed countries. For strong industrial base, establishment of basic industries like iron and steel industry, heavy chemical industry, etc., is must. But, as this requires huge investments and have long gestation period, the private investors do not come forward to take up such projects. Therefore, the development of such basic industries depends upon the initiative taken by the government. The state also extends support to the industrial sector by:

- Creating proper transport and communication facilities.
- Adequate supply of institutional credit.
- Setting up of power projects.
- Establishing technical and management institutions.
- Providing tax concessions for export units, etc.

In India too, the state has established various specialised financial institutions like IFCI, IDBI, etc. The government has also provided infrastructure facilities to the industrial sector like transport and communication, distribution of power, etc.

Removal of Inequalities in Income and Wealth: Income inequalities is the problem which almost every country of the world encounters some or the other time in its economic history. So in almost all the countries of the world, it is found that a small number of persons possess most of the properties and wealth and in turn get major benefits from the national income. This situation is harmful to the society as a whole, because this inequality reduces the utility of income. An amount of ₹10 may have no significance for a rich person, but has great importance for a poor person. A rich person will spend it for his pleasures or luxury, but a poor man will buy food or cloth for himself or his family. Thus, the economists view that success of social welfare will be maximum when the inequalities of income and wealth are reduced.

In a capitalistic economy, where accumulation of private property is allowed, the absolute equality of income and wealth cannot be achieved, but the government can adopt measures to bring out this equality. These measures may be progressive taxation, provision for social security, labour intensive development programme, infrastructural development of backward and rural areas, etc.

Rapid Agricultural Development: Agricultural sector absorbs the maximum portion of work force in less developed countries and contributes substantially to the national income. It forms the backbone of these nations and much of the economic development of these countries depends upon the agricultural development. State can play an important role in improving the productivity and production of this sector. it could undertake various institutional and technological reform policies as land reform, introduction of improved variety of seeds, irrigation, credit and marketing facilities.

Stability of Price Level: The living standard, happiness and comforts depend upon the quantum of goods and services one can get in exchange of the money he has earned. However, the quantum of goods and services depends upon the price level. When prices increase, purchasing power of the money decreases. A wage earner cannot get his wages increased every time when prices go up. Also the prices usually do not fall once they go up, and the workers and wage earners are the worst affected.

When prices fall tremendously, the industrialists resort to curtailing of production, rendering many people unemployed. Thus, we see that both rise and fall in prices are harmful to the society as well as to the nation's economic progress. The government cannot remain a silent spectator and has to initiate actions to keep the prices stable within a narrow range. The *Central Bank* of the country (The *Reserve Bank of India*) adopts certain measures to stabilise the price level as well as foreign exchange rate, because it affects the *International Trade*.

Sound Banking and Currency System: The entire economic activity and progress is related to the money and currency system. The banks of the country are intimately connected with its industry, trade and commerce. The banks mobilise the savings of the people, which in turn are invested for further capital formation. The government, therefore, has to make all possible efforts to establish and maintain efficient banking and a good currency system.

Control on Monopoly: The monopolistic practices generally lead to the exploitation of the customers by way of charging higher prices and lower supplies. The monopolist also exploits the labour by paying low wages. As such, monopolistic practices cause excessive profits and add to the inequalities of income and wealth. The monopolist may create an artificial scarcity in times of economic exigencies. All such activities are very harmful for economic development of a country and the government must be careful in its policies to curb unfair monopolies.

Better Terms and Conditions of Work: In general, the labourers/employees are financially weak and have low bargaining powers and invariably accept the terms and conditions of work offered and decided by the employer. Thus, the government is required to protect the interests of the workers. In advanced countries, there are laws about the working conditions in the factories. In our country also there are specific laws relating to working hours, leave, factory conditions, overtime, etc. The basic objective is to provide a healthy environment and better working conditions to the workers, so that their efficiency is improved and exploitation is avoided. The happy and efficient workers are real assets to any nation and can make a great contribution in economic progress.

Thus, we see that the state, by virtue of its immense enforcement powers and legal authority; has to play a very vital and significant role in the economic development of a country.

LESSON AT A GLANCE

Meaning of Economic Development: Economic development is the opposite of underdevelopment and implies that a country has a highly developed economic system. This, in turn, means that it has a highly effective organisation both of agricultural and of industry, a highly developed banking and credit system and an adequate development of transport and communication system.

Role of State in Promoting Economic Development: (i) Promoting capital formation; (ii) Development of economic infrastructure; (iii) Improvement in the standard of living; (iv) Full employment; (v) Social security; (vi) Rapid industrialisation; (vii) Removal of inequalities in income and wealth; (viii) Rapid agricultural development; (ix) Stability of price level; (x) Sound banking and currency system; (xi) Control on monopoly; (xii) Better terms and conditions of work.

PROJECT WORK

Prepare a "Report on the role of the State in the economic development of a particular region":

(a) Select any particular Region/State/District/Town for this purpose, and visit different government departments. For instance, the department of agriculture, industry, urban development, State planning board, etc. You should also visit the head offices of different public sectors like banks, post and telegraph offices, state transport corporation, railways and airlines offices, etc.

(b) Try to collect various types of information on the projects undertaken by such different Government departments/offices to promote economic development of the said region.

(c) Evaluate the role of the state and its agencies engaged in promoting the economic development of the said region.

QUESTIONS

A. Short Answer Type Questions:

1. Mention two economic functions of the State.
2. What do you understand by 'Full Employment'?
3. How full employment can be achieved?
4. Mention the role of Government in any two of the following:
    (i) Ensuring employment.
    (ii) Reducing inequalities of income and wealth.
    (iii) Social insurance.
    (iv) Establishing sound banking system.
    (v) Stabilisation of value of money.
    (vi) Improving the terms and conditions of work.
5. Explain the role of government in agricultural development.
6. State two ways in which the government can promote economic development.
7. State any two functions of government in achieving economic development.
8. How does a state contribute to the economic development of the country?
9. How the government maintains regional balance in the country?

Recent Year Questions:

1. How can the State help in generating income in the economy? [ICSE 2006]
2. Why is government support necessary to build up economic infrastructure in a developing economy? [ICSE 2008]
3. Mention one way by which government policy can ensure social justice. [ICSE 2013]

4. 'The role of the state is important in developing the economic infrastructure of a developing economy.' Give two reasons to support your answer. [ICSE 2015]

B. Long Answer Type Questions:
1. Define the term economic development. Mention six relevant functions of state which accelerate economic development in a country.
2. Discuss the following economic functions of the Government:
    (i) Control of monopoly.
    (ii) Providing full employment.
    (iii) Establishing a sound currency system.
    (iv) Stabilisation of prices.
3. Explain the role of the state in fostering industrial and agricultural growth of a country.
4. Discuss the role of state in economic development with reference to industrialisation and reducing inequality of income.
5. Discuss any four functions or roles of the State or government in economic development.
6. Reduction of inequality in income and wealth and full employment are the two functions which every society tries to attain. Discuss.

Recent Year Questions:
1. In less developed countries, the state has an active role to play in establishing social justice. Explain four methods adopted by the government to fulfill this objective. [ICSE 2009]
2. Explain clearly four ways by which the state can promote economic growth and development. [ICSE 2016]

13 Instruments of State Intervention

As desired by our Constitution, the government is asked to intervene in the economy to achieve economic and social goals. The following are the major instruments of intervention by the state:

- Fiscal policy
- Monetary policy

FISCAL POLICY

Fiscal policy refers to the policy of the government with regards to taxation, public expenditure and public borrowings so as to promote economic development of a country. Thus, there are three instruments of fiscal policy, viz., (i) taxation policy, (ii) public expenditure policy and (iii) public borrowing policy. A good and effective fiscal policy uses these three instruments in a proper combination and in the right balance.

> **OVERVIEW**
>
> Any country may adopt a particular type of economy, suiting to its socio-economic objectives, but economic efforts are to be carefully directed for the overall benefit of its people. As such, the Government of that country cannot remain as a silent spectator and allow the market forces to play in their own way.
>
> The Government, thus, exercises various types of monetary, fiscal and physical controls to regulate and direct the economic factors and forces to accomplish the socio-economic objectives and well being of its people.

"Fiscal policy means public expenditure and tax policy." —**Paul Samuelson**

"Fiscal policy is a policy under which the government uses its expenditure and revenue programmes to produce desirable effects and avoid undesirable effects on the national income, production and employment." —**Arthur Smithes**

"Fiscal policy involves changes in government expenditure and taxation designed to influence the pattern and level of activity." —**Harvey and Johnson**

The fiscal policy of the country actually determines the *exact manner and pattern of economic progress and stability*. The fiscal policy is an important tool to bring rapid economic growth of under-developed and developing economies. However, the objectives of fiscal policy for developed capitalistic economy may be different from those for under-developed economy.

Objectives of Fiscal Policy in a Developed Economy

Since the developed economies have already made substantial economic progress, their basic aims now is:

- to achieve and maintain full employment.
- to achieve economic stability by controlling both inflation and deflation.

The above mentioned objectives can be accomplished by adopting a fiscal policy of compensatory spending by the state. This refers to the compensatory variations in the public expenditures by the state in certain proportions according to changes in private expenditures. This can be understood like this : if the conditions of depression (recession) or unemployment has to be overcome, the total aggregate effective demand can be increased by government by way of increasing public expenditure. Thus, it can be stated that the decline in public expenditure (causing depression or unemployment) must be compensated for, by an increase in public expenditure.

Similarly, during the inflation period, the private expenditure is usually high, which results in excessive increase in total effective demand in an economic system. The only way to resolve this situation is to apply drastic cuts to public expenditure by the state under the compensatory fiscal policy.

Thus, it is clear that the main objective of the fiscal (budgetary) policy in developed economy is to maintain full employment with economic stability.

Objectives of Fiscal Policy in an Under-developed Economy

Since such economies are in a developing stage in which resources are still unemployed or underemployed, the main thrust of the fiscal policy should be to have quick and accelerated economic growth by employing the resources. All the objectives are, therefore, decided and devised with this main consideration. The main objectives of the fiscal policy may be the following:

- The first and foremost objective should be to encourage the people to maximise the level of aggregate savings by applying a cut to actual and potential expenditure at present.
- The next objective, naturally, should be to maximise the rate of capital formation by investing the savings of the people so as to break the economic stagnation and to pave the way for economic progress and growth.
- The third objective should be to divert the capital resources to more productive and socially more desirable uses. The less productive and less desirable plans and schemes may be taken afterwards, if resources permit.
- The situation of inflation should be avoided as far as possible because it adversely affects the economy.
- The fiscal policy should be so framed and implemented that all the sectors of economy get proper opportunities to develop and grow. The sectoral imbalances should be eliminated from time to time.
- The industries, providing higher employment potential without adversely affecting the economy and price structure; should be encouraged.
- The fiscal policy should be such that brings about an equitable redistribution of income and wealth in the society, because the economic inequalities cause greater setback to the under-developed economies. The desired economic progress cannot be achieved, if economic inequalities exist.

General Objectives of Fiscal Policy

- To achieve economic stability in the country.
- To achieve and maintain full employment in the country.

- To bring price stability.
- To reduce inequalities in income and wealth.
- To achieve high rate of economic growth in the country.
- To break the vicious circle of poverty.
- To encourage investment—both internal and external.

Thus, we see that the objectives of fiscal policies will be different for different economies and the state has a very important role to play in this direction.

INSTRUMENTS OF FISCAL POLICY

The instruments of fiscal policy like Taxation, Public Expenditure, Public Debt and Deficit Financing adopted by the government to raise adequate finance for economic growth are discussed as under :

Taxation

A tax is one of the important sources of public revenue. A tax is a compulsory charge or payment levied by the government on an individual or corporation. Therefore an element of compulsion is involved in taxation. Other sources of public revenue are excluded from this compulsory element. There is no direct give and take relationship between a taxpayer and the government.

"A tax is a compulsory contribution from a person to the government to defray the expenses incurred in the common interest of all without any reference to the special benefit conferred."

—**Prof. Seligman**

"A tax is a compulsory contribution imposed by the public authority, irrespective of the exact amount of service rendered to the taxpayer, in return for which no specific and direct quid pro quo is rendered to the payer."

—**Dalton**

From these definitions, it is clear that tax is a compulsory contribution. It means that the State has the right to tax. Refusal to pay the tax is punishable. The phrase 'without *quid pro quo*' means the absence of direct and proportional benefit to the taxpayer from the government.

Types of Tax

Taxes may be classified in various categories on different basis, such as the form, nature, aim and method of taxation. The most important classifications are :

(I) Direct and Indirect Taxes.

(II) Progressive, Proportional, Regressive and Degressive Taxes.

(I) Direct and Indirect Taxes

According to **J. S. Mill**, whether the tax is direct or indirect, depends upon the fact who ultimately pays the tax. If the tax is paid by the person on whom it is imposed, it is called direct tax and if the tax is paid by some person and the final burden or incidence is borne by some other person, the tax would be an indirect tax. Some modern writers classify taxes into direct and indirect taxes on the basis of tax on income received and expenditure incurred on commodity and service. Taxes imposed on receipt of income are called direct taxes. For example, income tax, profit tax, capital gain tax, etc. Taxes which are imposed on expenditure incurred on a commodity and a service are regarded as indirect taxes. For example, excise duty, custom duty, commodity tax or sales tax, service tax, etc. In the recent period all these indirect taxes except custom duty have been merged into a single Goods and Services Tax (GST).

Advantages of Direct Taxes

Equitable: A direct tax is an equitable tax. It is equitable in the sense that it is levied according to the taxable capacity of the people. The rates of direct taxes, like the income tax, can be fixed in such a way that higher the income of a man, the greater is the rate at which he has to pay the tax. Such a system is known as progressive taxation.

Economical: Direct taxes are economical in the sense that the cost of collecting them is low. They are mostly collected "at the source". For instance, the income tax is deducted from an officer's pay every month. This saves expense. The employer acts as an honorary tax collector. This means great economy.

Certainty: The taxpayers know how much they are going to pay and at what time they are going to pay the tax. The authorities also know the amount of revenue they can expect. There is certainty on both sides. This minimises corruption on the part of collecting officials.

Elasticity: A direct tax can be varied according to the needs of the government and changes in the income of the people. When the income of the people goes up, the rate of income tax can also be increased. If the income of the people falls, the rate of income tax can be lowered.

Productivity: Direct taxes constitute an important source of government revenue. Their collection charges are low. Therefore, direct taxes are more productive.

Increases Civic Sense: A person knows that he is paying a tax, he feels conscious of his rights. He claims the right to know how the government uses his money. Civic sense is thus developed. He behaves as a responsible citizen.

Disadvantages of Direct Taxes

Inconvenient: The greatest drawback of direct taxes is that they put the taxpayer to a lot of botheration and inconvenience. Sometimes, the taxpayer is called to pay the entire tax in one installment. Besides, the taxpayers have to maintain elaborate accounts for the satisfaction of the tax officials.

Evadable: By submitting false return of income, some people evade the tax. That is why a direct tax is called as "A Tax on Honesty".

Disincentive: Direct taxes reduce the desire to work and save. The rates of direct taxes in our country are usually high. Many business ventures are not undertaken on the ground that a large part of the income earned will have to be given to the government in the form of taxes. Thus, direct taxes reduce incentives to work and save.

Advantages of Indirect Taxes

Convenient: They are mostly levied on commodities and services and are paid by consumers when they buy them in the market. The amount of the tax is included in the price of the commodity and service and the consumer pays the tax without experiencing its pinch.

Equitable: Indirect taxes are equitable in the sense that they are paid by all the sections of the community at the time of making purchases of goods and services in the market, in the form of sales tax, service tax or custom duty.

Productive and Elastic: By increasing the rate of taxes, the government can secure an adequate income from such taxes. The income from such taxes goes on increasing with the increase in population and production in the country.

Socially Desirable: Indirect taxes are levied on intoxicants, like wine or opium, etc., and it serves a great social purpose because they limit the consumption of such harmful commodities by the public.

No Possibility of Evasion: No person can evade the indirect taxes, because they are collected in the form of higher prices of goods sold to the consumers.

Disadvantages of Indirect Taxes

Regressive: Indirect taxes are not equitable as they are regressive in nature. It affects the poor more than the rich man. For example, a commodity tax imposed on foodstuffs will affect a poor family to a much greater extent than a rich family.

Uncertain: As soon as the tax is levied on a commodity, its price rises in the market and, consequently, its demand declines. It cannot be said with certainty as to which extent the demand of the commodity has declined consequent upon the imposition of the tax. Hence, there is always uncertainty about the income occurring from the indirect taxes.

Absence of Civic Consciousness: Since the taxpayers do not feel that they are paying a tax at the time of purchasing a commodity, these taxes do not promote civic consciousness among the citizens.

Uneconomical: The cost of collection is quite heavy. Every source of production has to be guarded. Large administrative staff is required to administer such taxes. This turns out to be a costly affair.

Distinction between Direct and Indirect Taxes

Two different types of taxes are defined, depending on whether the burden of the tax is being shifted or not (*i.e.,* whether the 'impact' and the 'incidence' of the tax burden are on the same person). If the initial impact and the final incidence is on the same person, (*i.e.,* if the person on whom the government has imposed the tax, carries the burden of the tax), the tax is called a 'direct tax'. On the other hand, if the burden of the tax is shifted (*i.e.,* if the impact and the incidence are on different persons), the tax is called an 'indirect tax'. We have already seen that the burden of income tax cannot be shifted. Hence, income tax is a direct tax. On the other hand, a sales tax is an indirect tax.

(II) Proportional, Progressive, Regressive and Degressive Tax

Considering the relation between the tax rate and the base, there can be four types of taxation, viz. : 1. Proportional taxes, 2. Progressive taxes, 3. Regressive taxes and 4. Degressive taxes.

Proportional Taxes

Taxes in which the rate of tax remains constant, though the tax base changes, are called proportional taxes. Here, the tax base may be income, money value of property, wealth, or goods, etc. Income is, however, regarded as the main tax base, because it is the determinant of taxable capacity of a person.

In a proportional tax system, thus taxes vary in direct proportion to the change in income. If income is doubled, the tax amount is also doubled. It can be understood through the following *figure 13.1.*

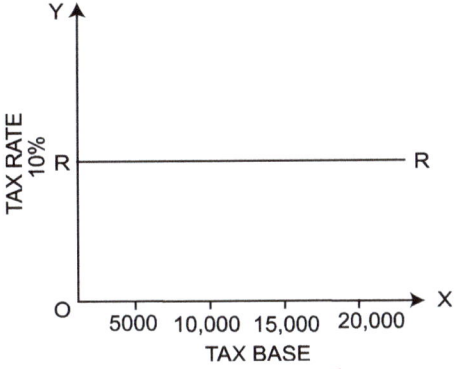

Fig. 13.1 : Proportional Taxes

Merits of Proportional Taxes

- Proportional taxation leaves the taxpayer in the same relative economic status.
- Proportional taxation is simple to calculate and to administer. Since it is uniformly levied, it is very convenient to estimate.
- Proportional taxation is not as repugnant to taxpayers as regressive taxation.
- The effect on willingness to work hard and save is not adverse in the case of proportional taxes. So it is free from the harmful effects of taxation.

Progressive Taxes

Taxes in which the rate of tax increases, with the increase in tax base are called progressive taxes. Thus, in a progressive tax, the amount of tax paid will increase at a higher rate than the increase in tax base or income, for the taxation amount is the product of multiplying the base by the rate and both these are increasing in a progressive tax. Thus, a progressive tax extracts an increasing ratio of rising income *(figure 13.2)*.

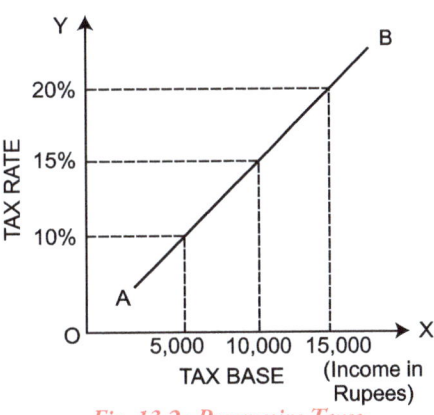

Fig. 13.2 : Progressive Taxes

Merits of Progressive Taxes

- A proportional tax is inequitable, as it falls relatively heavily on poor incomes. A progressive tax is more equitable, as a larger part is taxed on higher incomes. It is justifiable just as the law of diminishing marginal utility operates in the case of money. Hence, the disutility of paying a high tax by rich is not as much as that of poor in paying even a low tax. Therefore, the rich should be taxed at a higher rate than the poor.
- Progressive taxes may be justified on the ground that higher incomes contain surpluses, which have cent percent capacity to bear taxes. Thus, progressive taxation fully complies with the principle of capacity to bear or ability to pay the tax.
- Progressive taxes are more economical, as the cost of collection does not rise when the rate of tax increases.
- Progressive taxation has greater revenue productivity than proportional taxation.
- Progressive taxation is helpful in curbing inflationary trends.

Regressive Taxes

When the rate of tax decreases as the tax base increases, the taxes are called regressive taxes. It is represented through *figure 13.3.*

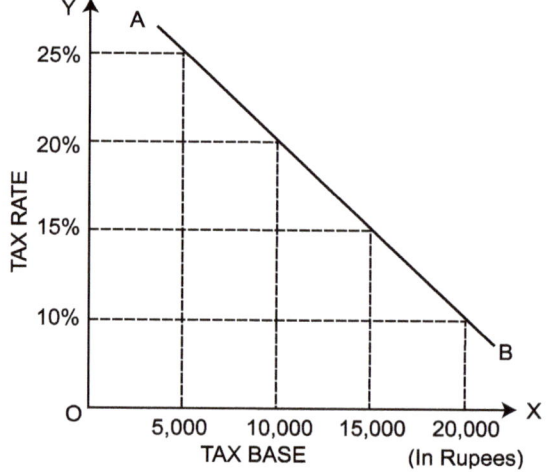

Fig. 13.3 : Regressive Taxes

Merits of Regressive Taxes

It must be noted that in regressive taxation, though the total amount of tax increases on a higher income in the absolute sense, in the relative sense, the tax rate declines on a higher income. Thus, a regressive tax extracts a declining proportion of the rising income. As such relatively a heavier burden (sacrifice involved) falls upon the poor than on the rich. Generally, taxes on necessaries are regressive as they take away a greater percentage of lower incomes as compared to higher incomes.

Thus, regressive taxation is unjust and inequitable. It does not comply with the canon of equity. It tends to accentuate inequalities of income in the community.

Degressive Taxes

In degressive taxation, a tax may be progressive up to a certain limit; after that it may be charged at a flat rate. It is a mixture of proportional as well as progressive tax system. This can be illustrated in *figure 13.4.*

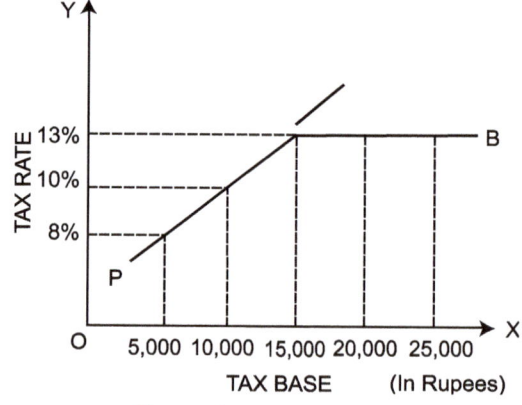

Fig. 13.4 : Degressive Taxes

Objectives of Taxation

The following are the main objectives or purposes of taxation:

Raising Revenues: In order to meet the state expenditure for carrying out its functions, the government levy taxes of different types so that its revenue may increase.

Equal Distribution of Income: Taxes are also imposed to reduce the inequality of income distribution in an economy. This can be done by levying taxes on the income of the rich community because their taxable capacity is more than that of the poor and the middle class.

Regulation: Taxation policy specially regulates consumption and production and also regulates economic activities in general.

Higher Growth: Taxes are used to interact in the market, so as to induce a greater output of goods and services resulting in higher growth to the economy.

Pushing Up Rates of Saving and Investment: The rate of saving and investment can be pushed up through tax policies. The government can design its tax system in such a way that investors and savers are taxed at lower rates than others in society.

Social Justice Through Taxation

Social justice refers to the concept of a society in which justice is achieved in every aspect of society, rather than merely the administration of law. It is generally thought of as a society which affords individuals and groups fair treatment and a just share of the benefits of society. It can also refer to the distribution of advantages and disadvantages within a society.

Social justice is both a philosophical problem and an important issue in politics, religion and civil society. Most individuals wish to live in a just society, but different political ideologies have different conceptions of what a 'just society' actually is. The term "social justice" is often employed by the political left wing to describe a society with a greater degree of economic egalitarianism, which may be achieved through progressive taxation, income redistribution, or property redistribution. The right wing also uses the term social justice, but generally believes that a just society is best achieved through the operation of a free market, which they believe provides equality of opportunity and promotes philanthropy and charity. Both right and left tend to agree on the importance of rule of law, and human rights.

Social justice is also a concept that some use to describe the movement towards a socially just world. In this context, social justice is based on the concepts of human rights and equality.

A progressive tax is a tax imposed so that the effective tax rate increases as the amount to which the rate is applied increases. The term "progressive tax" describes a distribution effect, which can be applied to any type of tax system (income or consumption) that meets the definition. It is frequently applied in reference to income taxes, where people with more disposable income pay a higher percentage of that income in tax than do those with less income. The term progressive refers to the way the rate progresses from low to high. The term can also apply to adjustment of the tax base by using tax exemptions, tax credits, or selective taxation that would create progressive distributional effect.

For example, a tax on luxury goods and the exemption of basic necessities may be described as having progressive effects as it increases a tax burden on high end consumption and decreases a tax burden on low end consumption. The opposite of a progressive tax is a regressive tax, where the tax rate decreases as the amount to which the rate is applied increases. In between is a proportional tax, where the tax rate is fixed as the amount to which the rate is applied increases. Progressive taxes attempt to reduce the tax incidence of people with smaller incomes, as they shift the incidence disproportionately to those with higher incomes.

Early Proponents

The idea of a progressive income tax has garnered support from economists and political scientists of many different ideologies–ranging from **Adam Smith** to **Karl Marx.** Many authorities trace the origin of modern progressive taxation to Adam Smith, who wrote in *The Wealth of Nations.*

The necessities of life cause great expense to the poor. They find it difficult to get food, and the greater part of their little revenue is spent in getting it. The luxuries and vanities of life causes the principal expense of the rich, and a magnificent house embellishes and sets off to the best advantage all the other luxuries and vanities which they possess. It is not very unreasonable that the rich should contribute to the public expense, not only in proportion to their revenue, but something more than that in proportion.

A century later, **Karl Marx** argued for a progressive income tax in *The Communist Manifesto* : "In the most advanced countries the following will be pretty generally applicable …a heavy progressive for graduated income tax."

Reasons for Implementation

(i) If the utility gained from income exhibits diminishing marginal returns, as many psychologists assert, then for the tax burden to be shared in an utilitarian way, the tax-bill must increase non-linearly with income.

(ii) As income levels rise, levels of consumption tend to fall. Thus it is often argued that economic demand can be stimulated by reducing tax burden on lower incomes while raising the burden on higher incomes.

(iii) It is also argued that people with higher income tend to have a higher percentage of that in disposable income, and can thus afford a greater tax burden (this is the "vertical equity" argument). Some would claim that a person making exactly enough money to pay for food and housing cannot afford to pay any taxes without it causing material damages, while someone making twice as much can afford to pay up to half their income in taxes.

(iv) A progressive tax is an automatic stabiliser in the sense that if a person were to suffer a decrease in wages due to a recession then the money regained by being in a lower tax bracket lessens this blow.

(v) It is inherent in tax policy that it implements economic and social policy. People, who are concerned about a runaway, cancerous character in the global economy, greenhouse gases, etc., see benefits in progressive taxation, both in its braking effect on the economy and in helping to shape economic activities towards necessities more effectively than purely monetary or fiscal policies.

MONETARY POLICY

Monetary policy is the policy of the government with regard to monetary matters. Such a policy involves influencing the aggregate supply of money in circulation by an effective credit control system.

This refers to the policies designed and adopted to ensure that entire economic system operates efficiently for which supply, cost and availability of money are responsible to accomplish it. Various measures to achieve this objective involve deliberate and calculated manipulation of bank rate, open market operations, variations in reserve requirements and credit controls. The objectives of monetary policy vary from time to time depending upon the types of problems prevailing in the country and the general economic policies adopted by the government of that country. Sometimes, the objectives are quite incompatible with each other and under those circumstances, the monetary policy needs to be modified according to the priorities.

"The management of the expansion and contraction of the volume of the money in circulation for the explicit purpose of attaining a specific objective such as full employment."
—**Prof. R. P. Kant**

According to this definition, the monetary policy means regulation of money supply by the monetary authority.

"Policy employing the Central Bank's (Reserve Bank's) control on the supply of money as an instrument for achieving the objectives of general economic policy." —**Harry G. Johnson**

"By monetary policy we mean any conscious action undertaken by the monetary authorities to change the quantity, availability and cost (rate of interest) of money." —**G. K. Shaw**

The fundamental basis of the monetary policy is proper functioning of the economic system. In modern days, the functioning of economy is influenced, to a great extent, by the *national debt* also and a broad definition may include composition and age profile of national debt. The monetary policy may then be framed keeping this aspect along with measures of open market operations designed to purchase short-term securities and variation in rates of long-term bonds.

OBJECTIVES OF MONETARY POLICY

The main objectives of the monetary policy may be any or all of the following:

Exchange Rate Stability: The main objective of monetary policy is to maintain stability in the exchange rates. This was the main objective under Gold Standard among different countries. When there was disequilibrium in the balance of payment of the country, it was automatically corrected by movements of gold. It was popularly known as, *"Expand currency and credit when gold is coming in; contract currency and credit when gold is going out."* This system used to correct the disequilibrium in the balance of payment and stability in the exchange rate was maintained. It must be noted that if there is instability in the exchange rates, it would result in outflow or inflow of gold, resulting in unfavourable balance of payments. Therefore, the main objective of monetary policy is to maintain stability in the exchange rate of currency of the country. It always tries to eliminate those adverse forces which tend to bring instability in exchange rates.

Price Stability: The objective of price stability has been highlighted during the thirties of the present century. **Cassels** and **Keynes** suggested price stabilisation as the main objective of monetary policy. Fluctuations in price either upward or downward direction distorts economic system which affect different sections of the society. Stable prices repose public confidence because cyclical fluctuations are totally eliminated. It promotes business activity and ensures equitable distribution of income and wealth.

Neutrality of Money: Economists like **Wicksteed**, **Hayek** and **Robertson** hold the view that monetary authority should aim at neutrality of money in the economy. According to them, the monetary change causes distortion and disturbances in proper operation of the economic system of the country. If neutral monetary policy is followed, there will be no cyclical fluctuations, no trade cycle, no inflation and deflation in the economy. Under this system, money is kept stable by the monetary authority.

Full Employment: According to **Keynes**, the objective of monetary policy should be to ensure the maximum utilisation of productive resources in the economy. Monetary policy should be used in such a manner so as to promote full employment of resources in the country. Monetary policy, as an instrument of full employment; should aim at securing an increase both in consumption and investment expenditures to deal with the problem of mass unemployment.

Economic Growth: In recent years, some economists have suggested economic growth as the main objective of monetary policy in a country. It implies utilisation of all the productive resources; *i.e.*, natural, human and capital resources in such a manner so as to ensure sustained increase in national and per capita income over time. Therefore, monetary policy promotes economic growth by maintaining equilibrium between the total demand for money and total production capacity and further creating favourable conditions for saving and investment.

Credit Control: Another objective of monetary policy is credit control in order to influence the patterns of investment and production in the economy. The credit control is needed to control inflationary pressures arising in the process of economic development.

Tools (Schemes) of Monetary Policy

Various measures adopted by the 'Central Bank' (Reserve Bank) can be classified into two main categories to implement the exact monetary policy.

Quantitative Control Measures like changes in cash reserve ratio, bank rate modifications and open market operations, etc. These measures are effective in regulating the volume of money circulating in the country. However, such methods have greater influence in countries where proper monetary markets exist like U.S.A. and U.K. The quantitative measures have very little or no effect in developing countries, because a large non-monetised sector exists there, *i.e.*, a market which does not depend too much on the supply or volume of money.

Qualitative Control Measures like restricting the credits for those industrial units or business sectors which are not beneficial to the economy. Such measures are effective in directing the investments into the desirable economic sectors. The qualitative control measures are useful to the economic development in following ways:

- The qualitative control measures curb the inflation without affecting the economy, because during inflation, the bank's advances increase rapidly. The monetary authorities can exercise check and restrict bank's advances to units which are not desirable, *i.e.*, which are not helpful in accelerating economic growth. As such, the bank's advances are directed towards essential commodity sectors and total restrictions can be imposed on other non-desirable sectors. Thus, the available money can be re-directed depending upon the exigencies and priorities of the nation.

- The qualitative measures can be utilised to prevent and restrict the investments into unproductive units.
- The qualitative credit control measures can encourage and help the flow of savings (available money) into any specific economic sector for investment.

Thus, we see that in under-developed or developing economies, the qualitative credit control measures are effective in influencing the volume and pattern of investment. The monetary policies by way of calculated manipulations can be effectively utilised for developments in desirable economic sectors of the nation.

DISTINCTION BETWEEN MONETARY AND FISCAL POLICY

One should clearly understand the distinction between fiscal and monetary policies. The fiscal policy affects either the revenue or the expenditure of the government, by monetary policy. In other words, it is the set of policies that affect the functioning of the economy by changing monetary variables, for instance, the total amount of money circulating in the economy or the money rate of interest (*i.e.*, the rate of interest at which money can be lent or borrowed). If the monetary authorities lower the rate of interest, this will stimulate investment in the economy. However, the same effect on investment can be achieved by giving tax concessions to investors. the former is an example of a change in the monetary policy, while the latter is a change in fiscal policy.

Distinction between Monetary Policy and Fiscal Policy

Basis	Monetary Policy	Fiscal Policy
1. Meaning	It refers to policy of the central bank of a country to control the supply of money and its cost, *i.e.*, rate of interest.	It is a policy under which the government implements to direct its revenue and expenditure programme to produce desired effects.
2. Instruments	Its main instruments are: (i) Bank Rate (ii) Open Market Operations (iii) Cash Reserve Ratio (iv) Selective Controls	Its main instruments are: (i) Taxation Policy (ii) Public Expenditure (iii) Deficit Financing
3. Impact	It mainly affects the producing sector of the economy.	It usually affects the entire economy.

LESSON AT A GLANCE

Instruments of State Intervention: The following are the major instruments of state intervention : (i) Fiscal policy; (ii) Monetary policy.

Fiscal Policy: Fiscal policy refers to the policy of the government with regards to: (i) taxation; (ii) public expenditure; and (iii) public borrowings.

A. Smithes defined it as, "A policy under which the government uses its expenditure and revenue programmes to produce desirable effects and avoid undesirable effects on the national income, production and employment."

Objectives of Fiscal Policy: In developed economy it is to achieve full employment; and to achieve economic stability. In under-developed economy it is to maximise the level of aggregate saving; to maximise rate of capital formation; divert the capital resources to more productive and socially more desirable uses; to avoid inflation; elimination of sectoral imbalances; and higher employment potential.

Instruments of Fiscal Policy:

Taxation: Direct and Indirect taxes; and Proportional, Progressive, Regressive and Degressive taxes.

Advantages of Direct Tax: (i) Equitable; (ii) Economical; (iii) Certainty; (iv) Elasticity; (v) Productivity; and (vi) Increases civic sense.

Disadvantages of Direct Taxes: (i) Inconvenient; (ii) Evadable; and (iii) Disincentive.

Advantages of Indirect Taxes: (i) Convenient; (ii) Equitable; (iii) Productive and elastic; (iv) Socially desirable; and (v) No possibility of evasion.

Disadvantages of Indirect Taxes: (i) Regressive; (ii) Uncertain; (iii) Absence of civic consciousness; and (iv) Uneconomical.

Proportional Taxes: Taxes in which the rate of tax remains constant, though the tax base changes.

Progressive Taxes: Taxes in which the rate of tax increases, with the increase in tax base.

Regressive Taxes: When the rate of tax decreases, as the tax base increases.

Degressive Taxes: In degressive taxation, a tax may be progressive up to a certain limit; after that it may be charged at a flat rate.

Objectives of Taxation: (i) Raising revenues; (ii) Equal distribution of income; (iii) Regulation; (iv) Higher growth; and (v) Pushing up rates of saving and investment.

Monetary Policy: Prof. R. P. Kant defined monetary policy as, "The management of the expansion and contraction of the volume of the money in circulation for the explicit purpose of attaining a specific objective such as full employment." According to this definition, the monetary policy means regulation of money supply by the monetary authority.

Objectives of Monetary Policy: (i) Exchange rate stability; (ii) Price stability; (iii) Neutrality of money; (iv) Full employment; (v) Economic growth; and (vi) Credit control.

PROJECT WORK

Collect the copy of budget proposals of Union Government and circulars of Reserve Bank of India. From the above make a brief report regarding various measures taken or proposed for effecting fiscal control and monetary controls. Take proper guidance from your subject teacher.

QUESTIONS

A. Short Answer Type Questions:

1. What is fiscal policy?
2. Write two objectives of fiscal policy in developed countries.
3. State two objectives of fiscal policy in under-developed countries.
4. What do you understand by taxation?
5. State two objectives of taxation.
6. What is the difference between 'a tax on income' and 'a tax on commodity'?
7. Give two advantages of direct taxes.
8. State two disadvantages of direct taxes.
9. Give two advantages of indirect taxes.
10. Define monetary policy.
11. Mention two objectives of monetary policy.
12. What are the quantitative measures to control credit?
13. Mention any two fiscal measures that the government can adopt to fight economic and social inequality.
14. Which form of tax discourages consumption expenditure? Give an example.
15. How can tax be used as an instrument to bring about equitable distribution of wealth and income?
16. Can direct taxes reduce income inequality?
17. Differentiate between direct and indirect tax.
18. Distinguish between fiscal and monetary Policy.

Recent Year Questions:

1. Mention one way by which fiscal policy can be used to control economic recession. [ICSE 2010]
2. Mention one way by which the government can reduce the disparity in income and wealth distribution of its citizens in a developing economy. [ICSE 2010]
3. State the difference between income tax and expenditure tax. [ICSE 2011]
4. Define a degressive tax. [ICSE 2012]
5. Citing reasons state the advantage of:
    (a) Progressive tax over proportional tax.
    (b) A direct tax over an indirect tax. [ICSE 2012]

6. What are indirect taxes? Give an example. [ICSE 2013]
7. Distinguish between the fiscal and monetary policy of the government. [ICSE 2013]
8. State whether the following statements are true or false. Give reasons for each:
   (i) In a developing country like India public expenditure should not be incurred on infrastructural development.
   (ii) An indirect tax can be made progressive by imposing higher tax rates on luxury goods. [ICSE 2013]
9. State whether the following statement is true or false. Give reasons.
   "Rate of taxation depends upon the income groups in a progressive tax structure." [ICSE 2014]
10. State two measures taken by the government to reduce income inequality in an economy. [ICSE 2014]
11. An indirect tax is not always equitable. Give two reasons to support your answer. [ICSE 2014]
12. Define fiscal policy. [ICSE 2015]
13. What is meant by shifting of tax burden? To which tax is this relevant? [ICSE 2015]
14. Classify the following types of tax into direct and indirect taxes : [ICSE 2015]
    (i) Entertainment tax
    (ii) Income tax
    (iii) House tax
    (iv) Sales tax
15. Briefly explain why direct taxes foster civic consciousness among people. [ICSE 2016]
16. What are progressive taxes. Give on example. [ICSE 2018]
17. How does direct tax reduce income inequality. [ICSE 2019]
18. Name any two instruments of fiscal policy. [ICSE 2019]

B. Long Answer Type Questions:

1. Explain the various tools of fiscal policy? How can fiscal policy be used for economic development?
2. Explain the main objectives of fiscal policy in under-developed economy.
3. Describe any four purposes of taxation.
4. How does taxation policy assist in achieving the objectives of social justice in a country? Briefly explain three ways of achieving the objectives of social justice through taxation.
5. Differentiate between direct and indirect taxes. What are the advantages and disadvantages of direct taxes?
6. What is meant by monetary policy? Explain, how the qualitative controls by government, as tools of monetary policy measures of credit control adopted in India; are effective in influencing the volume and pattern of investment?
7. Explain the tools of monetary policy.
8. Explain four objectives of monetary policy.

9. Discuss any three merits and demerits of indirect taxes over direct taxes.
10. Define fiscal policy. Explain the instruments of fiscal policy used by the government to control inflation.
11. Define fiscal policy. Discuss four of its objectives with references to India.

Recent Year Questions:
1. Define a tax. State two differences between income tax and commodity tax.
   [ICSE 2010]
2. Explain how tax can be used as an instrument to regulate consumption and production in an economy. [ICSE 2010]
3. State the following:
   (i) Four merits of a direct tax.
   (ii) Three demerits of an indirect tax. [ICSE 2011]
4. How does the state fulfil following socio-economic objectives:
   (i) Reducing income inequality.
   (ii) Promoting industrial growth.
   (iii) Environment protection. [ICSE 2011]
5. Explain the terms impact, shifting and incidence of a tax. Explain in brief two merits of direct tax. [ICSE 2012]
6. Define a tax. Explain the following with examples: [ICSE 2014]
   (i) Regressive tax,
   (ii) Proportional tax,
   (iii) Degressive tax.
7. With reference to the taxation policy: [ICSE 2015]
   (i) Mention three differences between direct taxes and indirect taxes.
   (ii) Differentiate between progressive and regressive taxes giving an example for each.
8. Give a reason for each of the following statements : [ICSE 2015]
   High rates of taxes reduce the savings capacity in an economy.
9. What is meant by an indirect tax? Give two examples. Explain briefly two merits and two demerits of Indirect tax. [ICSE 2016]
10. State two merits and two demerits of direct taxes. [ICSE 2019]

14
Public Sector Enterprises

Prior to 1947, there was virtually no 'Public Sector' in the Indian economy. The only instances worth mentioning were the Railways, the Posts and Telegraphs, the Port Trusts, the Ordnance and Aircraft Factories and a few State managed undertakings like the government salt factories, quinine factories, etc. The idea that economic development should be promoted by the state—actually managing industrial concerns—did not take root in India before 1947.

At the time of Independence, the activities of Public Sector were confined to irrigation, power, railways, ports, communications, etc. Since Independence, the activities of Public Sector expanded considerably. But simultaneously, it was assured by Industrial Policy Resolution of 1948 and 1956 that Private Sector will also be allowed to grow and therefore, the industries were divided into different categories and their fields were also specified. Some of the fields were reserved for public sector and some for private sector and remaining ones were left for both the sectors.

OVERVIEW

Public sector enterprises have expanded significantly after independence. At the time of independence these enterprises were confined to very limited spheres and areas. Public sector enterprises play a very significant role in economic development by way of generation of employment, capital formation, development of infrastructure, etc. Need for public sector in India is realised due to many factors like: (i) for the growth of heavy goods industries, (ii) for the establishment of socialistic pattern of society, (iii) for balanced regional growth, etc.

However, the public sector enterprises are not free from the inherent defects. Many public sector enterprises are suffering from heavy losses.

A glance on the division of fields between the Public Sector and Private Sector clearly brings out a fact that the Heavy and Basic Industries are reserved only for Public Sector. The consumer goods industries have been left for Private Sector (These have high and early returns). Agriculture, *i.e.*, the largest sector of our economy is in private sector, whereas the other social and infrastructure activities are in public sector like banks, financial institutions, railways, air-services, posts and telegraphs, telephones and communications.

Public Sector include Departmental enterprises like, Railways, posts and Telegraphs; Financial Institutions like, Industrial Finance Corporation of India (IFCI), Industrial Development Bank of India (IDBI); Non-departmental enterprises viz. Public Corporation and Government companies like Steel Authority of India Limited (SAIL), National Thermal Power Corporation (NTPC).

Public sector enterprise is an enterprise which is owned, controlled and managed by the government. It may be central government, state government or local government. By local government, we mean municipal corporation, municipality, district board, panchayat samiti or even village panchayat.

"Public enterprise is meant by such government institutions which provide goods and services to people in that form which private enterprises provide in absence of these public enterprises."
—**Encyclopaedia Britannica**

"State enterprises in business denotes an undertaking which is controlled and operated by the Government as its sole owner or major shareholder." —**Ray, Chaudhary and Chakravarty**

"By Public enterprises is meant the industrial, commercial and economic activities carried on by the Central Government or by a State Government or jointly by the Central Government and a State Government and in each case either solely or in association with private enterprise, so long as it is managed by a self-contained management." —**S. S. Khera**

Distinction between Departmental Enterprise, Public Corporation and Government Company

Basis of Difference	Departmental Enterprise	Public Corporation	Government Company
1. Formation	It is formed as a department or ministry of the government.	It is formed by the special act of the parliament or legislature.	It is formed under the Indian Companies Act.
2. Capital	Capital is provided by the budgetary provisions of the government.	Capital is provided by the government.	At least 51% of the capital is provided by the government and the rest by the private sector.
3. Legal position	It has no separate legal existence.	It has separate legal existence.	It has separate legal existence.
4. Management	It is managed by the government.	It is managed by separate board of directors.	It is managed by separate board of directors.
5. Autonomy	There is no autonomy.	There is substantial autonomy.	There is little autonomy.

ROLE OF PUBLIC SECTOR ENTERPRISES

Public sector enterprises play a dominant and dynamic role in the economic development of a country which is evident from the following:

Establishment and Development of Basic Heavy Capital Goods Industries: Public sector enterprises take the responsibility of establishing and developing basic heavy capital goods industries which require huge capital and high risk and have a long gestation period, such as atomic energy, heavy machines, fertilizers, coal mining, iron and steel, arms and ammunitions, ship building, aircraft building, etc. If these industries are left in the hands of private sector, they can make them the tools of exploitation of masses and endanger the safety of the country.

Establishment of Socialistic Pattern of Society: India aims at setting up a socialistic pattern of society where equal opportunities to work and earn will be provided. If all the industries are left in the hands of private entrepreneurs, they would be able to concentrate with more economic power and income disparities will widen more. Private entrepreneurs work with the profit motives. The ownership of industries will entail them the right to exploit the consumers and wage-earners on the one hand and the suppliers of raw materials and finished products on the other. In order to check the exploitative practices, the government must take the control of certain industries of strategic importance.

Balanced Regional Growth: Public undertakings are also set-up to remove the regional imbalances in the economy. While some of the regions in India are highly developed, others are still backward. Private entrepreneurs do not take any interest in establishing industries in those backward regions. They are guided by profit motive, therefore they set up industries in those area where the location and availability of other factors are favourable. The public undertakings are therefore set up in the backward regions not only to exploit the local or regional resources but also to have balanced development of the country.

The need for growth of public sector also arises because of the fact that it effectively and efficiently achieves the social and economic objectives. It is an effective tool to mobilise public savings for investment purposes.

Generation of Employment: Public sector enterprises are the most important source of employment. In India, more than 70% workers are employed in public sector. They generate lakhs of new jobs every year. As per the economic survey 2015-16 the number of persons employed in public sector industries was 176.09 lakh.

Capital Formation: Capital formation is considered the key factor in the economic development of a country. Public sector enterprises are a significant tool of capital formation in the country. For example, total financial investment in all CPSE (Central Public Sector Enterprise) was ₹16,40,628 crores in 2019 as compared to ₹253977 crores in 2018 showing growth of 8.55%. The profits of 178 CPSE's is 1,74,587 crores in 2018-19 which increases to 1,55,931 crores in 2017-18 showing growth in profit by 11.96%.

Infrastructure: Rapid industrialisation of a developing country like India depends upon the creation of infrastructure in terms of economic overheads, such as power, transportation, communications, irrigation, education, technical training, etc. It was left to Central Government to develop them and most of the public sector enterprises were set up in these industries. Public sector investment in the infrastructure sector has paved the way for both agricultural and industrial development of the country. Private sector investments also depend on such infrastructural facilities developed by the public sector of the country.

Export Promotion and Import Substitution: A large number of public enterprises have been established to promote India's exports. The state Trading Corporation and the Minerals and Metal trading Corporation have done admirable job of export promotion, especially in the East European Countries. Some public sector units were started specially to produce goods which were earlier imported, thus resulting in the saving of foreign exchange.

Contribution to Central Exchequer: Public enterprises have been making substantial contribution to the government exchequer through payment of corporate taxes, excise duty, custom duty and other duties. In this way they help in mobilising funds for financing the needs for the planned development of the country.

Control over Defence Industries: If the defence requirements are under the complete control of private sector, then it can be harmful for the country at any time. Government, in modern times, should control the defence sector because abundant amount is being spent on the establishment of this industry.

Economies of Large-scale: Large-scale industries, which require heavy capital investments and modern high level technology, need to be established in public sector only because if these large-scale units are set up in private sector, the possibility of concentration of economic powers in private hands cannot be ruled out. It is a well-known fact that when large-scale economies prevail, the free market does not produce good results. Therefore, for appropriate economic efficiency, the government regulation of public ownership becomes essential.

Check on Economic Powers: In a capitalist economy, where the public sector is practically non-existent, the economic powers get concentrated gradually in the hands of private persons, causing an increase in the inequalities of income and wealth. The existence of Public Sector in mixed economy acts as a deterrent for the tendency of concentration of wealth and economic powers in few private hands. India is a social welfare state having a fundamental policy of reducing disparities of income and wealth and bringing about social equality for which PEs are essential.

Economic Planning: Public sector enterprises play a crucial role in the field of economic planning of a country. Planning is a device for achieving and implementing economic development plans.

Thus, we find that the public sector has been playing a very significant and positive role in fulfilling social obligations of the state, as well as in bringing about balanced economic development of the different regions of the country.

PROBLEMS OF PUBLIC SECTOR ENTERPRISES/REASONS FOR DECLINING POPULARITY OF PUBLIC SECTOR

Public sector enterprises suffer from certain limitations as described below:

Lack of Clear-cut Objectives: PEs are required to fulfill a large number of objectives, economic as well as non-economic, which may be conflicting with each other. The objectives are not made clear and often there is a lack of policy clarification on various matters.

Labour Problems: PEs in general face the shortage of skilled, experienced and competent workers because of relatively lower salary and perquisites, etc. This has led to the inefficient management of these enterprises.

Political Interference: Theoretically, PEs are provided autonomy in their working. In practice, the government, the ministers, the politicians and other government agencies constantly interfere in their day-to-day activities. This results in inefficient functioning and poor performance of the enterprises.

Lack of Direct Incentive: The management of these enterprises, even if they are competent enough, do not show keen interest in their efficient working as they do not have any incentive or financial stake. Moreover, unlike private enterprises, they do not feel insecure about their jobs also. So, neither they have incentive of reward nor fear of losing their jobs.

Cost Over-run: Construction cost of many public sector projects increased due to their non-completion within the stipulated time period. Thus, an additional burden is put on the scarce resources of the country.

Delay in Decision-making: PEs do not believe in individual decisions. Committees are formed to take decisions relating to the operational requirements. This process leads to delay in the decision-making and advantages of quick decision-making, so essential for a business enterprise, are not availed of. Often, in practice the decisions in PEs are based on political rather than economic grounds. Their very location is also decided on political basis rather than economic expediency.

Unremunerative Pricing/Administered Price Policy: PEs do not function purely on the basis of commercial considerations. Lack of commercial approach by their executives leads to wastages, inefficiencies and resultant lower productivity. The prices of the products of public sector enterprises are generally kept low, keeping in mind the needs and purchasing power of the general people. Thus, they are not profit making enterprises and generally suffer losses.

Low Capital Return: The performance of any sector can be represented with the notion of profitability. In this respect, the performance of most of the public sector enterprises comes negative.

Bureaucratic Delays: Often, in practice, bureaucratic style of management is followed in PEs which leads to rigidity, strictness, adherence to rules and procedures and impracticability. This leads to inefficient functioning of these enterprises.

Permissive Atmosphere: PEs are often very weak in labour relations. For several reasons, the employees' aspirations go on increasing, even though they may be better placed, and even on petty issues, they resort to undesirable practices creating hurdles in production and sales, etc. They are, often guided by political leaders and neither they have any intuition to work hard nor any fear of losing jobs.

Under-utilisation of Capacity: Public sector enterprises are suffering from the problem of under-utilisation of installed plant capacity. It leads to an increase in average cost of production and adversely affects their profit earning capacity and thus results in low profitability.

Excessive Man Power: The number of man-power employed in the public sector enterprises are much more than the actual requirements. This increases the burden of payment of their wages and salaries.

Sick Units Burden: Public sector enterprises are suffering from the problem of existence of a large number of sick units which have been showing continuous heavy losses since several years. They become the burden on the economy of a country.

SUGGESTIONS TO IMPROVE THE EFFICIENCY OF PSU

On account of inefficient working of PEs, it has been felt very necessary that certain positive measures must be taken to remove the causes of inefficiency, so that PEs are beneficial to nation as a whole. Some of the suggestions can be outlined as below:

Reforms in the Board of Directors: Because of indifferent attitudes, the Directors do not take active interest in working of PE. Hence, it is advised that Board of Management be suitably reformed by giving appropriate representation of workers and financial directors.

Price Policy : Instead of adopting an ad-hoc price structure, it is considered appropriate that price policy should be based on existing price structure and market responses.

Commercial Outlook: It is must that PEs must generate surplus to make them self supporting. Hence, there needs to be a proper balance between National Interest and Profitability.

Check on Extravagance: The unwanted expenditures like that on foreign trip, entertainment, meetings and symposium must be curtailed.

Proper Auditing: For this purpose, the Administrative Reforms Committee has recommended that three or four Audit Boards should be established under the control of comptroller and Auditor General.

Sector Corporations: The Administrative Reform Committee has recommended for the establishment of various sector corporation so that each type of industries are under one sector corporation. Thus, all engineering units should be under one corporation and similarly all fertilizer units should be under another corporation.

Efficient Management: The appointment of efficient managers should be based on merits and not on political grounds.

Improvement in Working Efficiency: For this, there must be some incentives for raising the level of production and productivity. The persons must be appointed on the basis of ability, expertise and administrative capabilities.

Autonomy: PEs must be granted full autonomy in their day-to-day working. The political interference must be stopped. However, competent and able politician can be considered as honorary consultant.

Capacity Utilisation: All PEs must make a full utilisation of installed/ available capacity. The Bureau of Public Enterprises has also given various suggestions on similar lines for active consideration by the government.

Conclusion

Thus, the role of public sector in promoting economic development cannot be over emphasized. The Late Prime Minister Indira Gandhi advocated the public sector so as to gain control of the commanding heights of the economy; and to provide commercial surpluses with which to finance further economic development. But subsequently the approach is fast changing, most probably on political grounds.

LESSON AT A GLANCE

Meaning of Public Sector Enterprises: Public sector enterprise is an enterprise which is owned, controlled and managed by the government.

Role of Public Sector Enterprises: (i) Establishment and development of basic heavy capital goods industries; (ii) Establishment of socialistic pattern of society; (iii) Balanced regional growth; (iv) Generation of employment; (v) Capital formation; (vi) Infrastructure; (vii) Export promotion and import substitution; (viii) Contribution to central exchequer; (ix) Control over defence industries; (x) Economies of large scale; (xi) Check on economic powers; and (xii) Economic planning.

Problems of Public Sector Enterprises: (i) Lack of clear-cut objectives; (ii) Labour problems; (iii) Political interference; (iv) Lack of direct incentive; (v) Cost over-run; (vi) Delay in decision-making; (vii) Unremunerative pricing/Administered price policy; (viii) Low capital return; (ix) Bureaucratic delays; (x) Permissive atmosphere; (xi) Under-utilisation of capacity; (xii) Excessive man power; and (xiii) Sick units burden.

Suggestions to Improve the Efficiency of PSU: (i) Reforms in the board of directors; (ii) Price policy; (iii) Commercial outlook; (iv) Check on extravagance; (v) Proper auditing; (vi) Sector corporations; (vii) Efficient management; (viii) Improvement in working efficiency; (ix) Autonomy; and (x) Capacity utilisation.

PROJECT WORK

Make a survey of Government enterprise which is engaged in manufacturing sector and collect information in respect of production, work, efficiency, labour problems, etc. Check whether it is making profits or suffering from losses. Also point out the defects in its functioning. Make a similar type of survey in respect of some departmental undertakings like Post Office or Indian Telephone Industry or Water Supply Department.

QUESTIONS

A. Short Answer Type Questions:
1. Define public sector enterprise.
2. State any three points depicting the role of public sector enterprises.
3. Mention any three reasons for declining popularity of public sector.
4. Give two examples of public corporations.
5. Mention two causes responsible for the inefficiency of public sector enterprises.
6. What role does the public sector play in reducing regional disparities in industrial growth?
7. Give any two consequences of declining popularity of public sector.
8. How do public enterprises exercise control on economic powers?

Recent Year Questions:

1. Give two reasons to show how public enterprises are desirable in mixed economy.
   [Hint: (i) To build infrastructure, (ii) Welfare objectives.]
2. Mention two important roles played by PSU's in economic development. [ICSE 2007]
3. State two ways in which the public sector is important even at the present times. [ICSE 2009]
4. What are public sector units? Mention one problem faced by public sector units in India. [ICSE 2013]
5. Explain how an improper price policy results in the poor performance of public sector enterprises. [ICSE 2019]
6. What are public sector enterprises. Give two examples of public sector enterprises in India. [ICSE 2019]

B. Long Answer Type Questions:

1. Give a brief classification of public enterprises.
2. What are the problems of public enterprises? Explain.
3. What are the reasons of declining popularity of public sector?
4. How can the working efficiency of public sector units be improved? Give suggestions.

Recent Year Questions:

1. Discuss any four problems faced by public sector enterprises and suggest the remedies to overcome these problems. [ICSE 2006]
2. Public sector units made a commendable contribution to the Indian economy in the early phase of planned development. What are public sector units? Explain any four contributions of PSUs to the Indian economy. [ICSE 2010]
3. What are PSU? Give two of its examples. Explain any four problems faced by PSUs in recent times. [ICSE 2011]
4. What is a public sector undertaking? Explain three problems faced by public sector undertakings in India? [ICSE 2012]
5. Explain any four ways by which public sector enterprises plays a dominant role in an economy. [ICSE 2018]

15. Privatisation of Public Enterprises

Privatisation (alternately "denationalisation" or "disinvestment") is the transfer of ownership of a concern from the public sector (government) to the private sector (business). A transfer in the opposite direction could be referred to the nationalisation or municipalisation of some property or responsi-bility. The term is also sometimes used to refer to government sub-contracting a service or function to a private firm.

The term "Privatisation" also has been used to describe an unrelated, non-governmental interaction involving the buyout, by the majority owner, of all shares of a public corporation or holding company's stock, privatising a publicly traded stock.

A clear definition helps in avoiding ambiguity and facilitates a comprehensive analysis for an in-depth investigation of the issue in all its aspects. In the literature, several authors define privatisation differently. Some authors define privatisation narrowly to mean the sale of state-owned assets.

OVERVIEW

In view of comparatively huge investments and low returns, an opinion is generally expressed and argued for privatisation of the public sector units. With the growing problems of large-scale fiscal deficit faced by government in recent years, the issue of privatisation has been brought to the forefront. However, it cannot be denied that the public sector is suffering from various deficiencies and shortcomings in its functioning.

Privatisation programme is gaining momentum throughout the world. Now privatisation has become a worldwide phenomenon. Root cause for the interest in privatisation programme is the inefficiency of public enterprises.

"The transfer of a majority ownership of state-owned enterprises to the private sector by the sale of ongoing concerns or assets following liquidation." —**Kikeri, Nellis And Shirley**

"Refers to the sale of all or parts of a government's equity in state-owned enterprises to the private sector." —**Ramamurti**

"The divestiture by the state of enterprises, land or other assets." —**World Bank**

Several other authors see privatisation as a wider phenomenon encompassing interconnected activities that reduce the government ownership and control of enterprises and that promote private sector participation in the management of state-owned enterprises.

"An umbrella term for a variety of different policies that are loosely linked by the way in which they are taken to mean the strengthening of the market at the expense of the state."

—**Vickers And Wright**

"The introduction of market forces into an economy in order to make enterprises work on a more commercial basis." —**Hartley And Parker**

They argue that privatisation embraces denationalisation or selling-off state-owned assets, deregulation (liberalisation), competitive tendering, as well as the introduction of private ownership and market arrangements in the ex-socialist states.

"A range of different policy initiatives intended to change the balance between the public and private sector and the services they provide." —**Cook And Kirkpatrick**

They distinguish three main approaches to privatisation:
- A change in the ownership of the enterprise,
- Liberalisation or deregulation,
- A transfer of goods or services from the public to the private sector even if the government retains ultimate responsibility for supplying the service.

From a transition point of view,

"Any transfer of ownership of a state enterprise to other agents which results in their effective private control of the business." —**Blommestein, Geiger And Hare**

They argue that privatisation does not require a majority stake to be held by any private owner or group of owners; it is also compatible with some shares being retained by the ministry of finance (or another body charged with holding state assets). Figure below shows the classification of activities associated with privatisation.

Activities Included in Defining Privatisation

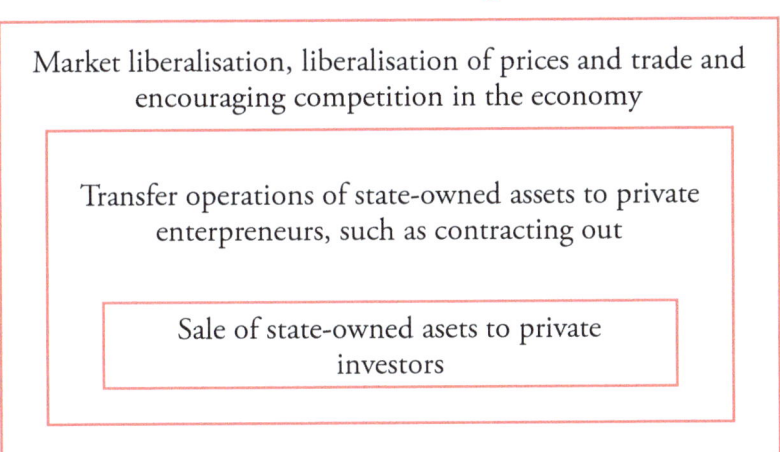

NEED FOR PRIVATISATION

Demand for privatisation can be considered on following grounds:

Control on Budgetary Deficits: In most of the developing countries, budgetary deficits have been increasing. These deficits lead to inflation and become a hurdle to economic growth. The slowing down of the process of economic growth is a direct blow to the rising hopes of common man. These deficits can be checked through privatisation of PEs.

Resource Mobilisation: Government consumption expenditure has been growing rapidly and thereby leaving less resources for development and plan expenditure. Not only this, but also the increasing revenue deficit is met through public borrowing. This public borrowing reduces the availability of resources for private enterprises and thereby the chances of getting more consumption goods are weakened. This process can be reversed only through privatisation of PEs.

Reduction in Extra Tax Burden: Continuous losses in PEs forces the government to bear this extra burden. Thereafter government compensates this loss through the new doses of taxes. It adversely affects the purchasing power of the public. In case of privatisation, there is no need for the government to bear the losses of PEs and imposing of extra tax burden does not arise.

Flow of Funds to Public Exchequer: The process of privatisation directly contributes to the flow of funds to the public exchequer in the form of realisation of money on the sale of shares of PEs to private sector.

Improvement in Production: The process of privatisation will lead to more economies in various costs through increased efficiency and productivity and control of waste. This means more availability of resources for the implementation of development and welfare programmes.

Increase in Competition: The privatisation process will result in more domestic and international competition and thereby making management more responsive towards the needs of customers and changing technology.

RATIONALE OF PRIVATISATION IN INDIA

In India the privatisation strategy has been adopted in the form of disinvestment of government's equity in public sector undertaking and also through the opening up of reserved areas for the participation of private enterprises. With the growing problem of large scale fiscal deficits faced by the government in recent years, the issue of privatisation has been brought to the forefront. In 1990-91, the huge fiscal imbalance and growing balance of payments crisis have forced the country to approach the IMF for huge repurchase facilities and also to World Bank for structural adjustment loan. Both IMF and World Bank had put certain 'conditions' covering different sectors of the economy for their gradual opening up and liberalisation. Accordingly, the new industrial policy, 1991 was formulated to meet some of these conditions. This new policy has emphasized the increasing role and importance of the private sector in developing the industrial sector of the economy and thereby adopted various measures. Some of these important measures included abolition of licensing in all industries excepting 18 industries (subsequently reduce to 15 industries), reducing the number of industries reserved for the public sector from 17 to 8 and now only 2 (Railways and Atomic energy), scrapping of the Monopolistic and Restrictive Trade Practice limit, free entry of foreign investment and technology transfer, etc. In recent years, the most specific step that has been identified and adopted by the Government of India is the divestiture, *i.e.,* through selling of equity of public sector enterprises to mutual funds, financial institutions and finally to the private sector. Recently, again IMF has made it clear that India is expected to go ahead with its disinvestment and privatisation programme in more ambitious manner. Public sector undertakings will go in for a massive dose of disinvestment and more infrastructure projects will be handed over to the private sector. In respect of infrastructure sector, privatisation will be carried over from power to telecommunications to roads, ports, railways and airways. Privatisation will be needed because the government has been lacking the required resources to build up such infrastructure on the required scale.

REASONS IN FAVOUR OF PRIVATISATION

Privatisation is being favoured on account of following arguments:

Creation of Competitive Environment: It is argued that if the ownership of public sector enterprises is transferred to private sector, then the monopoly of public sector enterprises will come to an end. But in fact, it will create a competitive environment which is must for industrial development of a country. For example, we have allowed private sector to the insurance, electricity, telecommunication, etc. In these sectors, a competitive environment has been created which is proving a boom in increasing competitive strength and efficiency.

Clarity of Objectives: In several PSUs, there is no clarity in corporate objectives. There exists a high degree of confusion among the managers of PSUs regarding the profit objectives as well as social responsibility. Many PSUs failed on both fronts. Thus, after privatisation profit becomes the foremost social responsibility of PSUs.

Reduction in Budgetary Deficits: There would be no question of budgetary deficit, if the PSUs yielded a 10 percent return on investment. But in reality it is not so. The budgetary deficit have risen sharply from year to year. For instance, the budgetary deficit which was 1,417 crores in 1983-84, has increased to 1,51,000 crores in 2005-06. Therefore, the government can control its staggering budgetary deficit by using the sale proceeds on the shares in PSUs.

Reduction in Public Debt: Prof. Hoover has rightly observed, "Blessed are the young for they shall inherit the national debt". A very common dictum is, 'Be not made a beggar by banqueting upon borrowing.' The public debt has increased in astronomical proportions. In 1950-51 public debt was of 290 crores which in 2004-05 increased to 19,86,167 crores. In 2015-16, the total outstanding liabilities of central government were estimated at 68.94 lakh crores. This rapid increase in public debt is an alarming problem and if such an increase in public debt is not drastically reduced, India will have to face economic retardation.

Greater Investment, Employment and Income Opportunities: Privatising will open new areas of greater investment, greater employment opportunities and more income opportunities. As a matter of fact, higher investment would mean greater capital formation and expansion of employment and income opportunities with the economy.

Greater Flexibility in Decision Making: Usually public sector suffers from red tapism in decision-making, whereas the private sector leads to quick decision-making. Moreover, in general the public sector does not enjoy sufficient autonomy as compared to private sector.

Improvement in Managerial Efficiency: Privatisation is a means of improvement in managerial efficiency because the private sector is almost free from political interference.

Increase in Accountability : Once the PSUs are privatised and the shares are listed on the stock exchange, market forces would compel these units to become accountable. The discipline of the balance sheet is the most effective index of all corporate disciplines.

Solution to Shortage of Resources: According to French proverb, a man without money is like a wolf without teeth. As the modern governments are wasting their precious resources on armaments and subsidies, even the few successful PSUs are facing the problem of funds. However, after privatisation, the profit-making and dividend paying companies can approach the capital markets in the country to raise additional resources for growth. In such conditions, there will be no need to depend on budgetary allocations.

Reduction in Unproductive Expenditure: Due to unproductive expenditure, most of the public sector units are running under heavy loss. Hence, the government has to incur huge sum of subsidy every year to keep them running. It increases financial burden on the government. Hence there is a move of privatisation–particularly that of loss making units in India.

PRIVATISATION IN INDIA

The main steps adopted and encouraged by the Central government towards privatisation are:

Table 15.1

Disinvestment in Public Sector Undertakings in India

Year	Budgeted Receipt (₹ crore)	Total Receipts (₹ crore)
2019-20	1,05,000	50,298.64
2018-19	80,000	84,972.16
2017-18	72,500	1,00,056.91
2016-17	56,500	46,246.58
2015-16	69,500	23,996.80
2014-15	43,425	24,348.71

Source : Dept. of Investment and Public Asset Management (Ministry of Finance, Govt. of India)

- Some basic policy announcements are delicensing of a number of industries, raising of licensing limit, legalisation of additional capacities which were illegally increased by business units, broad banding, relaxations from MRTP/FERA regulations, liberalisations in export-import policy, etc. Declaration and implementation of these liberalisation programmes are the moves towards privatisation. The liberalisation process (1986) published by the Centre for Monitoring Indian Economy, Bombay gives an excellent account of privatisation in our country. The thrust of liberalisation programmes has been to give relatively more freedom to individuals for faster growth and higher efficiency.

- The government has been manipulating the Industrial Policy Resolution of 1956 in favour of private sector even in regard to industries listed in schedules A and B. For instance, generation and distribution of electricity is in schedule A, but the Bombay (Mumbai) suburban Electric Supply's proposal for setting up 500 MW thermal power station has been cleared. The Resolution of 1991 has opened up a few more areas (steel, telecommunication, air travel) for Private Sector.

- The government has been more and more relying and seeking the services of private sector talents to manage the PEs. The government has preferred the private sector managers for the Board level appointments in PEs and this can be described as privatisation of public sector management. some appointments worth mention are of Ratan Tata as Chairman of Air-India, Rahul Bajaj as Chairman of Indian Airlines, R. C. Bajpai of Tata's as the Chairman-cum-Managing Director of National Industrial Development Corporation.

- Public enterprises which are chronically sick and which are unlikely to be economical may be referred to the BIFR or other similar high level institutions, created to protect the interest of workers which are to be affected by such rehabilitation packages.

PRE-REQUISITES FOR PRIVATISATION

The success of the privatisation measures depends upon certain pre-requisites:

- Sound fiscal and financial policies to enable stable prices and creating a congenial macro-economic environment;
- Removal of barriers to entry, exit, expansion, diversification and modernisation of industrial enterprises to eliminate monopolies and to allow efficiency to be imparted;
- Elimination/minimisation of public sector monopolies and de-canalisation of import/export items;
- Removal of subsidies and protection; and
- Open trade and exchange rate policies to enable the economy to integrate with the globalised framework.

LIMITATIONS OF THE PRIVATISATION

The privatisation process has following limitations:

- Privatisation leads to the opening of flood gates to foreign capital. This will result in wiping out of the national private sector ultimately.
- Proper evaluation of the assets is a difficult process and business.
- Privatisation has seven precautions to be taken:
    (i) Do not only maximise reverence but create a competitive environment.
    (ii) Do not replace public monopolies with private monopolies.
    (iii) Do not sell through discretionary, non-transparent procedures, which invite allegations of corruption and nepotism.
    (iv) Do not use sales proceeds to finance budget deficits and to retire national debt.
    (v) Do not 'burdened' financial markets with public borrowings at a time of public disinvestment.
    (vi) Do not make false promises to labour. Instead retain them for new industries.
    (vii) Do not rely merely on exceptive orders. Instead create a political consensus.
- Privatisation needs strategic planning efforts as well as appropriate administrative machinery to carry it out. However, in developing economy like India this one is not feasible due to cumbersome bureaucratic system.

SUGGESTIVE FRAMEWORK FOR PRIVATISATION

The following are a few suggestions in this regard:

- A programme of proper and systematic privatisation should be chalked out.

- Existing core sector and essential public sectors units should continue. Energies should be directed to reform these PEs to make them cost efficient so that they do not have to depend on tax payer's money for their sustenance. However, private sector be allowed to compete on equal terms.
- Incremental privatisation is already allowed in energy, steel, minerals, transport, communication, aviation and other sectors. The scope could be enlarged. Also, foreign companies must be provided incentives to enter these areas with capital and technology.
- Chronically sick public sector units should be sold and the displaced workers should be taken care by NRF.
- Service sectors like transport, banking and insurance be thrown open to Indian and foreign enterprises.
- The government should freeze future investment in public sector except in selected infrastructure or in socio-economic projects. Such investment should only be made as a last resort.
- The policy of transferring sick private sector units to the public sector be totally dispensed with.
- Exclusive reservation of areas for the public sector be done away with.
- A rational and reasonable exit policy be formulated to provide flexibility in adjustment of work force because it is crucial for the success of any privatisation programme.

LESSON AT A GLANCE

Privatisation: Privatisation is the transfer of ownership of a concern from the public sector to the private sector.

Need for Privatisation: (i) Control on budgetary deficits; (ii) Resource mobilisation; (iii) Reduction in extra tax burden; (iv) Flow of funds to public exchequer; (v) Improvement in production; (vi) Increase in competition.

Arguments in Favour of Privatisation: (i) Creation of competitive environment; (ii) Clarity of objectives; (iii) Reduction in budgetary deficits; (iv) Reduction in public debt; (v) Greater investment, employment and income opportunities; (vi) Greater flexibility in decision making; (vii) Improvement in managerial efficiency; (viii) Increase in accountability; (ix) Solution to shortage of resources; and (x) Reduction in unproductive expenditure.

PROJECT WORK

Make a detailed study of recent privatisation of any public sector undertaking. For the purpose of your project you may collect information from newspapers, and/or other economic publications.

QUESTIONS

A. Short Answer Type Questions:
1. Define privatisation.
2. Why has privatisation been adopted in India?
3. Give two arguments in favour of privatisation.
4. What is privatisation of management?
5. What are the pre-requisites of privatisation? Mention any two.
6. Mention any four limitations of privatisation.
7. Give two suggestions to make privatisation fruitful.

Recent Year Questions:
1. Give two reasons for privatisation of public sector units in India. [ICSE 2008]
2. What is meant by privatisation of public sector units? Explain four benefits of privatisation. [ICSE 2009]
3. State whether the following statement is true or false. Give reasons for each of the following:
   The privatisation of PSUs do not guarantee social welfare. [ICSE 2011]
4. Citing reasons state the advantage of private sector over public sector. [ICSE 2012]
5. Give two reasons in favour of privatisation of public sector enterprises. [ICSE 2016]

B. Long Answer Type Questions:
1. What is privatisation? Why is privatisation needed in developing countries?
2. Give your critical comments on privatisation.
3. What arguments can be given in favour of privatisation?
4. Explain the rationale of privatisation in India.

Recent Year Questions:
1. "Privatisation has failed to solve crucial problems like poverty in India." Discuss two arguments each in support of and against the statement. [ICSE 2008]
2. What is meant by privatisation of public sector units? Explain four benefits of privatisation. [ICSE 2009]
3. What is meant by privatisation? Explain in brief three arguments against privatisation of public sector units in India. [ICSE 2012]
4. Define privatisation. Discuss two arguments each in favour of and against privatisation. [ICSE 2013]
5. What is privatization? Explain the following arguments favouring privatization:
   (i) Greater flexibility in decision making.
   (ii) Better utilization of resources.
   (iii) Greater employment opportunities. [ICSE 2018]

16
Money and Inflation

In ancient times, man's wants were very few. He led a simple nomad life and mainly lived on hunting and fishing and satisfied all his wants himself. As time passed, man started developing various goods to overcome the difficulties of life. This resulted into the division of labour and specialisation. This also resulted into the human living in communities by making settlements. So, now his wants started increasing and his self-sufficiency disappeared because he was not in a position to produce everything by himself and became dependent on others for the goods they were producing. So, he started to exchange the things he produced for those which other possessed. Such direct exchange of things without the use of money is called Barter. It means buying goods in exchange of goods. Today barter is carried on only in some highly backward areas.

> **OVERVIEW**
>
> *Money originated to overcome the difficulties of barter system. It plays a significant role in the modern economy. A convenient exchange cannot be imagined without the participation of money. The production of goods and services and their distribution among a large number of unknown consumers involve a large number of processes in which many different factors of production take part. This is possible only through exchange of money.*

IN-CONVENIENCES OR DIFFICULTIES OF BARTER SYSTEM

The barter form of exchange was possible and successful only in the primitive days when people had only limited wants. But in the modern times, people have innumerable wants, and the goods to satisfy them are of very large types. As such, the people cannot fulfill their wants by having the barter form of exchange. The modern society gave up the barter form of system, because of so many inconveniences. We briefly mention some of them below:

Need for Double Coincidence of Wants: The barter form of exchange can take place only when the two parties need each other's goods in the form of exchange. For example, if a farmer produces rice and a weaver produces cloth, then the exchange can take place only when the weaver wants rice and farmer wants cloth. The exchange will not take place if one party wants a commodity which the other party does not have and vice-versa.

Difficulty of Division and Sub-division of Goods: The barter form of exchange can take place only when it is possible to divide and sub-divide goods. Suppose a man has a cow, and he wants sugar, utensils and cloth. Then he cannot divide the cow in order to exchange for three things. Further, suppose he exchanges his cow for only one commodity, say for sugar, then, since the price of his cow is much more than few kilograms of sugar, he will have to take several units of sugar in exchange for his cow, which are of no use to him at present.

Difficulty in Calculating the Value of Goods: In the absence of common measure of value, it is very difficult to decide how much rice has to be given for an amount of wheat. Thus, there is a great difficulty in calculating the value of goods.

Difficulty in the Case of Services: In the Barter System, it is very difficult and inconvenient to calculate the worth of the services of a teacher, or an engineer, or a doctor, or a washerman.

Difficulty in Storing Value: In the barter system, it is difficult to store wealth for future use. Goods, like food-grains, cloth, cattle, sheep, etc., are sure to perish after sometimes. Thus, in the barter system of economy to store wealth for future use is impossible.

All the inconveniences of barter system compelled the people to try to find out a suitable medium of exchange, *i.e.*, something which the seller does not want for its own sake but which is acceptable to him because he knows that he himself can exchange it for the things which he wants for their own sake. That is why the money came into existence. Today we cannot think of life without money as the money plays that role in an economy which the blood plays in a body.

Now-a-days everybody recognises money, but usually does not know how to define money. Money has been defined differently by different economists. While some economists like walker have defined money in terms of the functions, others like keynes, cole, Robertson, etc., have emphasized the general acceptability aspect of it. To serve as money, the definition of money should be comprehensive enough to cover all the essential functions that money performs in the economy. Before we arrive at the most suitable definition, it is essential on our part to study a few definitions of money as given by some eminent economists.

"Anything which is widely accepted in payments for goods, or in discharge of other kinds of business obligations."
— **Robertson**

"As that by delivery of which debt contracts and price contracts are discharged."
— **Lord. J. M. Keynes**

"Money constitutes all those things which are at any time and place, generally current without doubt or special enquiry as a means of purchasing commodities and services, and of defraying expenses."
— **Dr. Marshall**

"Anything which is commonly used and generally accepted as a medium of exchange or as a standard of value."
— **Dr. Kent**

The above definitions of money are incomplete as they take into account only one or two functions. An appropriate definition of money has been given by **Crowther**.

"Anything that is generally acceptable as a means of exchange and, acts as a measure and store of value is money."
— **Crowther**

In other words we can say that "Money is anything which is generally acceptable as a medium of exchange and at the same time acts as the measure and store of value and standard of deferred payments."

FUNCTIONS OF MONEY

Money performs several important functions. **Prof. Kinley** has classified the functions of money into three group:

FUNCTIONS OF MONEY

Function of Money

Primary Functions	Secondary Functions	Contingent Functions
1. Medium of Exchange.	1. Standard of Deferred Payments.	1. Maximisation of Utility.
2. Measure of Value.	2. Transfer of Value.	2. Employment of Factor Inputs.
	3. Store of Value.	3. Credit System.
		4. Distribution of National Income.
		5. Liquidity of Capital.

These functions are elaborated below:

(I) Primary Functions

The essential and fundamental functions that money should perform in every economy, are regarded as primary functions of money.

Medium of Exchange: Money serves as a medium of exchange. This is the main and most important function of money. Money carries the capacity to purchase goods and services which people need. Money is normally accepted as a medium through which all the sales and purchases takes place. As the money is being accepted as a common medium of exchange, it has eliminated the difficulties of barter system. It has avoided the wastage of time and resources and has eliminated the need for double coincidence of wants involved in the barter.

Measure of Value: Money is accepted as a common measure of value or unit of account. Under the barter system, the price of a commodity was expressed in terms of other commodity. As price of rice can be expressed in terms of piece of cloth, but after the evolution of money, price of any commodity can be expressed in terms of money. For example, as price of rice, now can be expressed in terms of money. So money is also called the numeraire or the measure of value. In modern economies, it is money, which acts as a numeraire, *i.e.*, prices of all goods are expressed in terms of money.

(II) Secondary Functions

This category of functions refers to those, which are derived from the primary functions. Secondary functions of money are as follows:

Standard of Deferred Payment: Money acts as a standard of deferred payment. In other words money can be used in the settlement of debts. It means payment to be made in future can be assessed and expressed in terms of money. This function of money has been derived from medium of exchange function of money. In modern economy, many transactions involve the deferred payment. It is possible to accept money as a standard of deferred payment because money has a general acceptability and it can be expressed in definite and standardised units. For example, A lends ₹1,000 to B for a year. He knows well what he will receive after a year or two years or ten years.

Transfer of Value: Money also acts as a means to transfer of value. This function of money has evolved from the general acceptability of money as a medium of exchange. Value can be transferred from one person to another with the help of money. When we pay the price of any commodity to its owner, we transfer the value to the owner. Similarly, money is a quick and efficient means of transferring value from one place to another. Price of any commodity can be paid in terms of money from one city to another or from one state to another or even from one country to another.

Store of Value: Money acts as a store of value. It means people can store their wealth in the form of money. Before the evolution of money, it was not always possible to store the wealth. As the perishable commodities, *i.e.*, wheat, rice, vegetables, which were not needed at a time, could not be stored for a long time. Money has facilitated the store of value. Though there are some other things which can be stored like money as gold, bond, shares, debentures, etc. But money is considered to be a better storage of value in terms of its liquidity and longevity. It possesses the immediate purchasing power which other goods does not. Similarly it can be saved for very long period. Thus, in the form of money, purchasing power can be stored and can be used, at any time as and when needed.

(III) Contingent Functions

The contingent functions of money were not the contemplated functions rather they emerged or evolved with the expanded scope of facilitating functions of money. Money can be used in assisting various economic entities, such as consumers, producers, etc., in arriving at economic decisions relating to consumption, production, etc. These are the contingent functions of money. The main contingent functions are as below:

Maximisation of Utility: As we know a rational consumer wants to maximise his utility (or satisfaction) while purchasing various goods and services. Consumer will be able to maximise his total utility, if the ratios of marginal utilities of different commodities are equal to the price ratio of different goods. For equalising the marginal utilities, money plays an important role, because prices of all commodities are expressed in terms of money.

Employment of Factor Inputs: Money helps the producer in deciding how many unit of a factor of production be employed. Every producer wants profit maximisation while employing various factors of production. A producer with maximum profit capacity will equate marginal productivity (expressed in value terms) of a factor with its price (rate of remuneration) and remunerations are expressed in money terms. Thus, money is helpful in taking decisions regarding employment of units of factors of production.

Credit System: Money has facilitated the application of credit system in the economy. In modern economy, various commercial and business transactions take place on credit. It is the money which provides the basis of entire credit system. Without the existence of money, important credit instruments like cheques, bills of exchange, etc., cannot be used.

Distribution of National Income: Distribution of national income among the various factors of production can be easily made with the use of money. various factors of production help in the process of production. Thus, production is the outcome of the contribution of the numerous units of these various factors. Without the use of money, the distribution of national income among these factors of production would have become impossible.

Liquidity of Capital: Anything can be converted into money which has general acceptability. Other things are not acceptable in their physical form as cloth, car, house and land. Money is more liquid than anything mentioned.

IMPORTANCE OF MONEY

Money plays a significant role in modern economy. It plays an active role in economic activities. Importance of money in an economy can be discussed as below:

Removal of the Difficulties of Barter: There were some difficulties attached to barter system of exchange, *i.e.*, lack of double coincidence of wants, problem of measurement of value, problem of future payment, etc. Invention of money has overcome all the difficulties of barter system. There is no need to find coincidence of wants and the value can be measured easily in terms of money.

Money and Production: Money helps in various ways in the process of production. It can easily be ascertained with the help of money what is and how much is to be used as input in the production. Moreover, the existence of money helps the producers to discover what people want and how they want.

Money and Consumption: Money has a great importance in consumption. With the help of money, the consumer can easily decide what they need and how much. They have a ready command over the goods and services. Moreover, they can postpone their demand as per the needs.

Money and Distribution: Money has made it possible to distribute accurately and conveniently the reward among the various factors of production. The reward of factors like wages, rent, interest and profit can be distributed in the form of money.

Money and Capital Formation: Money is essential to facilitate capital formation. Savings of people can be mobilised in the form of money and these mobilised savings can be invested in more profitable ventures. Financial institutions are the part of this process. They mobilise the savings and channelise them in productive process through the process of loans and investments.

Money and Public Finance: Public finance deals with the income and expenditure of the government. Government receives its income in the form of money through taxes and other means and makes expenditure in development and administrative processes.

External Trade: Money has facilitated trade not only inside the country but also between countries. With the use of money, goods and services can easily and rapidly be exchanged. Though in external trade foreign currencies are used in receipts and payments but they are exchanged with the help of domestic currencies.

Money and Economic Development: Supply of money in country affect its economic development. If the money supply is more than what is required then it may lead to inflationary situation in the economy which may hamper growth. Similarly, if the supply of money is lesser than what is required then there will be shortage of liquidity, which will lead to lesser investments and hence lesser employment.

Helps in National Integration: Money is helpful in encouraging national unity. People living in far off places meet for commercial purposes or social purposes or recreational purposes. This has reduced the social isolation. This became easier with the invention of money.

Increase in Standard of Living: Money has facilitated the increase in overall production and fair distribution of income and wealth. This has raised the standard of living of the people in the country.

TYPES OF MONEY

Currency: The currency is a country's unit of exchange issued by their government or central bank, whose value is the basis for trade. Currency includes both metallic money (coins) and paper money that is in public circulation.

(i) Metallic Money: Metallic money refers to the coins which are used for small transactions. These coins are issued by the government. Examples of coins are 50 paise coins, and 1, 2, 5 and 10 rupee coins.

(ii) Paper Money: It refers to paper notes and are used for large transactions. Each currency note carries the legend, 'I promise to pay the bearer the sum of 50/100 rupees' depending on the amount of note. The currency notes are duly signed by the Governor of RBI. Simply, the meaning of legend is that it can be converted into other notes or coins of equal value. Examples of currency notes are 1, 2, 5, 10, 20, 50, 100, 500 and 2,000 rupee notes.

Deposit Money: It refers to money deposited by people in the bank on the basis of which cheques can be drawn. Customers of the bank deposit coins and currency notes in the bank for safe-keeping, money transferring and also to get interest on the deposited money. This money is recorded as credit to the account of the bank's customer which can be withdrawn by him on his wish by cheques. Cheques are widely accepted these days because transfer of money through cheques is convenient.

Legal Tender Money: Legal tender money is the currency which has got legal sanction or approval by the government. It means that the individual is bound to accept it in exchange for goods and services; it cannot be refused in settlement of payments of any kind.

Both coins and currency notes are legal tender. They have the backing of government. They serve as money on the fiat (order) of the government. But a person can legally refuse to accept payment through cheques because there is no guarantee that a cheque will be honoured by the bank in case of insufficient deposits with it.

Currency is the most common form of legal tender. It is anything which when offered in payment extinguishes the debt. Thus, personal cheques, credit cards, debit cards and similar non-cash methods of payment are not usually legal tender. Coins and notes are usually defined as a legal tender. The Indian rupee is also legal tender in Nepal and Bhutan, although the Nepalese rupee and Bhutanese ngultrum are not legal tender in India.

Near Money: It is a term used to describe highly liquid assets which are not cash but can easily be converted into cash on short notice such as bank deposits, gold and shares.

Near money does not function as a medium of exchange in everyday purchases of goods and services.

Fiat Money: Fiat money is any money whose value is determined by legal means. The terms fiat currency and fiat money relate to types of currency or money whose usefulness results not from any intrinsic value or guarantee that it can be converted into gold or another currency, but instead from a government's order (fiat) that it must be accepted as a means of payment.

Credit Money: Credit money (*i.e.* cheques issued against demand deposits or credit card payments) in fact, is not money, it only performs the function of money. Credit money is therefore regarded as near money.

INFLATION

Inflation is phenomena which generally affects each one of us at some or the other time. It is not the problem which is confined to only one economy. Rather it's a worldwide problem. Different economists have offered different definitions of inflation. The layman, however, understands the term 'inflation' as a rapid increase in the general price level. Inflation, in simple words, indicates rising prices which cause a decline in the purchasing power of money.

Inflation is defined as, *"A sustained rising trend in general price level or a rate of expansion of money income greater than the rate of growth of real output."* Similarly *Prof. Coulbourn* defined inflation as *"Too much money chasing too few goods"*. Under such circumstances, the general prices increase and in turn the value of money decreases. Although, the circulation of money increases, the availability of goods is limited, and this results in price rise.

"Inflation is a state in which the value of money is falling, i.e., prices are rising."

—**Prof. Crowther**

Here it must be understood that all price rise is not inflation. In this context Prof. Hawtrey defined inflation as, "the issue of too much currency." But in this definition, the exact meaning of "too much currency" is not clear. In fact, it should be co-related with some economic condition of the country or economic progress.

"The rise in price-level after the point of full employment, is true inflation."

—**J. M. Keynes**

"Inflation exists when money income is expanding more, than in proportion to income earning activities." —**Prof. A. C. Pigou**

CHARACTERISTICS OF INFLATION

Main characteristics of inflation are as listed below:
- Inflation is always associated with a rise in prices which is continuous and persistent. It is a process of rising prices. It should be distinguished from price rise which may occur temporarily or during a cyclical swing.
- Inflation is a dynamic process which can be observed only over a more or less lengthy period.
- Inflation is basically an economic phenomenon which originates within the economic system and is fostered by interaction of economic forces.

- Excess of demand over the available supply is the hallmark of inflation. It is a condition of economic disequilibrium.
- Inflation is generally considered a monetary phenomenon as it is normally characterised by an excessive money supply. All increases in the stock of money may not be inflationary, but a persistent rise in prices cannot be sustained, unless the quantity of money rises as well.
- Inflation may be caused by 'demand-pull' factors or 'cost-push' factors or both working together.
- Inflation is always cumulative in the sense that a mild inflation in the first instance gathers momentum leading to rapid price rises. Its effect on an economy depend on how rapid it is.

TYPES OF INFLATION

There are various types of inflation which are generally observed in an economy. They are following:

Creeping Inflation: Creeping inflation occurs when there is a sustained rise in prices over time at a mild rate, say around 2 to 3 percent per year. It is also known as mild inflation. This type of inflation is not much of a problem. Rather this much of inflation is considered healthy for an economy because this gives an extra impetus to businessmen to invest more.

Walking or Trotting Inflation: When the rate of rise in inflation is of international standard of 3 to 8 percent per annum, it is called walking or trotting inflation.

Running Inflation: When the sustained rise in prices is over 8 percent and generally around 20 percent per annum, it is called running inflation. It normally shows two-digit inflation. Running inflation is a warning signal indicating the need for controlling it.

Hyper or Galloping Inflation: Hyper inflation occurs when increase in prices is 20 percent to 100 percent or more per annum. At this stage there is no limit to price rise, and price line goes out of control. Money becomes almost worthless causing severe hardship to people. There is complete collapse of currency and economic and political life is disrupted.

Open Inflation: Inflation is open when there is no barrier to price rise. It occurs in the economy where there are no control and checks by the government on price rise. Rising prices by large magnitude is the symptom of open inflation.

Repressed Inflation: Repressed inflation refers to a situation when there exist inflationary pressures in the economy, but prices are controlled by certain administrative measures such as price control and rationing. Price increase is suppressed here. However, prices rise by large magnitude after the price controls are removed.

Stagflation: It is a situation where high level of unemployment is accompanied by high rate of inflations. This type of inflation is peculiar in India.

Sectoral or Sporadic Inflation: This arises initially out of excess demand in particular industries or few commodities but it may results in general price rise.

Comprehensive Inflation: It is that type of inflation in which prices of all commodities register a rise in the economy.

CAUSES OF INFLATION

There are two types of factors which are responsible for inflationary pressure:

(I) Demand pull factors.

(II) Cost push factors.

These two types of factors may be in operation independently or simultaneously. The factors arising out of demand are called Demand Pull Factors and those relating to supply are termed as Cost Push Factors. In our country as well, both these have inflationary effects, which will be clear from the following explanations:

(I) Demand Pull Factors

Increase in Supply of Money and Change in Real Income: When a disequilibrium exists between increase in the supply of money and the increase in real income and the increase in supply of money is in excess of increase in the real income or output, inflation takes place. For example, in our country, the supply of money has been much greater than the increase in real income (or say output), and this has been the main cause of price rise. This is also true on the basis of Quantity Theory of Money which states, "the increasing supply of money directly affects the price levels." For example: since 1950-51 to 1990-91, the real national income of India increased by four times only as against the money supply which increased by 46 times. This has resulted in the situation of more money chasing less goods.

Expenditure of the Government: The government expenditure results in the income of the people. This tremendous increase in such expenditure leads to the increase in demand of goods and services. If the availability of these goods does not increase proportionately, under such conditions, the price rise is natural.

High Rate of Investment: The heavy investments made by the government as well as private industrialists, results in continuous rising demand for capital goods and raw materials which increases the prices of capital goods and other items of production.

Growth of Population: The rapid growth of population results in a large increase in demand for the goods and services. The demand for food, clothes, medicines, education, fuel, housing, etc., increases instantaneously with the increase in population. The natural outcome is increase in prices.

Deficit Financing: Besides plan expenditures, the government adopts the measures of deficit financing. This method increases the money supply in public hands, thereby increasing the demand of goods and services, resulting in the increase in their prices.

Black Money: Black money means unaccounted money. It is created through tax-evasion and is also responsible for price-rise. Black money is spent on non-productive activities like buying real estate, gold smuggling, luxurious living, etc. Black money generates hoarding of goods in the economy.

(II) Cost Push Factors

Fluctuations in Output and Supply: The wide fluctuations in production and supply of food grains and other raw materials are mainly responsible for price rise. Fluctuation in production accompanied by artificial scarcity created by hoarding by middlemen and producers may result in an increase in price of food grains and raw materials.

The power breakdowns, strikes and lockouts result in lower production of manufactured goods.

Natural Disasters: Natural calamities whether it is flood or draught or cloud burst or earthquake, etc., contribute significantly in increasing cost push inflation. The net impact of all these happenings take place on the production of raw material in terms of reduced production. This has very big impact on cost push inflation.

Enhanced Taxation: With every budget, the government may impose fresh commodity taxes. It leads to an increase in prices of different commodities in general which push up all the prices in general. The railway budget, sales tax, excise duty, etc., directly affect the prices of all types of commodities.

Oil-Price Hike: Global inflation and hike in oil prices continuously results in higher import costs for importing crude oil from abroad. It results in rise in prices of diesel, petrol and other petroleum products and leads to higher costs of transport and electricity generation.

Distinction between Demand Pull and Cost Push Inflation

Demand Pull Inflation	Cost Push Inflation
1. The excess demand conditions cause the price level increase.	1. The increased cost of production results into the cost push inflation.
2. Basic factors for demand pull inflation are increase in population, rise in income level and less supply as compared to increased demand.	2. Increase in the price of various factors of production like fuel, wages, transport, etc., are some of the factors causing cost push inflation.

EFFECTS OF INFLATION

The main effects of inflation are discussed below:

Effect on Producers: During inflation, the producers and businessmen gain in the short-period. Usually the cost of production does not rise as fast as the price of their product in the first wave of inflation and so there is artificial margin of profit. But they may also be affected adversely in the long run. If the price level goes on increasing, the total consumption of their product will fall. The reduced consumption will ultimately raise the cost of production per unit and reduce the profits.

Effect on the Working Class: labour is the lowest paid class. This class is badly affected by inflation, especially if the prices of necessities of life rise steeply, affecting adversely the family budgets of the working class. Their consumption level goes down telling upon their health and lowering their efficiency. It may also create unrest. No doubt, through trade unions, workers may manage to get increased dearness allowance but this does not provide them desired relief, for price hike generally precedes any increase in dearness allowance. In turn, the increased wages further push up the price level owing to increased demand. A vicious circle sets in, resulting in wage-push or cost-push inflation.

Effect on Fixed Income Groups: This group includes pensioners, government servants, owners of government securities and promissory notes and others who get a fixed money income in terms of salary, pension or interest on deposits, etc. They are known as rentiers. This class is worst affected by inflation because the purchasing power of their fixed income goes on decreasing with rising prices.

Effect on Debtors and Creditors: Debtors gain when they pay back their debt during inflation. It is because the value of money was high when they borrowed but came down when they repaid their debts. As against this, the creditors are losers during inflation. However, if debtors take loans during inflationary period, the position is reversed. In that case, the debtors are losers and the creditors are gainers.

Cost Increases: As prices increase, cost of projects both of private and public sectors go up. Consequently, the total outlay of each plan exceeds, the one provided for originally set physical targets are not fully achieved.

Wage Spiral: A rapid increase in prices is not suitable as workers demand more wages. Under such circumstances, wages are raised to compensate the workers. Thus, price spiral inflicts the economy.

Inequality in Distribution of Wealth: During inflation, producers and traders are the gainers. As a result, rich becomes richer and poor becomes poorer. It leads to concentration of wealth in the hands of few rich.

Effect on Foreign Investment: A rapid increase in prices has an adverse effect on the foreign investment in the country. Foreign investors do not invest in those countries where the value of money is falling on account of rise in prices. Value of money falls and the investors suffer losses.

Adverse Balance of Payment: Price rise has an adverse effect on the export of the country. As the commodities to be exported become costlier in the country, so exporters fail to increase the exports to the desired extent. Therefore, balance of payment continues to be unfavourable.

Effects on Employment: Rising prices increase the profits of producers and function as incentive for wider and expanded investment. This type of effect prevails till full employment is attained.

ANTI-INFLATIONARY MEASURES

Inflation is harmful for the economy if not checked on time. Primarily there are two categories of measures *i.e.*, Monetary measures and Fiscal measures which are to be taken by government to control inflation but there are other measures also which can be taken by government to curb inflation. They are following:

Monetary Measures: Monetary measures are taken by a country's Central Bank (Reserve Bank of India in India) on behalf of the government. The monetary measures in detail will be discussed in the next chapter. Monetary measures work through changes in the quantity of money and rates of interest. For example, Reserve Bank of India or RBI frequently changes the repo rate and reverse repo rate to bring changes in the lending rate of interests of the banking system. The rise in repo rate makes the borrowing from RBI costlier for commercial banks, which makes lending by commercial banks costlier.

So the demand for credit by bank customers falls and so the excess demand. This reduces the inflation. Similarly by increasing Cash Reserve Ratio, Statutory Liquidity Ratio and Margin requirements, the supply of money is reduced and loans are made costlier. This controls the inflation.

Fiscal Measures: Fiscal measures are taken by the government directly. Fiscal measures work through the government expenditure and tax rates. When the government spends money on various heads like road and dam construction, subsidies, salaries of ministers and administrative employees and many other heads, etc., it supplies money in the form of incomes. Thus by reducing expenditure, the government may reduce the supply of money and inflationary pressure. Similarly, by increasing taxes government may also reduce the purchasing power in the hand of the people, hence reducing the inflationary pressure in the economy. Government may resort to surplus budget in which government incomes are more than government expenditure. Government may also promote the savings in the country. Various schemes like compulsory deposit schemes, national savings schemes, etc., have been introduced to encourage the people to save more. This will reduce the effective demand of the people and prices will remain under control to some extent.

There are other measures also which can be employed by the government to curb inflation. They are following:

Rationing and Price Control: The government can introduce rationing system for essential commodities, so as to ensure proper supply. In India a large number of fair price shops have been opened. This enables the poorer sections of the people to purchase the commodities on controlled price.

Increase in Agricultural and Industrial Production: To induce the farmers to grow more food grains, the government can announce procurement prices for several items. Loans and credits can be granted to improve their lands and to procure good seeds, fertilizers, etc. The increased production would ensure adequate and proper supplies and control the prices within limits. Moreover, maintenance of buffer stocks also helps in checking the rising prices and in meeting the demand of the people. Similar steps can also be taken for increased industrial production.

Control on Population Growth: In order to control the demand for consumer goods, it is essential to curb the rapid rise in population. This check is also necessary to reduce the expenditure of the government on housing, civic amenities, public health, education, etc.

Other Measures: Trade and tariff policies must be modified to make the domestic prices of industrial products, reasonably competitive. Excise duties on several industrial products should be reduced to accelerate the pace of industrial growth.

Punishment for Hoarding: Government must take stringent steps to stop hoarding of essential commodities. For this purpose proper administrative mechanism should be devised and put in place.

Check on Speculation: Government must control speculation in essential commodities. Though future markets have been organised and online trading of commodities has been allowed by the government but it should be kept in mind that speculation in online trade has contributed significantly in increasing inflation which should be stopped at any cost.

LESSON AT A GLANCE

Definition of Money: Anything which is widely accepted in payments for goods, or in discharge of other kinds of business obligations, is called money.

Functions of Money: Functions may be classified into:

Primary Functions: (i) Medium of exchange; (ii) Measure of value.

Secondary Functions: (i) Standard of deferred payments; (ii) Transfer of value; (iii) Store of value.

Contingent Functions: (i) Maximisation of utility; (ii) Employment of factor inputs; (iii) Credit system; (iv) Distribution of national income; and (v) Liquidity of capital.

Importance of Money: (i) Removal of the difficulties of barter; (ii) Money and production; (iii) Money and consumption; (iv) Money and distribution; (v) Money and capital formation; (vi) Money and public finance; (vii) External trade; (viii) Money and economic development; (ix) Helps in national integration; (x) Increase in standard of living.

Types of Money: (i) Currency; (ii) Deposit money; (iii) Legal tender money; (iv) Near money; (v) Fiat money; (vi) Credit money.

Meaning of Inflation: A sustained rising trend in general price level or a rate of expansion of money-income greater than the rate of growth of real output.

Types of Inflation: (i) Creeping inflation; (ii) Walking or Trotting inflation; (iii) Runn-ing inflation; (iv) Hyper or Galloping inflation; (v) Open inflation; (vi) Repressed inflation; (vii) Stagflation; (viii) Sectoral or Sporadic inflation; and (ix) Comprehensive inflation.

CAUSES OF INFLATION:

Demand Pull Factors: (i) Increase in supply of money and change in real income; (ii) Expenditure of the government; (iii) High rate of investment; (iv) Growth of population; (v) Deficit financing; (vi) Black money.

Cost Push Factors: (i) Fluctuations in output and supply; (ii) Natural disasters; (iii) Enhanced taxation; (iv) Oil price hike.

Effects of Inflation: (i) Effect on producers; (ii) Effect on the working class; (iii) Effect on fixed income groups; (iv) Effect on debtors and creditors; (v) Cost increases; (vi) Wage spiral; (vii) Inequality in distribution of wealth; (viii) Effect on foreign investment; (ix) Adverse balance of payment; (x) Effect on employment.

Anti-inflationary Measures taken by Government: (i) Monetary measures; (ii) Fiscal measures; (iii) Rationing and price control; (iv) Increase in agricultural and industrial production; (v) Control on population growth; (vi) Other measures; (vii) Punishment for hoarding; (viii) Check on speculation.

PROJECT WORK

Prepare a list showing value of Indian rupee with respect to value of other currency prevailing in other countries. Note down fluctuations in value of Indian rupee with respect to US dollar during the period of last six months and show it graphically.

QUESTIONS

A. Short Answer Type Questions:
1. Define money. Write three primary functions of money.
2. State two inconveniences of barter system.
3. State two importance of money.
4. What do you mean by inflation?
5. State any four characteristics of inflation.
6. What is open inflation?
7. Give any three reasons for the rise of inflation in the economy.
8. State the kinds of inflation.
9. Distinguish between hyper and running inflation.
   [Hint: In hyper inflation there is no limit to price rise and thus price line goes out of control. In running inflation, there is sustained price rise, say 8% to 10%]
10. What is the impact of inflation on the economy?
11. Mention any three causes of inflation.
12. How is deficit financing responsible for inflation?
13. Specify two measures to control inflation.
14. How does money help in the distribution of national Income?
15. Mention the effect of inflation on the value of money.
16. Give two reasons why deficit financing is inflationary in nature.
17. State two difficulties of the barter system.
18. How does increased money supply affect prices of a commodity?

Recent Year Questions:
1. A moderate dose of inflation is necessary for the development of an economy. Briefly explain. [ICSE 2011]
2. State the effect of inflation on creditors. [ICSE 2011]
3. What is meant by running inflation? State its impact on fixed income groups. [ICSE 2012]
4. Which section of the society is worst affected during inflation? Briefly explain. [ICSE 2013]
5. Define money. How does it act as a 'measure of value'? [ICSE 2013]
6. How does money act as a standard of deferred payment? [ICSE 2014]
7. State two primary functions of money. [ICSE 2015]
8. Give a reason for the following statement:
   "The fixed income group is adversely affected during periods of inflation." [ICSE 2015]

OR

Explain the impact of inflation on fixed income group of people. [ICSE 2019]
9. State whether the following statement is true or false. Give one reason for your answer.
   "During inflation the debtors gain and creditors lose." [ICSE 2016]
10. Which section of the society gains during inflation? Why? [ICSE 2018]
11. What do you understand by hyper inflation? [ICSE 2019]
12. Why is money referred to as legal tender money? [ICSE 2019]

B. Long Answer Type Questions:

1. Define term money. Explain its utility as a standard of deferred payment, in existing production decisions and measure of value.
   [**Hint:** Money now acts as the standard of deferred payments i.e., future payments.]
2. Discuss the main functions of money.
3. What do you understand by inflation? Explain various types of inflation.
4. State the main characteristics of inflation. How can it be controlled?
5. What are the main causes of inflation?
6. Discuss the impact of inflation on the various entities of a country.
7. What is the effect of inflation on businessman?
8. Explain the contingent functions of money.

Recent Year Questions:

1. Give reason for the following: Creeping inflation is regarded essential for economic growth. [ICSE 2009]
2. (i) Define money.
   (ii) What is legal tender money?
   (iii) Explain how money facilitates production and trade. [ICSE 2009]
3. What is meant by economic depression?
   For each of the following measures, state whether they are taken during inflation or depression. Give reason for your answer.
   (i) Direct taxes are reduced and public expenditure is increased.
   (ii) Government securities are sold by the Central Bank in the open market operations.
   (iii) Credit rationing. [ICSE 2009]
4. Distinguish between Fiat money and Bank money. Explain two primary functions of money. [ICSE 2010]
5. Define Money. Explain how money performs the following functions:
   (i) As a measure of value.
   (ii) As a standard of deferred payment.
   (iii) As a store of value. [ICSE 2012]
6. Define money. How does money perform its role as a:
   (i) Medium of exchange.
   (ii) Store of value. [ICSE 2014]
7. Read the extract given below and answer the questions that follow:

TNN, 15th August, 2013

Rising vegetable prices and the impact of a weak rupee pushed inflation to a five month high of 5·79% in July 2013, posing yet another challenge for Asia's third largest economy battling to defend the rupee and boost growth. Official data released on Wednesday showed inflation as measured by the wholesale price index, jumped to 5·79% in July from previous months 4·86%. Easing wholesale price inflation had fuelled expectations of a moderation in tight monetary policy but the slide of the rupee against the dollar has dashed hopes for now.

  (i) What is meant by running inflation?
 (ii) Mention two fiscal measures to control inflation.
(iii) Briefly explain the effect of a high level of inflation on the following:
    (a) Fixed income groups.
    (b) Producers.
    (c) Creditors and debtors.
(iv) Explain three monetary policies of the Reserve Bank of India to control credit.   [ICSE 2014]

8. Define money. Explain the secondary functions of money.   [ICSE 2019]

17
Banking : Commercial Banks and Central Bank

In modern economic and social activities, banks play a significant role. These attract savings from the people and thus encourage the investment in industry, trade and commerce. It will not be an exaggeration to say that for the economic progress of the country, a well-organised banking system is must. The bank can be defined as "financial institution, which deals in money and credit". People deposit their money with the bank to keep their money safe and to earn interest also. The bank accepts the deposits at a lower rate of interest and lends to others, at a higher rate of interest who are in need of it, and the surplus is the profit of the bank. These are actually the main functions of the commercial banks. This financial institution has been defined in many ways, some of which shall be presented here.

> **OVERVIEW**
>
> *In modern days, the banking organisation plays a very significant role in economic development of the nation by way of providing financial assistance to various economic sectors like industry, agriculture, transport, communication, etc. various types of functions are being performed by banking network so as to encourage and facilitate the commercial activities of industry and trade, besides serving the common people in their day-to-day economic activities.*

"Bank is an establishment which makes to individual such advances of money as may be required and safely made and to which individuals entrust money when not required by them for use."
—**Kingsley**

"The term 'Bank' generally applies to an institution, which receives deposits of money before it and which seeks profits through the extension and sale of its own deposit."   —**E.E. Agger**

"The accepting, for the purpose of lending or investment of deposits of money from the public, repayable on demand or otherwise and withdrawal by cheque, draft, order or otherwise."
—**The Banking companies Act of India**

"Nobody can be a banker who does not take deposit accounts, current accounts, issue and pay cheques and collects cheques-crossed and uncrossed for its customers."   —**John Paget**

"A bank collects money from those who have it to spare or who are saving it out of their incomes and it lends this money to those who require it."   —**Crowther**

COMMERCIAL BANKS

Commercial bank is an institution which deals in money, *i.e.*, borrowing and lending of money. The lending rate of interest is more than the borrowing rate of interest and the difference is the profit of a commercial bank.

The deposits are accepted from people, and other resources. The money so collected is provided in the form of short-term and long-term loans to customers, *i.e.*, industry, trade and general public. depending upon the functions performed and services rendered, the banks are known as deposit bank, industrial bank, mixed bank, exchange bank, etc.

FUNCTIONS OF COMMERCIAL BANKS

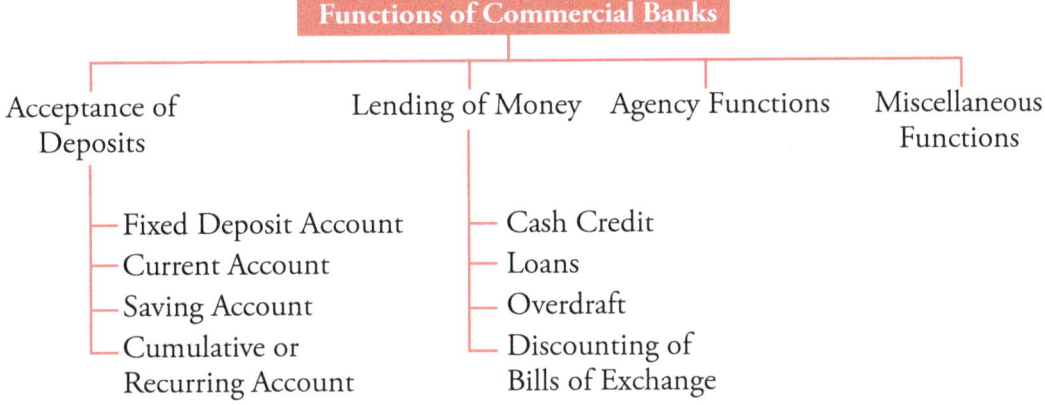

1. Acceptance of Deposits from the Public

A commercial bank accepts deposits from the people for the purpose of making investments and granting loans to various economic sectors. The money is deposited in banks for the sake of safety as well as to earn interest. Actually, the deposits are the basis of bank's 'Lending Business'. The money is deposited in different types of accounts with the bank as described below:

Fixed Deposit Account: In such deposits, the deposited amount can be withdrawn only after the period of time agreed upon by the bank and the depositor. The interest rates are higher in case of such deposits.

Current Account: The depositor can deposit into and withdraw money from such accounts at any time. Usually no interest is paid by the bank on such deposits, but the bank charges for the services rendered on maintaining such deposits. In some cases, the bank provides overdraft facility also to the depositor against certain securities or personal guarantee. Such deposits are mainly kept by traders and industrialists who are required to make large payments through banks.

Saving Account: This kind of account is opened by banks with the objective of collecting small savings from the people who have small earnings and money deposits in small amounts as they like or have the opportunity. The withdrawals are also allowed from the account. However, the rate of interest is less than that on fixed deposits. The common current saving account interest rate is 4% per annum but it varies from bank to bank.

Cumulative or Recurring Account: In case of such deposits, an account holder has to deposit certain fixed amount every month for a specified period. The amount accumulated with interest (cumulative deposits) is paid to the depositor after the specified period.

2. Lending of Money

This is the second basic function of the bank. The commercial banks lend out money to traders and businessmen, which it gets as deposits from the public. Various types of methods and procedures to lend money are described again:

Cash Credit: In cash credit, the bank advances a 'cash loan' upto a specified limit to the customer against a bond or other security. A borrower is required to open a current account and bank allows the borrower to withdraw upto the full amount of the loan. The interest is charged only on the amount actually utilised by the borrower and not on the loan sanctioned.

Loans: A loan is a specified amount sanctioned to the credit of a borrower for a fixed period. However, before sanctioning the loan, the bank is required to ascertain and satisfy itself about the ability of the borrower to repay according to the soundness of his scheme or business and the genuineness of his purpose. Invariably, a loan is granted against some kind of security of assets or personal security of the borrower and the interest is charged on the full amount sanctioned as loan, irrespective of the fact whether full amount or part of it has been used. In case of loans, the borrower is provided with the facility to repay the loan in instalments or as a lump-sum.

Overdraft: The overdraft facility is allowed to the depositor maintaining a current account with the bank. According to this facility, a borrower is allowed to withdraw more amount than what he has deposited. The excess amount so withdrawn has to be repaid to the bank in a short period and that too with interest. The rate of interest usually charged is more than that charged in case of loans. However, the overdraft facility is given only against security of some assets or on personal security of the customer.

Discounting of Bills of Exchange: The banks provide financial help to the merchants and exporters by way of discounting their bills of exchange. However, these merchants and exporters must be the customers of that bank. In such facility, the bank pays the amount of bill presented by the customer, after deducting the usual bank discount. This way, the customer gets the amount of the bill before the date of its maturity. As such the bank assists its customers to a great extent by accepting their bills and providing them with liquid assets (money). Usually a bill matures after 90 days or so and then the bank presents it to the acceptor and receives full amount of the bill.

Thus, we see that a bill of exchange is of great help both to exporters and importers. The exporter gets the amount from the bank immediately for his use, whereas the importer needs not to pay immediately. The importer pays after he has sold the goods and has funds in his hand (after the period of maturity of bill).

3. AGENCY FUNCTIONS

The commercial banks also render various types of services to their customers and act as agents of the customers in such functions. The services so rendered are termed as 'Agency Functions' of the bank, some of which are as below:

- The bank collects the payment of the bills of exchange, promissory notes, cheques, etc., on behalf of its customers.
- The bank collects the dividends, and interests on shares and debentures as per the instructions of its customers.
- The banks also buy and sell shares and debentures, on behalf of their customers (as per the instructions from the customers).
- The banks also transfer funds from one branch of the bank to another as per the instructions of the customers.

- The banks on behalf of the customers, arrange for the payment of loan instalments, interests, insurance premium, taxes, etc., in accordance with the requirements of the customers.
- The bank acts as a representative on behalf of its customers, for other banks and financial institutions as far as transactions of funds are carried out through that bank.
- The bank also performs the work of a trustee, and executor for its customers, in respect of financial matters related to other institutions.

4. Miscellaneous Functions

Besides providing the above mentioned functions, the banks perform several other functions of utility and miscellaneous services for their customers as well as for the society. Some of the functions are:

- Banks provide safety vaults and lockers to their customers for safe custody of their valuable articles and documents.
- Banks also issue letters of credit like circular notes and traveller's cheques, etc., for the use by the customers in manner of safety.
- The banks also provide various kinds of business and trade information, which may be beneficial to their customers.
- The banks give correct information to their customers about the credit of other customers and also about the financial position and status of their customers, whenever it is necessary.
- The transactions made between two customers through bank act as a third party guarantee and proof in case of disputes arising out subsequently.

Promotion of Cheque System: The commercial banks render a very useful service of exchange like cheques. According to prevailing circumstances, people find the cheque as a more convenient method to settle their debts than through the use of cash. In fact, it is the most developed credit instrument in the money market.

Purchase and Sale of Foreign Exchange: The commercial bank sell and purchase the foreign currencies. Ordinarily, this is done by the Foreign Exchange Banks, while in our country some commercial banks also do business in foreign exchange.

CREDIT CREATION BY COMMERCIAL BANKS

- Commercial banks are the unique financial institutions in modern economies which are able to create money in the form of deposit money. Banks are able to bring about a change in the amount of bank deposits. This power of the banks to change bank deposits is the basis of change in money supply, since bank deposits are one of the important components of money supply. Banks can create money by creating bank deposits and they can reduce money supply by reducing bank deposits.
- It is important to note two things here:
- Banks create deposits in the process of advancing loans to its customers. In fact, bank deposits are created in two ways. One, when customers deposit currency or cash with commercial banks. Such deposits are known as primary deposits. Banks play a passive role in creation of such deposits, since it is the decision of the customers who determine how much cash would be deposited in the banks. On the basis of

these deposits, banks' customers are able to make payments with the use of cheques. Creation of primary deposits, however, merely transforms the currency money into deposit money and there is no change in total volume of money in the economy.

- The second way by which banks can create deposits is when they grant loans, discount bills of exchange, provide overdraft facilities and make investments through bonds and securities. When banks advance loans or provide overdraft facilities, they do not pay amount in cash. But they open demand deposits (current account) in the name of the borrowers and allow them to withdraw the required sum by cheques. In this way, banks create deposits. These deposits are known as derivative deposits. These derivative deposits are actively created by banks by their lending and investing activities. They increase the volume of demand deposits without any decrease in the availability of currency with the public. Thus, derivative deposits increase the total amount of money supply in the economy. It is the creation of derivative deposits which is known as creation of credit by the commercial banks.

- Second important thing to be noted is that commercial banks are able to extend loans and advances by an amount which is many times more than the cash reserves they get by primary deposits. Apparently, it appears that an individual bank can lend only what has been deposited with it. But the banking system as a whole can give loans and make investments many times the cash reserves of the banks. Banks know by their experience that all depositors do not withdraw their money at the same time. On any normal day, some customers withdraw the cash while others deposit it, and the difference between withdrawals and the deposits is likely to be very small. Therefore, banks are able to meet the day-do-day cash requirements by keeping small cash reserves and using the surplus or the excess reserves in advancing loans. They keep a certain fraction or percentage of total deposits as cash reserves for this purpose. This fraction is called the cash reserve ratio. It is essential for the banks to maintain this reserve ratio because otherwise they will not be able to meet the cash demand of depositors which could result in the failure of banks. Thus, banks are able to create credit or deposits by keeping a small amount of cash in reserve and lending the remaining amount. If banks keep 100 percent cash against deposits, they would not be able to create credits. It is in this sense that credit is created by commercial banks.

Process of Credit Creation

Let us explain the process of credit creation by taking an imaginary but relevant example. While doing so, we make the following assumptions:

- We take a situation, as is the case in the real world, of multiple banking system. In other words, we assume that there are many commercial banks, such as Bank of Baroda, Canara Bank, Syndicate Bank, etc., in the country.
- It is assumed that minimum legal cash reserve ratio is 20 percent. Thus, each bank is required to keep 20 percent of its deposits in the form of cash reserves.
- Excess (of 20 percent) cash reserve is used in extending loans and advances.
- One particular bank, say Bank of Baroda, receives a cash deposit of ₹1,000 from its customers.

- For the sake of simplified presentation, it is assumed that the loan amount drawn by a customer of one bank somehow is transferred in full to the second bank and that of the second bank to the third bank and so on.
- Each bank starts with an initial deposit which is deposited by the borrower of the other bank.

When the customer of Bank of Baroda deposits ₹1,000 in it, a deposit of ₹1,000 in cash raises the liability as well as the assets by ₹1,000 each.

Excess of (20 percent) cash reserve *i.e.,* (1,000 – 200) is ₹800. Bank of Baroda gives loan of ₹800 to its customer.

The loan of ₹800 given by Bank of Baroda becomes the deposit of Canara Bank. Excess of (20 percent) cash reserve *i.e.,* (800 – 160) is ₹640. Canara Bank gives the loan of ₹640 to its customer.

The loan of 640 given by Canara Bank becomes the deposits of Syndicate Bank. Syndicate Bank now has the excess cash reserves of ₹512 (640 – 20 percent of ₹640 *i.e.,* (640 – 128) which is lent by it. After this transaction, an initial deposit of ₹1,000 with the Bank of Baroda has resulted in the creation of deposits by three banks amounting to ₹1,000 + ₹800 + ₹640 + ₹512 = ₹2,952 and the process of credit creation is still going on. But this is not a never-ending process.

Limits of Credit Creation

Commercial banks have power of credit creation. This power is not absolute. It is restricted by certain limitations. Some of these limitations are as given below:

Amount of Cash: The first important factor on which the extent of credit creation depends is the amount of cash which the commercial banks possess. The larger the amount of cash with the banking system, the greater will be the excess funds and hence larger will be the credit creation power of the bank. As **Crowther** puts it, *"The bank's cash is the lever with which the whole gigantic system is manipulated."* But the bank's cash is not any form of money that the bank itself can create or expand at will. The bank's power of creating money or credit is thus limited by the cash it can get through primary deposits.

Cash Reserve Ratio: As we have seen, credit multiplier co-efficient is the reciprocal of the cash reserve ratio. The higher the percentage of cash reserve ratio to be kept, the smaller the relative excess funds and smaller the volume of credit creation, and vice-versa.

Cheque Clearances: It is not possible for banks to receive and draw cheque of exactly equal amount. Often some banks have their reserve. Increase or decrease in reserves through cheque clearances expands and contracts credit creation on the part of banks. Accordingly the credit creation varies.

External Drain: The most important factor, according to **Whittlesey**, which restricts credit expansion, is "external drain". As we have seen, on the basis of the excess reserve, commercial banks can expand their credit by creating demand deposits. Some of the borrowers from these banks are likely to withdraw part of their deposits in currency. Every rupee in cash that is withdrawn from the banking system lowers the reserves of the banks, and thus checks further deposit expansion. In short, external drains refer to the cash withdrawal from the banking system by the public which lowers the reserves of the banks and partly destroys the power of banks to create credit.

Willingness of Customers to Borrow: Bankers cannot create credit at will. The amount of credit is conditioned by the needs and will of the borrowers. The amount of borrowing by the customers sets a limit to the expansion of credit; if no customer comes forward to borrow, there is no expansion of credit. This may happen in times of depression when even a sufficient reduction in the interest rate may prove to be ineffective for credit expansion. Credit creation depends on the demand for loans, which in turn, depends upon the nature of business conditions. Credit creation, therefore, will be larger during a period of business prosperity, and smaller during a depression.

Supply of Collateral Security: The availability of good securities places one more limitation on the power of banks to create money. Every loan made by a bank is secured by some valuable form of wealth—bills, shares, stocks, etc. "Thus, the bank does not create money out of thin air; it transmutes other forms of wealth into money." Hence, what a bank really does when it creates credit is to extend liquidity to holders of liquid securities. Clearly then, the power of the bank to turn liquid assets into money depends on the volume of such assets or securities with the borrowers. If approved securities are not available, the bank cannot create credit without inviting trouble.

Banking Habits and Banking System: Development of the banking system and banking habits among the people is an important factor. If people prefer to transact by cash and not by cheques, then multiple credit creation by the banks will not be possible. The banking habit will become popular only if there is a sound, developed banking system.

Monetary Policy of the Central Bank: In the modern economy, the extent of credit creation will largely depend on the monetary policy of the Central Bank. The Central Bank has the power to influence the volume of money in the country and from time to time, uses various methods of credit control and these methods influence the banks to expand or contract credit.

CENTRAL BANK

The 'Central Bank' of a country is called 'Central' because it is at the apex of the entire banking system of the country. It has certain special rights, powers and privileges, so that it can regulate the activities of other commercial banks and can exercise control over the monetary and credit policies of the nation.

"Central bank is a bank which constitutes the apex of the monetary and banking structure of its country." **—De Kock**

"Central Bank is an institution charged with the responsibility of managing the expansion and contraction of the volume of money in the interest of general public welfare." **—R.P. Kent**

The Central Bank has a very major role in stabilising the economy of the country, besides setting right the balance of payment and foreign exchange problems. In view of growing interdependence of economic activities between the countries of the world and because of the element of planning and regulations involved in the economic system of the nations, the role of the Central Bank has become very important.

The organisation, powers and the regulation of Central Bank differ from country to country, but the functions are almost same. Prior to World War–II, the Central Banks were established and managed by private people and the government used to exercise some powers over the management. But to avoid misuse of powers and to streamline the working of banking system and also to bring harmony between different countries in respect of trade and commerce, the Central Banks of almost all the countries have been nationalised and the government of the country has full control on it.

In India, the Reserve Bank of India (The Central Bank of the Country) was the shareholders' bank from 1939 to 1949. The government nationalised it in 1949 by paying off the shareholders. It is now totally owned and controlled by the Government of India and its chief managing and controlling authority is called as the Governor.

FUNCTIONS OF A CENTRAL BANK OR THE RESERVE BANK OF INDIA

This is an apex body of the entire banking system of the country and as such its functions are different than those of a commercial bank. The difference is because of the basic objectives of the two. The main objective of a 'Central Bank' is to promote and stabilise the economy in the country. It has nothing to do with profit. The 'Commercial Banks' are, however, concerned mainly with profit in all their business activities. Therefore, it can be very conveniently said that the Central Banks have socio-economic objectives in their functions. Some of the important functions of the Central Bank are described below:

Issuing Paper Currency: The Central Bank has the monopoly of issuing paper currency of the country. For issuing the notes, the Central Bank has to maintain a reserve of gold, silver and foreign securities in certain fixed proportion, so as to inspire and retain the confidence of the people in the paper currency.

Since 1957, the Reserve Bank of India (Central Bank of the Country), has to maintain a reserve of ₹200 crores, out of which ₹115 crores is in the form of gold and remaining in the form of other securities. The RBI can issue currency notes from ₹2 to ₹10,000 denominations.

Banker, Agent and Adviser to the Government: As a banker to the government, the 'Central Bank' makes and receives payments on behalf of the government whenever it becomes necessary. It also floats public debts and manages it for a shorter or longer period as the case may be, for the government.

As a fiscal agent of the government, it receives loans, taxes and other payments from the public and manages the public debt on behalf of the government. It also appoints its senior bank officials for the purpose of attending international conferences on monetary and economic matters and thus acts as a representative of the government on such occasions.

As a financial adviser to the government, the Central Bank gives advice to the government on economic, monetary, financial and fiscal matters, such as, deficit financing, devaluation, trade policy, foreign exchange policy, etc.

Banker's Bank: The 'Central Bank' is the bank for all the commercial banks in the country. In other words, the relations of 'Central Bank' with other banks of the country are similar to those of a bank with its customers. And as a matter of legal obligation, the commercial banks have to keep certain portion of their deposits with the 'Central Bank' as cash reserves. These cash reserves enables the Central Bank to exercise control on the issue of credits by the commercial banks, thereby keeping the entire credit-system elastic.

As a banker's bank, the Central Bank also allows the facility of short-term loans and discounting of the bills to the commercial banks. The 'Central Bank', by notification also advises the commercial banks of the country in matters relating to their business, like fixation of rate of interests on deposits and loans, etc.

Lender of the Last Resort: The 'Central Bank' provides financial help to the commercial banks in times of emergency. Sometimes, a number of depositors may withdraw large sums at the same time and the commercial bank will opt to borrow from other banks to fulfill the needs of the customers. But other banks may not be in a position to help that particular bank on account of some reason. Under such circumstances, the 'Central Bank' either grants loan or purchases the securities of that commercial bank to help it out. Thus, the 'Central Bank' of the country acts as a 'lender of the last resort' for the commercial banks.

Custodian of Foreign Currency: This is one of the most important functions of the 'Central Bank' of a country. The 'Central Bank' is actually a sole custodian of the gold and foreign currency reserves of the country, so that these reserves can be utilised for making payments to foreign countries. The inflow and outflow of foreign exchange depends upon whether the position of balance of payments is favourable or otherwise. In view of the balance of payment position, the 'Central Bank' advises the government to take appropriate measures in respect of exports and imports, so that the balance of payments may be favourable to the nation.

Maintenance of Exchange Rate: In order to maintain and promote the country's trade with other countries, the 'Central Bank' makes every effort to maintain stable exchange rate with foreign currencies. For this purpose, it keeps a watch over country's exchange rates in relation to that of other countries. These efforts of the 'Central Bank' also help and encourage the inflow of foreign currency in the country.

Credit Control: This is the most important function of the 'Central Bank'. For the stabilised and smooth working of the economy of the county, it is very essential to regulate the credit granting capacity of the entire banking system and this task is assigned to the 'Central Bank' of the country.

The commercial banking system may lend too much or too little or the lending of money may be to wrong parties or may be issued for unproductive purposes or the rate of interests may be either too high or too low. All such activities cause wide fluctuations in the price structure, business dealings and the level of employment and ultimately de-stabilise the economy of the country. The 'Central Bank', therefore, exercises qualitative as well as quantitative control on the credit-granting powers of the commercial banking system of the country. Some of the measures adapted to this effect include modifications and adjustments in bank rates, open market operations, change in cash reserve, credit rationing, moral suasions, warning, publicity, and specific instructions.

Clearing House Function: The 'Central Bank' provides a clearing house facility to the commercial banks by settling the claims of various banks by a process of book entries. The 'Central Bank' possesses the cash reserves of the commercial banks as such and obtains daily report of transactions and makes adjustments accordingly by means of debits and credits.

The following example will be sufficient to explain the function of a clearing house. Suppose, the Bank of Baroda has to pay ₹10 lakh to the State Bank of Indore and the State Bank of Indore has to pay ₹3 lakh to Bank of Baroda. Thus, net payment to be made to the State Bank of Indore by the Bank of Baroda is ₹7 lakh. Therefore, the Bank of Baroda will issue a cheque of ₹7 lakh to the State Bank of Indore and these entries of debit-credit will be made in the records maintained by the Bank performing clearing house functions. In India, the Reserve Bank offices are situated only at a few places. As such, where there is no Reserve Bank office, the function of clearing house is being performed by the *State Bank of India.*

The provision of clearing house facility settles the claims between commercial banks by a very simple operation of making entries in the book. Thus, it economises the use of money in these operations. Besides this, it stabilises the operation of banking system of the country by way of minimising the possibilities of cash withdrawals during the period of economic crisis.

Development Functions: In some countries, particularly in underdeveloped and developing nations, the 'Central Bank' performs developing and promotional functions also. For this objective, special financial institutions are established for the development and progress of different sectors like agriculture, industry and commerce.

In our country, the Reserve Bank of India has special department for agricultural credits. This work is being done by NABARD. The Reserve Bank also provides funds to various financial institutions for granting loans and other financial facilities to various sectors of the economy.

Miscellaneous Functions: The 'Central Bank' also performs some optional functions, which are not obligatory and the 'Central Bank' may or may not perform them.

- The 'Central Bank' makes a study of the economic problems of the country and after analysis, publishes data, information and reports for the use by banks and the public.
- The 'Central Bank' also acts as a representative to the International Financial Institutions like International Monetary Fund (IMF), World Bank, etc., on behalf of the government.

Difference between Central Bank and Commercial Banks

Basis of Difference	Central Bank	Commercial Bank
1. Principal objective	The principal objective of the 'central bank' is to maximise economic welfare of the country.	The principal objective of 'commercial banks' is to earn profit.
2. Banker	The 'central bank' acts as a banker to all commercial banks.	The 'commercial bank' acts as a banker to all his customers.
3. Right to print currency	The 'central bank' has a right to print currency on behalf of the government.	The 'commercial banks' do not possess such right.

4. Loan facilities	The 'central bank' gives loan facilities to the government.	The 'commercial banks' can also provide loan facilities to the government units.
5. Credit facilities	The 'central bank' does not provide loan facilities to the public.	The 'commercial banks' provide loan facilities to the public.
6. Acceptance of public deposit	The 'central bank' does not accept public deposit.	The 'commercial banks' accept public deposits.

VARIOUS ASPECTS OF CREDIT CONTROL MEASURES

The credit control function is very important as far as economic interests of the country are concerned. The commercial banks lend money and create credit. The credit in itself is a very powerful factor that can be beneficial as well as detrimental for the economy. So it becomes necessary to exercise full and effective control on credit operation, so that it cannot be misused.

OBJECTIVES OF CREDIT CONTROL

Objectives of credit control may be listed as follows:

Stabilisation of the General Price Level: The traditional objective of credit control was that of keeping exchange rates stable through the medium of a mono-metallic or bi-metallic standard. But, in recent times, greater importance is attached to the stabilisation of prices as the ultimate goal of a Central Bank's credit control policy. Stabilisation of the general price level and hence stability of the value of money have been considered essential for the smooth operation of the economic system and for national economic welfare.

Stabilisation of the Money Market: Some economists stress that the credit control policy of a 'Central bank' should aim at the stabilisation of the money market. Credit control should be such that demand and supply be adjusted at all times. However, this objective has not been widely recognised because it is incompatible with the goal of stabilising the other phases of economic activity.

Promoting Economic Growth: It is widely realised that credit control should be conducive to economic growth. It should not act as an inhibitory factor. It should promote and maintain a high level of employment and income.

METHODS OF CREDIT CONTROL

Various methods are adopted by the 'Central Bank' of the country for achieving these objectives. However, the methods or instruments of credit control can be classified into two parts; viz., (I) General or Quantitative Methods, and (II) Selective or Qualitative Methods.

1. GENERAL OR QUANTITATIVE METHODS

Bank Rate: The bank rate is defined as *"the rate, at which the 'Central Bank' is ready to rediscount the first-class securities and bills produced before it by the commercial banks."*

The changes in bank rate affect the changes in all local market interest rates because of the reason that the 'Central Bank' of the country is the lender of the last resort. With the increase in bank rate, the market rates and other lending rates of the money market also go up and vice-versa. As a result, these changes affect the supply and demand of the money in the market. When the market rates and lending rates are higher, the borrowing is discouraged and the credit becomes costly and there is contraction of credits. Similarly, when the market rates are lower, the borrowing is encouraged, the credit becomes cheap and expansion of credit takes place. Thus, overall credit control can be manipulated by Central Bank by changing the bank rate. The trend in Bank Rates in India can be seen by following table:

Bank Rates in Our Country

Month/Year		Bank Rate (%)
October	2016	6.75
August	2017	6.75
August	2018	6.25
April	2019	6.25
June	2019	6.0
August	2019	5.65
October	2019	5.40
March	2020	4.65
May	2020	4.25

Source: RBI

Open Market Operations: This refers to the purchase or sale of government securities, in an open market by the 'Central Bank'. It is the direct method of credit control but it is more effective where big and active market exists for purchase and sale of government securities for short as well as for long periods, like in U.S.A. and U.K.

In the open market operations, when the 'Central Bank' sells the securities, the money supply in the market is reduced and so the credit granting capacity also decreases. On the other hand, when the 'Central Bank' purchases the securities from the open market, the money supply to the market increases and credit-granting (lending) position improves.

Change in Cash Reserves of the Commercial Banks: All the commercial banks have to keep certain ratio of cash reserves with the 'Central Bank'. By increasing the cash reserve ratio, the excess reserve of the commercial banks is reduced which restricts the credit-granting capacity of the commercial banks. Similarly, the reduction in cash reserve ratio increases the capacity of commercial banks to expand credits.

Changes in the Cash Reserve Requirements (CRR)

Year		CRR (%)	Year		CRR (%)
August	2017	4.00	June	2019	4.00
October	2018	4.00	August	2019	4.00
December	2018	4.00	October	2019	4.00
February	2018	4.00	February	2020	3.00
April	2019	4.00	March	2020	3.00
			May	2020	3.00

Source: RBI

Changes in SLR: Under the original Banking Regulation Act 1949, banks are required to maintain liquid assets in the form of cash, gold, govt. securities, etc., as a certain percentage of their total demand and time deposit liabilities. It is called Statutory Liquidity ratio (SLR). Its current rate is 18 percent in May 2020. For reducing the flow of credit, the central bank increases this liquidity ratio. For increasing the flow of credit, the liquidity ratio is reduced.

2. Selective or Qualitative Methods

Credit Rationing: In this method, the 'Central Bank' imposes restriction on demand of accommodation for more credits by the commercial banks. The 'Central Bank' limits the credit available to each of the commercial banks. Thus, this method of credit rationing directly affects the credit-granting (lending) capacity of the commercial banks.

Moral Persuasion: Under certain circumstances, the 'Central Bank' requests and persuades the commercial banks not to grant credits for speculative and non-essential activities. Since the 'Central Bank' is the symbol of financial authority and sovereignty, the commercial banks honour such requests. This method proves very effective under normal conditions of market and economy.

Publicity and Notifications: The 'Central Bank' publishes weekly reports, periodicals, reviews, the statement of assets-liabilities and balance sheets for the guidance and reference of commercial banks. These publications provide the latest information of the money market, public finance activities, trade and industries. From this data, the commercial banks can plan and adjust their credit activities.

Thus, we see that 'Central Bank', because of special financial powers resting with it, exercises the credit control measures on commercial banks and in turn helps in stabilising the economic system of the country. The Central Bank in our country is known as the 'Reserve Bank of India'.

Fixation of Margin Requirement on Secured Loan: The margin is the difference between the "loan value" and the "market value" of securities offered by borrowers against secured loan. By prescribing the margin requirements on secured loans, the 'Central Bank' does not permit the commercial bank to lend to their customers the full value of securities offered by them but only a part of their market value.

Direct Action: The method of direct action is most extensively used by 'Central Bank' to implement its credits policies. This method can be used to enforce both quantitative as well as qualitative credit control by the Central Bank. Under this method the Central Bank may impose punishment on those banks which do not comply with the declared credit control policies of the Central Bank.

THE RESERVE BANK OF INDIA

The 'Central Bank' of India is Reserve Bank. It is at the apex of the entire banking system. It was established in 1935 under the Reserve Bank of India Act of 1934. At that time, it was a shareholders' bank with a share capital of ₹5 crores divided into ₹5 lakh shares, each of ₹100. The RBI was taken over by the Government of India in 1949 by purchasing all the shares at 118 and 10 annas (62 paise) per share of ₹100 each.

MANAGEMENT OF THE RESERVE BANK OF INDIA

It is managed by a Central Board of Directors of 20 members, which consists of one Governor, four Deputy Governors, one official from Ministry of Finance, ten Directors nominated by the Central Government (to give appropriate representation to important elements of economic life of the country) and four Directors nominated to represent four local boards. The Governor, Deputy Governors and all Directors are nominated by the Central Government. The Governor is the Chairman of the Board and Chief Executive Authority of the Reserve Bank of India. The main office is situated at Mumbai (Bombay) and branches are at Delhi, Kolkata, Kanpur, Chennai, Nagpur, Bangalore, Jaipur, etc.

NEEDS FOR HAVING THE RESERVE BANK OF INDIA

The RBI can be considered as the monarch of the Indian money market and several activities in the money market centers around the RBI. Let us now point out the needs for having the RBI in the Indian money market:

Need for a Central Bank: Like the Bank of England, India also required Central Bank which would occupy the pivotal position in the monetary and banking structure of the country. The economy needed a leader bank in the money market which would supervise, control and regulate the activities of the commercial banks. Hence, the RBI was established as the Central Bank of India.

Need for State Control over the Issue of Currency Notes: For maintaining proper uniformity, elasticity and security in the issue of currency notes, the country needed a central bank. With the continuous growth in trade and commerce within the economy, the demand for currency notes, *i.e.*, the common exchange medium, was also increasing. Hence, it was necessary to increase the supply of the 'legal tender' or the currency notes issued by the monetary authority. For maintaining proper uniformity in note circulation and its better regulation, our economy needed the establishment of a central bank.

Need for Proper Maintenance of the Banking Accounts of the Government: In view of the mixed economy system and growing importance of the public sector, it was necessary to establish a banker which would render useful banking services to the Government of India. In different countries, the central bank acts as the banker to the government. Hence, the RBI, as a Central Bank, had to function as the banker to the Government of India.

Need for Maintaining a Centralised Cash Reserves by Commercial Banks: If all the commercial banks maintain a cash reserve with the 'central bank', it improves the confidence of the general public in commercial banks. This centralised cash reserve also enables the 'central bank' to provide additional funds to those banks which face temporary difficulties. This also helps the commercial banks in settling down their claims against each other through the Central Bank, which acts as a 'clearing house'.

Need for Proper Control Over Credit Creation by Commercial Banks: We know that commercial banks, through their loan-giving operations, can create credit. In these cases, more demand deposits are created by commercial banks, *i.e.*, the individual or the institution which has taken loans from any commercial bank, can withdraw money from the bank by drawing cheques on his bank accounts.

Thus, the expansion of credit means the expansion of purchasing power, and hence, expansion is the effective demand within the economy. Given the supply condition, this may lead to an excess demand for goods and services, and hence, there will be an inflationary pressure within the economy. The social and economic consequences of such inflationary pressures (or a continuous rise in the price level), are far-reaching. On the other hand, continuous contraction in credit facilities may lead to a deflationary or slump condition (*i.e.*, a continuous fall in the price-level), within the economy. Hence, it is necessary to control this process of credit creation through the monetary policy or the credit control policy implemented by the central bank.

Need for the Promotion of a Well-organised Money Market: If a large segment of the money market is unorganised and consists of indigenous bankers, then credit control policies cannot work in an effective manner. Indian money market also suffered from this drawback, and hence, our economy needed the establishment of a central bank, viz., the RBI, that would help in making the money market much more organised and well-knit in nature.

LESSON AT A GLANCE

Banks: The *Banking Companies Act of India* has defined banking as follows: "The accepting, for the purpose of lending or investment, of deposits of money from the public, repayable on demand or otherwise and withdrawal by cheque, draft, order or otherwise."

Commercial Banks: Commercial bank is an institution which deals in money, *i.e.*, borrowing and lending of money.

Functions of Commercial Banks: (i) Acceptance of deposits from the public; (ii) Lend-ing of money to commerce, trade and industry; (iii) Agency functions related to commerce and trade; and (iv) Miscellaneous functions.

Credit Creation: Creation of credit is a major function of commercial bank. When a bank creates credit or advance loans, there tends to be a multiple expansion of credit in the banking system.

Limits of Credit Creation: (i) Amount of cash; (ii) Cash reserve ratio; (iii) Cheque clearances; (iv) External drain; (v) Willingness of customers to borrow; (vi) Supply of collateral security; (vii) Banking habits and banking system; and (viii) Monetary policy of the Central Bank.

Central Bank: According to De Kock, "Central bank is a bank which constitutes the apex of the monetary and banking structure of its country."

Functions of Central Bank or The Reserve Bank of India: (i) Issuing paper currency; (ii) Banker, agent and adviser to the government; (iii) Bankers' bank; (iv) Lender of the last resort; (v) Custodian of foreign currency; (vi) Maintenance of exchange rate; (vii) Credit control; (viii) Clearing house function; (ix) Development functions; and (x) Miscellaneous functions.

Objectives of Credit Control: (i) Stabilisation of the general price level; (ii) Stabilisation of money market; and (iii) Promoting economic growth.

Methods of Credit Control:

Quantitative Methods: (i) Bank rate; (ii) Open market operations; (iii) Change in cash reserves of commercial banks; and (iv) Changes in SLR.

Qualitative Methods: (i) Credit rationing; (ii) Moral persuasion; (iii) Publicity and notifications; (iv) Fixation of margin requirement on secured loans; and (v) Direct action.

Reserve Bank of India: It is at the apex of the entire banking system in India. It was established in 1935 under the Reserve Bank of India Act of 1934.

Needs for Having the RBI: (i) Need for a Central Bank; (ii) Need for state control over the issue of currency notes; (iii) Need for proper maintenance of the banking accounts of the government; (iv) Need for maintaining a centralised cash reserves by commercial banks; (v) Need for proper control over credit creation by commercial banks; and (vi) Need for the promotion of a well-organised money market.

PROJECT WORK

Collect data, as to how many banks are operating in your town? Make a separate list of Nationalised Banks and other banks.

Select one nationalised bank office and one other bank office. Contact the Manager of each bank and collect information about various functions of that office being performed to serve common people, traders, industrial units and agricultural units.

Prepare a detailed note in respect of operating any one type of bank account, mentioning advantages of operating that bank account. Also give suggestions for improvement, if any, you feel possible in respect of operation of that type of Bank Account.

QUESTIONS

A. Short Answer Type Questions:
1. What is bank?
2. Explain briefly the following:
    (i) Fixed Deposit Account;
    (ii) Recurring Deposit Account;
    (iii) Overdraft.
3. Explain any one agency function of a commercial bank.
4. What do you mean by credit creation?

5. Explain the following:
    (i) Discounting of bills;
    (ii) Creation of credit;
    (iii) Agency function;
    (iv) Clearing house facility.
6. Mention any four limitations of credit creation.
7. What is meant by 'Central Bank'?
8. State the main objectives of credit control.
9. State any two ways in which the Central Bank can promote economic development.
10. Mention four functions of a Central Bank.
11. Briefly explain the following credit control methods adopted by the Central Bank:
    (i) Change in bank rate policy
    (ii) Open market operation
    (iii) Change in cash reserves of commercial banks
    (iv) Credit rationing
12. Name quantitative credit control methods of Central Bank of India.
13. State two differences between Central Bank and Commercial Bank.
14. What are the chief methods of lending available to commercial bank?
15. Mention any two functions of commercial bank.
16. State any two relevant differences between qualitative and quantitative methods of credit control adopted by the Reserve Bank of India.
17. Differentiate between current deposits and fixed deposits.
18. Give two reasons why the Central Banks enjoy monopoly of note issue.
19. What are savings bank accounts? Compare the rate of interest given to such an account to that of a current account and a fixed deposit.
20. How do commercial banks invest their surplus funds?

Recent Year Questions:

1. Give two advantages of depositing money with commercial banks. [ICSE 2010]
2. Mention two ways in which the RBI assists the commercial banks. [ICSE 2010]
3. State whether the following statement is true or false:
   Commercial banks act as the lender of the last resort. [ICSE 2011]
4. State the effect of inflation on creditors. [ICSE 2011]
5. What is meant by overdraft facility? [ICSE 2013]
6. What is meant by bank rate? How does it help in controlling the flow of credit in the economy? [ICSE 2013]
7. How does the Central Bank act as a 'lender of the last resort'? [ICSE 2014]
8. State an important difference between demand deposits and time deposits. [ICSE 2014]
9. What is the difference between a loan and an overdraft? [ICSE 2015]
10. State two advantages of opening a bank account. [ICSE 2015]
11. State the impact of an increase in Cash Reserve Ratio on loanable funds. [ICSE 2015]

12. Which of the following is a function of a commercial bank? Give a reason to support your answer.
    (i) Acting as a lender of last resort.
    (ii) Deciding what is legal tender.
    (iii) Determining monetary policy.
    (iv) Providing cash credit facility. [ICSE 2015]
13. State two agency functions of a commercial bank. [ICSE 2016]
14. Give any two reasons as to why a country, needs a Central Bank. [ICSE 2018]
15. Which bank is referred to as a 'Bankers Bank'? Why is it so? [ICSE 2018]
16. Differentiate between current and saving deposits. [ICSE 2018]
17. How does presence of banks in a country helps in capital formation? [ICSE 2019]
18. Briefly explain the following credit control methods adopted by the Central Bank:
    (i) Publicity, (ii) Moral persuasion [ICSE 2019]

B. Long Answer Type Questions:

1. Explain the functions of a modern commercial bank.
2. What is credit creation? What are the limitations of credit creation?
3. Which are the important methods of lending available to the commercial banks?
4. Describe two basic functions of commercial banks, giving suitable examples.
5. State briefly the various monetary measures adopted by the Reserve Bank of India.
6. State and explain any five important functions of a commercial bank.
7. Elucidate the quantitative credit control methods practiced by the Central Bank in the developing countries.
8. Explain the following functions of the Central Bank:
    (i) Monopoly of note issue.
    (ii) Clearing house facility.
9. (i) Give two reasons why the Central Bank controls price rise.
   (ii) Explain three selective methods of credit control adopted by Central Bank.
10. (i) Mention two ways in which commercial banks differ from the Central Bank.
    (ii) Explain four important agency functions of a commercial bank.
11. The following statement is correct or incorrect. Give reason to support your answer: 'To control inflation, the Central Bank lowers the bank rate.'
12. (i) Explain three important functions of a commercial bank.
    (ii) What is meant by Cash Reserve Ratio?
13. Explain clearly four differences between a Central Bank and a Commercial Bank.

Recent Year Questions:

1. Discuss the role of the Central Bank as the banker and fiscal agent to the government. [ICSE 2010]

2. The main functions of a commercial bank are to accept deposits and advance loans. Explain any two types of deposits accepted and two types of loans given by the commercial banks. [ICSE 2010]
3. Explain the role of the Central Bank as:
    (i) The Banker of the Government.
    (ii) Lender of the Last Resort.
    (iii) Custodian of Foreign Exchange Reserves. [ICSE 2011]
4. Name the bank which has sole authority to issue currency in India. Mention three ways by which it differs from a commercial bank. [ICSE 2012]
5. Explain the following functions of the Central Bank of a country:
    (i) Acting as a 'Banker to the government';
    (ii) Fixation of margin requirement on secured loans;
    (iii) Developmental functions. [ICSE 2013]
6. Define a commercial bank. Explain three methods adopted by commercial banks to mobilise funds from the public. [ICSE 2013]
7. Define a commercial bank. Explain three ways by which commercial banks advance loans to the public. [ICSE 2014]
8. With reference to the Central Bank of a country:
    (i) State two reasons for the need of a Central Bank in country.
    (ii) List two ways in which a Central Bank acts as a Banker to the Government.
    (iii) What is meant by open market operations? How does it act as a method to control credit? [ICSE 2015]
9. What are Commercial Banks? Explain clearly three methods adopted by Commercial Banks to borrow money from the public. [ICSE 2016]

OR

Explain the methods adopted by Commercial Banks to mobilize funds from Public. [ICSE 2019]
10. Who controls the Credit Supply in an economy? What is this policy called? Explain how the following can control inflation in an economy? [ICSE 2018]
    (i) Cash Reserve Ratio
    (ii) Statutory Liquidity Ratio.
11. Explain clearly four differences between a Cental Bank and a Commercial Bank. [ICSE 2018]

Case Study

CASE STUDY 1
Read the extract given below and answer the questions that follow:

Slow agricultural growth is a concern for policy makers as 2/3rd of India's population depend on rural employment for a living. Current agricultural practices are neither economically nor environmentally sustainable and India's yields for many agricultural commodities are low. Poorly maintained irrigation systems and lack of good extension services are among the factors responsible. Farmers access to market is hampered by poor roads, rudimentary market infrastructure and excessive regulation. [World Bank—India Country Overview 2008]

QUESTIONS:
(a) What is meant by productivity of land?
(b) Mention two factors that affect the productivity of land.
(c) State two ways in which the productivity of land can be increased.

CASE STUDY 2
Read the extract given below and answer the questions that follow:

[Factors of Production]

In India, the total number of persons in the labour force is unknown. According to official figures, from 1981-2001, the total number of workers grew more than 50% from approximately 245 million to 402 million persons. These figures count only those who are considered to have "engaged in economically productive work for 183 days or more". The actual number of persons in the labour force is likely to be much higher.

QUESTIONS:
(a) What is meant by labour?
(b) State any two characteristics of labour.
(c) What is meant by efficiency of labour?

CASE STUDY 3
Read the extract given below and answer the questions that follow:

Inflation fell for the second consecutive week, dropping by 6 basis points to 4·2 percent for the week ended May 1 mainly due to cheaper prices of vegetables, fruits, milk, maida and flour.

The point-to-point Wholesale Price Index (WPI) inflation fell from the previous week's level of 4·26 percent despite the soaring prices of sugar, tea, eggs, imported edible oils and fuel used in the manufacturing sector. The general price level was as high as 6·89 percent during the same period of the previous year.

The government has revised downwards inflation to 4·79 percent for the week ended March 6 against the provisional level of 4·91 percent. The final WPI stood corrected at 179·4 points during the first week of March compared to the provisional figure of 179·6 points.

The WPI remained unchanged at the previous week's level of 181·1 points, mainly due to the unchanged manufactured product's group index, even as prices of primary articles eased. The index stood at 173·8 points in the same period a year-ago. Notwithstanding the steep increase in global crude oil prices, fuel prices remained subdued during the week under review.

The index of the group of primary articles fell by 0·2 percent to 183·9 points due to a dip in the price of food articles. The index was 181·4 points during the previous year period. The group index of food articles was down 0·3 percent to 182·6 points due to cheaper jowar (2%) and milk, fruit, vegetables and bajra (1% each). However, there was a steep rise in the price of tea (13%), poultry chicken (7%), barley (6%) and a marginal rise in prices of maize (2%), eggs, ragi, and moong (1% each). The index of non-food articles group rose by 0·1 percent to 190·2 points due to costlier raw rubber (6%) and raw wool and gingelly seed (1% each).

QUESTIONS:

(a) What contributed to the fall in the inflation consecutively for the second week?
(b) What was the reason for WPI remaining unchanged?
(c) What has caused the group index of food articles to move downwards?

CASE STUDY 4

Read the extract given below and answer the questions that follow:

The scale of sell off in the equity markets after the fall of NDA government caught most investors by surprise. Although markets had expected a fall in indices in the event of the NDA government being voted out, the huge selling by FIIs was unforeseen by most market participants. What appeared to have rattled foreign investors was the statement from Left Front allies of Congress that they were completely opposed to the disinvestments of Public Sector Units (PSUs), particularly the profitable oils sector PSUs. This was seen as a signal that the economic reform process would be put on the back burner, therefore, some foreign hedge funds and FIIs decided to sell their holdings in India. Coupled with concerns on the political front, there have been pressures on FIIs for pulling out a part of their funds from emerging markets, after the US Fed declared that it intended to hike interest rates. The dual pressure of these redemptions and selling by FII created a huge selling pressure that triggered the short fall in indices.

The concern was reflected in the first comments coming from CLSA Emerging Markets, which said, "The Congress has maintained its pro-reform stance. However, with both congress and the leftist parties opposed to it, the privatisation thrust is clearly off. The new government is also less likely to support labour reforms and the easing of foreign ownership limits."

The fear that PSU sell off may be put off and reforms in the banking sector too may be put on the back burner led to a major offloading of position in public sector shares and banking stocks. Each of these sectors saw leading stocks fall by 15% to 20% during a single trading session. That set off a chain reaction among other lending counters, resulting in the meltdown of indices.

QUESTIONS:

(a) What is meant by disinvestments of Public Sector Units?
(b) When was the economic reform Process started in India?
(c) Give any three arguments in favour of Privatisation.
(d) What are the limitations of Privatisation?
(e) What made foreign funds sell heavily into Indian Markets?

CASE STUDY 5

Read the extract given below and answer the questions that follow:

The Reserve Bank of India proposes to re-introduce capital indexed bonds (CIB) with inflation linked returns to deepen the government securities market.

In December 1997, 6% CIB of five year tenure was initially introduced and now it is proposed, in consultation with the government, to reintroduce a modified CIB with structured features of similar instructions prevalent internationally. The RBI said in a discussion paper on CIB release here today. Subsequent to that issuance, there was no further issuance of CIB mainly due to lack of enthusiastic response of market participants of the instrument, both in primary and secondary markets, it said.

Some of the reasons cited for the lackluster response are that it only offered inflation hedging for the principal, while the coupons of the bond were left unprotected against inflation and complexities involved in pricing of the instrument.

The proposed CIB would offer inflation linked returns on both the coupons and principal repayments at maturity. The basic feature of bonds would be that the coupon rate for the bonds would be specified in real terms. Referring to the coupon, the RBI said the interest on CIB would be payable on a semi-annual basis at a fixed real rate of interest throughout the tenure of the bonds. The fixed real rate of interest would be applied not to the par amount of the security, but to the inflation adjusted principal.

The RBI said CIB would be sold through auction under which competitive bidders would be required to bid in terms of a desired real yield. Specific terms and conditions for the auction, including auction date, issue date, tenure and the notified amount would be announced prior to each auction. The first issuance of a CIB may be at par at 100. The price of re-issue bond would be determined in the auction and may be at, below par or above par.

Referring to taxation, it said the value of investment in the CIB and the coupon payable thereon would be governed by the provisions of tax laws as applicable from time to time.

QUESTIONS:

(a) What type of bank is Reserve Bank of India?
(b) What are the functions of Reserve Bank of India?

(c) Why was there no further issuance of capital indexed bonds by RBI?
(d) What is the purpose of issuing capital indexed bonds?

CASE STUDY 6

Read the extract given below and answer the questions that follow:

Yaga Venugopal Reddy has put his cards on the table. He has little choice amid hardening global rates, nervous markets, a slow recovering and livewire politics. The ample liquidity is a positive, but the negative is an underlying concern on inflation and another big imponderable is the possible deficit that a new government could cause. He did what any central banker should have done : keep key signaling rates like the bank-rate and repo-rate the rates at which banks borrow from and lend to RBI-unchanged.

In the Reserve Bank of India's annual policy statement presented on Tuesday, Governor Reddy has pegged the GDP growth for 2004-05 at a realistic level of 6.5-7%. This may look lower than the 8.1% in 03-04, but the RBI forecast has been made on a higher base.

The inflation forecast for the year is 5% which possibly reflects certain concerns on the price front.

"We have weighted structural vis-a-vis cyclical factors and external vis-a-vis domestic uncertainties", said Mr. Reddy.

While he maintained a status quo on rates, the financial markets felt that rates may have bottomed out, but it would not rise immediately. In market parlance, Mr. Reddy has shifted from a 'soft interest rate bias' to a 'neutral' stance without actually saying it in so many words.

QUESTIONS:

(a) Explain the term Bank-rate?
(b) What is the full form of GDP?
(c) Why is inflation considered a concern for the Indian Economy?
(d) How could the new government cause a possible deficit?

CASE STUDY 7

Read the extract given below and answer the questions that follow:

A clutch of Indian Banks led by the market leader State Bank of India are being drawn into commodity derivatives business which they think has a considerable business potential. SBI has sought the approval of the Reserve Bank of India to get into exchange traded commodity futures. A couple of other state owned banks are also gearing-up to get into this segment as institutional players, according to bankers. These include Punjab National Bank, which is one of the promoters of the National Commodity and Derivatives Exchanged Limited (NCDEX), besides Bank of India and Union Bank which are assessing the business prospects in this segment. SBI, for instance feels that there is a considerable business opportunity to be tapped across a swathe of clients-including farmers, manufacturers and traders.

QUESTIONS:

(a) What type of Bank is SBI?
(b) What are the various functions of a Commercial Bank?

(c) What is the difference between bank and financial institution?

CASE STUDY 8

Read the extract given below and answer the questions that follow:

Reformist Manmohan Singh rebooted himself to become left compatible today. The architect of economic reforms got off to a flying start this morning by displaying his socialist hues and raising comfort levels of the left parties. Prime Minister designate made it clear that ONGC and GAIL would not be privatised, interest of workers at divestment bounds PSUs would be protected and scope of Cross Subsidisation in areas like power for farmers would be explored. Reiterating his famous line that reforms would continue with a human face, he said the government was committed to build strong private and public sectors while performing selective disinvestment. "Development will be key priority, the aim of reforms would be to remove poverty, increased employment through relief to decentralised sectors" he said.

"PSUs like GAIL and ONGC will remain in the public sector. There is no intention to privatise them. Similarly, there are nationalised banks which will remain in public sector. These will not be privatised" he added.

Mr. Singh's comments were warmly welcomed by the left parties. "Sweet heart deals for public sector companies, in which there were allegations that some people close to certain political parties were favoured, should be probed," CPM spokesperson Sitaram Yechury said.

QUESTIONS:

(a) Name the person who started economic reforms in India.
(b) What would be the aim of reforms according to Dr. Manmohan Singh?
(c) Which companies have been kept away from disinvestment?

CASE STUDY 9

Read the extract given below and answer the questions that follow:

The last year totalled almost 6% of GDP, and painlessly financed the fiscal deficit. This has fed the illusion that deficits don't matter. But they do : history is littered with the wrecks of high-deficit economies. If India's fiscal deficit looks like shooting up, expect a reduction (and may be reversal) of flows from FIIs and overseas Indians. Two factors have the potential to reduce the fiscal deficit : the growing service tax and fall in interest rates. However, the service tax still has a small base, and cannot produce thousands of crores overnight. India's public debt has risen from 57% of GDP in the mid 1990s to 85% today. This has not raised debt service correspondingly since the interest rate on public debt has fallen, a consequence of reform and globalisation. However, global interest rates are certain to rise. The US Fed looks like raising its short-term rate from 1% to perhaps 4% over the next year or two. Indian rates will have to rise in tandem. So, falling interest rates will cease to provide budgetary relief.

CMP claims it will reduce the revenue deficit to zero by 2009. But it has no credible programme to raise enough revenue to meet even the current deficit, let alone one greatly expanded by explosive spending on education, health and employment. CMP assumes that a human face means two things : more subsidies and more public spending on antipoverty schemes. But dozens of studies show that such spending is mostly wasted. Three-quarters of subsidies go to the non-poor, and the announcement of free power for farmers by several states will worsen this ratio. Possibly 85% of funds in employment schemes fail to reach the poor, and 95% of funds spend on the public distribution system. Teachers and health workers do not attend schools or clinics.

FIIs have brought around $ 20 billion into Indian stock markets, half of that since the start of 2003. The withdrawal of a mere $ 700 million on black Friday caused a fall of over 500 points and 786·89 points on next Monday in the Sensex. Imagine what will happen if FIIs withdraw just a quarter of their investment ($ 5 billions). Indian investors will also follows suit Mr. Manmohan Singh needs to lose some sleep over this.

QUESTIONS:

(a) What evil effect will high deficit have on Indian economy?
(b) What is the claim of CMP relating to control of deficit?
(c) What have past experiences shown regarding the policies followed by new government to achieve the reduction in revenue?

CASE STUDY 10

Read the extract given below and answer the questions that follow:

The UPA government's commitment to keep price rise under check notwithstanding, inflation rose by 0·47% to 4·67% for the week ended May 15 due to surging prices of mass consumption items like vegetables, milk and edible oils.

The point-to-point Wholesale Price Index (WPI) inflation rose from 4·20% in the previous week even as prices of fuels remained unchanged despite violent gyrations in global markets and the general price level was as high as 6·58% in the same period during 2002-03.

The United Progressive Alliance (UPA), in its Common Minimum Programme released as before, stressed that it would take "effective and strong measures" to control the price hike of essential items.

The WPI rose by 0·2% to 181·5 points due to sharp rise in the prices of primary articles and marginal increase in heavy-weighted manufactured product prices and it was 173·4 points in the previous year period. Government revised upwards inflation to 4·53% for the week ended March 20 as against the provisional figure of 4·3%. The final WPI stood corrected at 179·9 points during the third week of March as compared to provisional level of 179·5 points.

The index of Primary Articles group shot up 0·6% to 184·9 points due to increasing prices of food, non-food and minerals and it was 180·8 points in the year-ago period. Food Articles group index was up by 0·7% to 183·9 points due to costlier fish-marine (8%), vegetables (4%), mutton and jowar (2% each) and maize, milk grams, eggs and ragi (1% each). However, prices declined in the case of barley and tea (3%), condiments and spices (2%) and bajra, poultry chicken, masur and wheat (1% each). The index of Non-Food Articles group moved up by 0·3% to 190·4 points due to higher prices for soyabean (4%), niger seed and rape and mustard seed (3% each) and copra (2 %).—PTI

QUESTIONS:
(a) Explain the term inflation.
(b) What type of inflation is the Indian Economy currently facing?
(c) Why is the inflation rate continuously gaining in the economy?
(d) Name few measures that United Progressive Alliance (UPA) government can adopt for controlling inflation.

CASE STUDY 11
Read the extract given below and answer the questions that follow:

RBI, in the Third Quarter Review of the Annual Statement on Monetary Policy for 2006-07 (January 31, 2007), reiterated its resolve to keep inflation as close as possible to the declared range of 5.00-5.50 percent at the earliest, while maintaining the medium-term goal to rein in inflation at 5.0 percent. The review also spelt out the following three important issues in the conduct of monetary policy : (i) demand pressures appearing to have intensi-fied, reflected in rising inflation, high money and credit growth, elevated asset prices, strains on capacity utilisation, some indications of wage pressures and widening of trade deficit; (ii) increased supply-side pressures evident from prices of primary articles; and (iii) the need of the policy to contend with lagged response of productive capacity and infrastructure to the ongoing expansion in investment. It was once again stated that to maintain price stability, RBI would use all policy instruments including CRR, LAF and MSS to modulate liquidity in the system so that all legitimate requirements of credit are met, particularly of the productive sectors of the economy.

QUESTIONS:
(a) Define the term 'Monetary Policy'.
(b) What do you mean by Demand?
(c) Give the full form of CRR.

CASE STUDY 12
Read the extract given below and answer the questions that follow:

Fiscal policy is the building block for an enabling macro-environment, which not only provides stability and predictability to the policy regime, but through its tax transfer mechanism, also ensures that national resources are allocated in terms of its defined priorities. Unproductive expenditure, tax distortions and high deficits are considered to have constrained the economy from realising its full growth potential. The medium-term fiscal policy stance of government, therefore, has been to reduce deficits; prioritise expenditure and ensure that these results in intended outcomes; and augment resources by widening the tax base and improving the compliance while maintaining moderate rates. At the beginning of the fiscal reforms in 1991, the fiscal imbalance was identified as the root cause of the twin problems of inflation and the difficult balance of payments position. The fiscal consolidation, which followed in response, in the absence of a defined mandate, however, failed to sustain itself.

QUESTIONS:
(a) Explain the term 'tax'.
(b) What is meant by Fiscal Policy?
(c) Which factors are responsible for the constraint of growth of an economy?

Assignment

LIST OF ASSIGNMENT

1. Take a fast moving consumer good (FMCG) like washing machine detergent. Analyse the factors that determine the demand of this product. Present your findings in form of a class presentation.
2. Develop a hypothetical table of information for coffee that shows quantity demanded at various prices and supply of coffee at these prices. Draw a demand curve and supply curve and show an equilibrium price at which market is cleared of its supplies.
3. Make a list of products for which you think demand is price inelastic and price elastic. Specify the reasons you may think relevant for your analysis.
4. Take a case of public enterprise which is about to be privatized or has been recently privatized. Analyze the pros and cons of such an exercise undertaken by the government. (The case of VSNL or BALCO can be taken up)
5. Take a case of a nationalised bank–visit any one of its branches in your city. Analyze the main functions of this bank's branch. Make a presentation to this effect.
6. Recently rates of interests have been reduced on all the saving instruments. Carry out a survey of 30 people in your area as to what is their reaction to this cut. The sample may consist of salaried people, business people and professionals.
7. Take a case of five FMCGs–fast moving consumer goods–bathing soaps, toothpastes, facial creams, shampoos, ball pens. Analyze as to how the market for these products is characterized by product differentiation.
8. Take the case of a company and analyze the production process in which all the factors that you studied in your class, are used by the company to produce a product.

We have suggested the guidelines for the students for completing the above assignments by taking the examples of assignment 2, 3 and 6. Students can complete other assignments in the same way.

Assignment 2

Develop a hypothetical table of information for coffee that shows quantity demanded at various prices and supply of coffee at these prices. Draw a demand curve and supply curve and show an equilibrium price at which market is cleared of its supplies.

Suggestive Hints

1. A rise in price of goods always decreases the quantity demanded assuming other variable remaining constant. Conversely the fall in prices will always increase the quantity demanded, for example if price of a coffee goes up, the quantity demanded for coffee falls. Economicst call this inverse relationship as the law of demand.

2. Students are advised to make a demand schedule in the form of table specifying a price of coffee (in rupees) and the quantity demanded over a period of time (per day/per year). From 10 households.

Example:

Quantity Demanded (per kg.)	Price (₹)
400	10
300	15
200	20

3. The positive relationship between price and quantity supplied is called law of supply. Where increase in price will lead to increase in quantity assuming other variables remaining constant. Students are advised to make a supply keeping the price figures same as above. For example.

Quantity Supplied (per kg.)	Price (₹)
200	10
400	15
600	20

4. With the help of demand schedule students can frame demand curve (points are graphed and the line connecting them is demand curve). Same exercise will be done with the help of supply schedule results in formation of supply curve.

5. For determining the equilibrium price both the graphs needs to be appear on the same graph as price on the vertical axis and quantity on the horizontal axis.

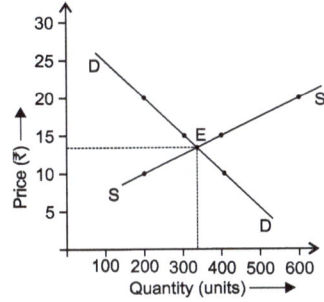

ASSIGNMENT 3

Make a list of products for which you think demand is price inelastic and price elastic. Specify the reasons you may think relevant for your analysis.

Suggested Hints

1. Product is considered as price elastic when a small change in price results in significant change in demand of a product. On the other hand products are considered to be price

inelastic when there is little or no change in demand of a product even with change of price of a product.

2. If demand is price elastic consumers are more sensitive to changes in prices and vice versa in case when demand is price inelastic.
3. If the substitute is easily available for the product the demand will be elastic.
4. If the product is termed as a necessity product the demand will be more inelastic.
5. If a product shares a major proportion in consumer's budget the demand of the product will be price elastic.
6. Goods that can only be produced by a single manufacturer generally have inelastic demand.

The table below indicates list of the commonly used products indicating the type of demand with reason.

Product	Type of demand	Reason
Laptop	Price Elastic	It is a luxury product, If the price of the laptop increases or decreases it will affect the demand of the product.
Life Saving Medicine	Price Inelastic	There is no substitute available for life saving drugs hence if the price of such medicines increases in future it will not affect the demand of the product.
Jewelry	Price Elastic	It is not a necessity product the demand of the jewelry can be deferred by the consumer if the price increases in future.
Air Conditioners	Price Elastic	It is a luxury product, If the price of the AC's increases or decreases it will affect the demand of the product.
Branded Clothes	Price Elastic	It is a luxury product, If the price of the branded clothes increases or decreases it will affect the demand of the product.
Railway Service	Price Inelastic	There is a monopoly of Indian Railway Services. Transportation is a necessity hence changes in price of rail tickets will have no effect on the demand of rail tickets.
Fuel	Price Inelastic	Fuel is non-renewable source of energy it is not easily available. There is no substitute of the product available hence the demand of fuel is price inelastic.

Milk, Salt, Rice, Wheat	Price Inelastic	Milk, Salt, Rice, Wheat are the necessity products. There are no substitutes available for the necessity products hence consumer will bound to buy the product if the prices got increased in future.
Electricity	Price Inelastic	There is no substitute available in market. We cannot live without electricity. Hence in future if the price will increase/decrease it will not affect the demand.
Cars/Bikes	Price Elastic	These are the examples of luxury products hence customer can deferred the demand if price increases in future
Tea/Coffee	Price Elastic	Tea and Coffee are substitute products hence if the price of coffee increases in future the consumer will switch to tea hence the demand is price sensitive.

ASSIGNMENT 6

Recently rates of interests have been reduced on all the saving instruments. Carry out a survey of 30 people in your area as to what is their reaction to this cut. The sample may consist of salaried people, business people and professionals.

Suggested Hints

1. Firstly the students are advised to identify the objective of the study that is we need to access the reaction of the people on reduced interest rate on all saving instruments.
2. The sample size in our study is 30. The method of sampling is convenience sampling. Students are advised to ask the questions to the selected set of people whether salaried, professional or businessmen in nearby area.
3. Students are advised to frame a questionnaire asking them about the information required. They will decide on question content and develop the question wording. (A small questionnaire is attached for the reference of the student).
4. The questions should be few, short, clearly worded, simple and easy to reply.
5. Choose the method(s) of reaching your target respondents.
6. After collecting the responses from the respondent's students are advised to do analysis of data collected.
7. Record the answers of each respondent question wise and are advised to make an analysis of the same.
8. Make Interpretations and are advise to derive and conclusion.

SAMPLE QUESTIONNAIRE:

Name: ....

Gender: ....

Designation: ....

Organization: ....

Age: Between 20-30 ☐   30-40 ☐   above 40 ☐

Qualification: ....

Occupation: ....

Annual Income:

    Below 2Lakh ☐   2-4 Lakh ☐
    4-6 Lakh ☐   Above 6 Lakh ☐

1. How do you spend your monthly income?
   - Shopping ☐   Investment ☐
   - Saving ☐   All ☐

2. What percentage of Income do you save?
   - 0-10 ☐   10-20 ☐
   - 20-30 ☐   30-40 ☐

3. How do you invest your saving?
   - Saving Account ☐   Shares / Bonds ☐
   - Pension ☐   Mutual Fund ☐
   - Real Estate ☐   Other ☐

4. What do you think are the best options for investing your money? (Rank in order of Preference) ....

5. Reason for selecting the option
   1. ....
   2. ....

6. Are you aware that Government reduces the interest rate on saving instrument?
   Yes ☐   No ☐

7. Is reducing interest rates affects your investment decision?
   Yes ☐   No ☐

8. After reduced interest rates, your preferred investment options are:
   1. ....
   2. ....

9. Any Suggestion /Recommendation for the decision of Government........................

Thank you for your responses

www.ingramcontent.com/pod-product-compliance
Ingram Content Group UK Ltd.
Pitfield, Milton Keynes, MK11 3LW, UK
UKHW050418240426
12048UKWH00014B/691